Land and Schooling

PUBLISHING FOR THE WORLD
125 Years
THE JOHNS HOPKINS UNIVERSITY PRESS

**Other Books Published in Cooperation with
the International Food Policy Research Institute**

IFPRI

Land and Schooling

Transferring Wealth across Generations

AGNES R. QUISUMBING, JONNA P. ESTUDILLO,
AND KEIJIRO OTSUKA

Published for the International Food Policy Research Institute

The Johns Hopkins University Press
Baltimore and London

The Johns Hopkins University Press
2715 North Charles Street
Baltimore, Maryland 21218-4363
www.press.jhu.edu

International Food Policy Research Institute
2033 K Street, NW
Washington, D.C. 20006
(202) 862-5600
www.ifpri.org

LIBRARY OF CONGRESS CATALOGING-IN-PUBLICATION DATA

Quisumbing, Ma. Agnes R. (Maria Agnes R.)
    Land and schooling : transferring wealth across generations / Agnes R. Quisumbing,
Jonna P. Estudillo, and Keijiro Otsuka.
      p.   cm. — (International Food Policy Research Institute)
    Includes bibliographical references and index.
    ISBN 0-8018-7842-X
    1. Land tenure—Developing countries. 2. Land use—Developing countries.
3. Income distribution—Developing countries. 4. Agricultural laborers—
Developing countries. 5. Sex discrimination against women—Developing
countries. I. Estudillo, Jonna P. II. Otsuka, Keijiro. III. Title.
IV. International Food Policy Research Institute (Series).
HD1131.Q57 2004
333.3′09172′4—dc21   2003013892

A catalog record for this book is available from the British Library.

Contents

Figures

Tables

Foreword

Eliminating gender disparities in well-being is one of the goals of development policy. Despite the progress made in reducing the gender gap in education, property rights of men and women remain unequal in much of the developing world. Attempts to achieve gender equity in these areas, however, will need to consider the motives of parents who make the critical choices of educating sons and daughters, and of transferring physical wealth to them. Parental decisions are influenced by cultural norms, but also by their own constraints and the changing economic and social environment.

This book examines parental decisions to transfer wealth through schooling investment and land inheritance in three developing countries with different cultural traditions: the Philippines, Indonesia, and Ghana. What underlies parents' decisions to invest differentially in sons and daughters? How do the adoption of new crops and growth in the nonfarm sector affect these investments? What are the consequences of gender differences in education and landownership on incomes of the next generation? Will improving gender equity create efficiency costs or gains?

This book brings together two originally separate IFPRI research programs —one on gender and intrahousehold issues and the other on property rights and collective action—to address these issues. At present, many of the challenging issues facing development economists are multifaceted, requiring researchers with different expertise to collaborate in order to undertake fruitful studies. The issue of transferring wealth across generations is no exception. A comprehensive knowledge of the accumulated evidence on gender issues and a clear understanding of intrahousehold decisionmaking behavior are critical components of this type of study. In addition, knowledge of institutional economics, including the issues of property rights, land tenancy, and collective action, is indispensable. Furthermore, detailed empirical knowledge on prevailing land-tenure institutions and technological characteristics of various farming systems is also necessary. It is easy to say that collaboration across subject areas is needed, but, as many of us know well, there are constraints to this kind of joint research even if it is potentially valuable. Therefore, I am pleased that the three coauthors successfully collaborated in bringing this book to publication, contributing new knowledge based on their respective areas of expertise in a variety of relevant research fields.

It is noteworthy that this study challenges the conventional wisdom that inheritance systems are unchanging. If parents bestow land on children who can make the best use of it, the adoption of new agricultural technologies and the growth of the nonfarm sector, by changing relative returns to land and schooling, can alter traditional inheritance patterns. Most heartening is the finding that a smaller gender gap in land and schooling is associated with higher lifetime incomes of both men and women, and with improved household welfare.

The efficiency gains resulting from the elimination of gender disparities can provide impetus to governments and policymakers to further reduce gender disparities in schooling and property rights. This study argues, quite convincingly, that policies should be directed toward developing labor-intensive agricultural technologies, which increase the demand for female labor; extending and strengthening schooling systems in rural areas; and promoting competition in nonfarm labor markets so as to eliminate discrimination against women.

In conclusion, I emphasize the importance of such cross-cutting research, which generates new insights and not only unveils the complexities of development problems but also contributes to the formulation of strategic policy solutions.

Joachim von Braun
Director General, IFPRI

Preface

This book reflects more than a decade of collaboration among the three authors. We first met in 1988: Agnes Quisumbing was at the Economic Growth Center, Yale University, on leave from her position as an assistant professor of economics at the University of the Philippines, Quezon City; Jonna Estudillo was her graduate student; and Keijiro Otsuka was a visiting scientist at the International Rice Research Institute (IRRI) in the Philippines. The three of us tried to understand why, in comparison with other countries in Asia, Filipino women are more educated than men. The most plausible hypothesis, given our understanding of Philippine culture, was that sons inherit more land and daughters receive more schooling. This hypothesis was based on several assumptions: (1) men have a comparative advantage in farming, whereas women have a comparative advantage in nonfarm jobs that require schooling; (2) land inheritance and schooling investments are substitutable ways of transferring wealth across generations; and (3) parents are egalitarian with respect to wealth transfers to daughters and sons. Whether these "stylized facts" were true in the Philippines and whether they were applicable to other countries were not at all clear to us at that time.

This intriguing question has remained with us for a long time. Quisumbing, with Estudillo's assistance, made a first attempt to understand this issue in 1989 by resurveying five Philippine villages that were first surveyed by Cristina C. David and Otsuka in 1985 for their book *Modern Rice Technology and Income Distribution in Asia* (1994). This research, which resulted in one of the first empirical papers to address the possibility that different forms of intergenerational transfers are substitutes, was published in the *Journal of Development Economics* in 1994. Although the paper confirmed our hypothesis in the Philippines, expanding our study to other countries had to wait until 1995, when Otsuka and Quisumbing were visiting research fellow and research fellow, respectively, at the International Food Policy Research Institute (IFPRI) in Washington, D.C. Otsuka was heading the multicountry research program on Property Rights and Collective Action, while Quisumbing headed the multicountry research program on Strengthening Development Policy

xviii *Preface*

through Gender and Intrahousehold Analysis. Otsuka then requested that Quisumbing join his land tenure project, which resulted in the book *Land Tenure and Natural Resource Management: A Comparative Study of Agrarian Communities in Asia and Africa* (2001). Otsuka found that in western Ghana, where wives traditionally did not inherit land from their husbands under the so-called uterine matrilineal system, husbands were increasingly giving land to their wives through gift transfers. Similarly, in Sumatra, where traditionally only women inherited land under the matrilineal system, men had more recently been inheriting some portions of parents' land. Why have such changes in land inheritance systems been taking place? What has been happening to the schooling of daughters compared with sons in these societies, if land inheritance and schooling investments are substitutes? These questions provided an unusual opportunity for interdivisional collaboration at IFPRI.

Otsuka and Quisumbing decided to undertake a comparative study of three countries—the Philippines, Ghana, and Indonesia—and invited Estudillo to join the project. Estudillo conducted a resurvey of the Philippine study villages in 1998, and later worked with Otsuka from 1998 to 2000 as a postdoctoral fellow at the Tokyo Metropolitan University, where Otsuka was a professor of economics.

Thus, this book is deeply rooted in our past research. Without valuable prior information on intricate land tenure institutions and the role of schooling in farm and nonfarm activities provided by earlier studies, it would not have been possible. The book also relies heavily on our informal collaboration for the past decade and a half, which has been sustained by mutual trust and respect.

A major message we would like to convey from this study is that using both qualitative and quantitative methods can contribute much to the study of gender issues. Although topics such as inheritance and family structure have long been studied by anthropologists, ethnographers, and sociologists, past research has been primarily descriptive, which has made generalization and replication difficult. Our studies have drawn heavily on the anthropological literature on these countries, on our own extensive field visits and semi-structured interviews, and on community interviews to gather information on norms and practices regarding land tenure and inheritance. We are hopeful that this will stimulate other work on gender equity issues in the developing world based on this combined method.

This book is a compilation of papers published by the three authors in numerous journals, including *Land Economics,* the *Journal of Development Studies, Agricultural Economics, Developing Economies, World Development, Economic Development and Cultural Change,* and *Environment and Development Economics,* as well as an IFPRI research report, *Land, Trees, and Women: Evolution of Customary Land Tenure Institutions in Western Ghana and Sumatra.*

We express our deepest gratitude to IFPRI, IRRI, Tokyo Metropolitan University, the Japan Society for the Promotion of Science, the Foundation for

Advanced Studies on International Development, the United States Agency for International Development, and the United Kingdom Department for International Development for supporting various phases of this research. We are greatly indebted to J. B. Aidoo and S. Suyanto, our collaborators in Ghana and Sumatra, respectively, who conducted the field surveys and translated many interviews with farmers and their families, giving us an insider's view of these societies. We also thank Ellen Payongayong, who provided technical assistance and continuity in the fieldwork and data analysis, and Jay Willis for word processing. We thank IFPRI's Publications Review Committee and two anonymous referees for their constructive comments and suggestions. We also acknowledge the support and encouragement we received from Jere Behrman, Michael Carter, Gelia Castillo, Cristina C. David, Marcel Fafchamps, Yujiro Hayami, Peter Hazell, Mahabub Hossain, Michael Kevane, John Maluccio, Ruth Meinzen-Dick, John Pender, Per Pinstrup-Andersen, Frank Place, Jean-Philippe Platteau, and T. Paul Schultz.

Finally, we dedicate this book to three generations of women—Agnes Quisumbing's daughter, Cecilia Q. Villaseñor; Jonna Estudillo's mother, Petronila dela Peña; and Keijiro Otsuka's wife, Kari—as an expression of our sincerest appreciation for the inspiration they have given us in the writing of this book.

Land and Schooling

1 Introduction: Scope, Framework, and Objectives

In rural societies, passing down land and providing an education are the main ways in which parents assure the future welfare of their children. Because land and human capital are both valuable resources, if parents educate their sons and not their daughters and if only sons inherit land, women will be worse off compared with men. However, gender gaps in land and schooling are not the same in all countries. Evidence from various sources, such as the Humana (1992) index, suggests that, in terms of social and economic rights, gender biases in favor of men are less significant in Southeast Asia than in Sub-Saharan Africa and South Asia. In much of Africa, for example, women have unequal access to land, more commonly gaining weak land rights through their husband upon marriage (Gray and Kevane 1999; Kevane and Gray 1999; Lastarria-Cornhiel 1997). Gender gaps in education follow a similar pattern: East Asia, Latin America, Europe, and Central Asia have the highest gender equality in education; South Asia has the lowest.

The value of land and education to future generations also depends on changing returns to these resources. Historically, land has been a major factor of production in agriculture and returns to land have accounted for the largest portion of farm income in developing countries. However, as new agricultural technologies and modern inputs are introduced and as income-earning opportunities emerge outside the farm sector, the importance of land as a source of farm household income tends to decline and that of human capital to increase (Schultz 1964). In the Philippines, for example, nonfarm labor income, which accrues largely to human capital, has risen significantly relative to the return to land over the past three decades (Estudillo, Quisumbing, and Otsuka 2001a; Estudillo and Otsuka 1999).

How do parents allocate land and education between sons and daughters? How do changing returns to land and human capital affect parental investments in children? What are the implications of gender differences in land and schooling for the welfare of men and women? This book aims to identify factors that affect the distribution of land inheritance and schooling between men and women across generations and to examine their consequences for the distribution of income and consumption expenditures within the household. Our analysis is based on specially designed household surveys undertaken in selected rural communities of the Philippines, Sumatra in Indonesia, and western Ghana in sites covered by our previous studies (David and Otsuka 1994; Quisumbing 1994; Otsuka and Place 2001; Quisumbing and Otsuka 2001). These provide rich and invaluable background information for this study. In this chapter, we begin with the motivation for the research and its relevance to policy. We then explain the conceptual framework of this study and provide descriptive information on gender differences in land and schooling, based on our study sites and the existing literature. We conclude by stating the empirically testable hypotheses of this study.

Background and Policy Relevance of the Research

Whereas there are many studies documenting the increase in women's education in developing countries (for example, King and Hill 1993), similar evidence on women's land rights is scarce. With the exception of a few studies and review papers by Agarwal (1994) for South Asia, and by Lastarria-Cornhiel (1997) and Gray and Kevane (1999) for Sub-Saharan Africa, studies tend to be descriptive and confined to a few small sites, and rarely provide the quantitative information needed for testing empirical hypotheses. The scarcity of gender-disaggregated information on land rights has made it impossible to examine whether, on balance, women's access to the two major income-earning resources—land and human capital—has deteriorated or improved through time.

It has often been argued that a shift in customary land tenure institutions toward individualized ownership systems erodes women's land rights (Lastarria-Cornhiel 1997). This argument is supported by the gradual disappearance of matrilineal inheritance and the rise of patrilineal inheritance systems such as those occurring in some parts of South Asia (Agarwal 1994) and Sub-Saharan Africa (Place and Otsuka 2001a, 2001b). Women's land rights, however, have not declined universally in the developing countries. In our study sites in the uterine matrilineal communities of the Akan tribe in western Ghana, landownership rights have traditionally been transferred from a deceased man to his brother or nephew (sister's son). As the demand for women's labor has increased in the process of the intensification of land use, women have received increasingly larger areas of land from their husbands and fathers as inter vivos gifts.

In Southeast Asia, parental preferences in land inheritance may favor sons in communities where farming is intensive in male labor (Estudillo, Quisumbing, and Otsuka 2001b, 2001c). Among the Ilocanos of the northern Philippines, for example, parents traditionally give a portion of their landholdings to a newly married son as a gift. The Ilocanos practice both primogeniture, in which the eldest child (usually the son) alone inherits the parents' property, and ultimogeniture, in which the youngest child inherits the property, depending on the availability of land. Among the Ilonggos of Panay Island in the middle Philippines, daughters and sons may receive land rights more equally and independently than the Ilocanos, although, for land-constrained households, children who help the parents in farming receive more land than do their siblings.

In our study sites in Indonesia, traditionally land has been bequeathed from mother to daughters in a matrilineal inheritance system. At present, however, daughters and sons inherit both paddy and cinnamon fields equally in areas where rice and cinnamon production are equally intensive in male and female labor, whereas sons inherit primarily rubber fields and daughters inherit paddy fields in areas where men work exclusively in rubber fields and women work primarily in paddy fields. We describe the current inheritance system as "egalitarian" rather than matrilineal.

We hypothesize that emerging gender patterns in land acquisition and schooling respond to changing perceived opportunities available to adult men and women. Parents who care about their children and their own well-being as they enter old age are careful in their choice of allocations of wealth to their sons and daughters. They consider the likely returns from investing varying amounts of schooling and land in their children. We argue that, in areas where markets and local social institutions reward male farmers and female human capital, parents allocate land to their sons and education to their daughters. We also postulate that gender differences in investments in schooling depend on the cost of sending children to school relative to parents' perceptions of the private returns to schooling. The costs of investing in girls' schooling may be higher because the opportunity costs of time are higher for girls who work longer hours at home and outside than boys do (Hill and King 1995). Although school fees are generally the same for boys and girls, distance may be a greater deterrent for parents who are concerned about their daughters' safety (for example, Lavy 1996 for Ghana; King and Lillard 1987 for the Philippines) and would then pay more for girls' transportation expenses because they do not want their girls to walk a long way to school.

Parents may consider investments in girls' schooling less attractive if women earn less than men and if they are expected to provide less old age support to their parents (Stark and Lucas 1988). Empirical estimates from 19 developed countries and 42 developing countries indicate that, on the average, women earn 77 percent as much as men in developed countries and 73 percent as much in developing countries (World Bank 2001: 55, Table 1.2). Only about 20 percent of the earnings differential is explained by differences in worker and job characteristics; 80 percent is explained by factors that are not easily observed such as innate abilities and gender discrimination in the labor market (World Bank 2001). Consequently, parents may act on lower returns to daughters' schooling. Even where the private returns to education do not differ systematically by gender, demand for girls' education could be affected by gender differences in the effective returns realized by parents. In societies where women move to their husbands' household and thus have limited ability to transfer resources to their parents, investments in daughters appear less desirable (World Bank 2001).

Attitudes of parents, teachers, and children themselves are also important influences on schooling attainment. A study in Kenya found that girls in primary school are particularly affected by negative attitudes and discrimination (Mensch and Lloyd 1998). For example, girls' (but not boys') propensity to stay in school is significantly affected by whether teachers think math is important for girls and whether boys and girls receive (and perceive) equal treatment in the classroom. Parents' attitudes have a similar effect: sons attain higher exam scores in households where parents think schooling is more important for boys than for girls, holding other factors constant. In the Philippines, in contrast, an ethnographic study by Bouis et al. (1998) indicates that parental decisions regarding schooling depend on the child's attitudes. According to this study, Filipino parents invest in the schooling of girls because they are "more studious," "patient," "willing to sacrifice," and "interested in their studies," which are traits that would make them succeed in school. Boys, on the other hand, are more prone to vices (such as drinking), are fond of "roaming around" and "playing with their *barkada*" (peer group), and have to be "reminded" and "scolded" to do their schoolwork.

Since household wealth is a binding constraint in parent–child intergenerational transfers, land inheritance and schooling investments are jointly determined. If parents have egalitarian preferences in making wealth transfers to children, there is likely to be a tradeoff between land inheritance and investment in schooling—those who get more land may be given less schooling. If men and women have different comparative advantages in farming (for example, lowland versus upland cultivation), a similar tradeoff may exist in intergenerational transfers of different types of agricultural fields. Whether or not parents are, in fact, egalitarian is an empirical matter that needs to be verified.

Parental decisions regarding wealth transfers can have a profound impact on the pattern of gender income inequality over time because returns to land and human capital are major components of rural household income. Moreover, greater access to land and increased schooling attainment by women may be translated into higher income and stronger bargaining power at home for women. This has implications for the distribution of welfare within the household because there is growing evidence that women and men spend income under their control in systematically different ways (Guyer 1980; Dwyer and Bruce 1988).

Women are observed to spend a higher proportion of their income on food and children's health care, whereas men spend a higher proportion of their income on tobacco and alcohol (Kennedy 1991; Thomas 1994; Haddad et al. 1996). In Brazil, the effect of women's unearned income on child survival probabilities is almost 20 times higher than that of men's unearned income (Thomas

1994). In Taiwan, women's income share has a significant and positive effect on the household budget shares of staples and education and a negative effect on the budget shares allocated to alcohol and cigarettes (Thomas and Chen 1994). In Bangladesh and South Africa, although women bring far fewer assets to the marriage, these assets play a significant role in household decision-making, particularly on the allocation of household expenditures to education (Quisumbing and Maluccio 2003). Even in patriarchal societies such as Bangladesh where husbands control most of the resources, women's assets have a positive effect on educational expenditures (Quisumbing and de la Briere 2000); they also reduce girls' rate of illness (Hallman 2000). Thus, differences in access to land and in schooling attainment by men and women may have important effects on household welfare.

Although the above studies have demonstrated high private returns to increasing resources under women's control, evidence of higher social returns to investing in women makes gender equity an issue of great interest to policymakers. Schultz (2002), for example, argues that the regions that have most successfully promoted equal education for men and women—East Asia, Southeast Asia, and Latin America—have also experienced the most economic and social progress in recent decades. In contrast, regions that have lagged behind in growth—South and West Asia, the Middle East and North Africa, and Sub-Saharan Africa—have lagged in relative investments in women's schooling (Schultz 2002: 207–208). The World Bank's (2001) policy research report on gender and development provides additional evidence in support of interventions to improve gender equality. For example, some studies suggest that gender inequalities have a cost in terms of forgone economic growth. One study estimates that, if the countries in South Asia, Sub-Saharan Africa, and the Middle East and North Africa had started with the gender gap in average years of schooling that East Asia had in 1960 and had closed that gender gap at the rate achieved by East Asia between 1960 and 1992, their per capita incomes could have grown by 0.5–0.9 percentage points more per year, a substantial increase over the actual growth rates of 0.7 percent per year in Sub-Saharan Africa, 1.7 percent in South Asia, and 2.2 percent in the Middle East (Klasen 1999a).

Closing the gender gap in education also lowers fertility and improves child survival.[1] Using data on 100 countries in 1990, Klasen (1999b) finds that an additional year of female education reduces the fertility rate by 0.23 births. Over a longer time period, Gatti (1999) finds that an additional year of women's schooling decreases the fertility rate by 0.32 births. This implies that a three-year increase in the average education level of women is associated with as much as one less child per woman. In countries where girls are only half as likely to go to school as boys, there are on average 21.1 more infant deaths per

---

1. This discussion draws on World Bank (2001).

1,000 live births than in countries with no gender gap, controlling for other factors (Hill and King 1995). Improving women's status also helps reduce child malnutrition. Smith and Haddad (2000) consider the underlying determinants of food security against data on child underweight rates between 1970 and 1995 from 63 developing countries, representing 88 percent of the developing world's population. The research results show that increases in women's education have made the greatest contribution to reducing the rate of child malnutrition, being responsible for 43 percent of the total reduction. Improvements in women's status, proxied by the ratio of female to male life expectancy, make up 12 percent. Improvements in food availability came a distant second to women's education, contributing 26 percent to the reduction rate.

The gains are not confined to investments in women's education. Reducing inequalities within the household in human capital, land, and inputs used by women can increase crop yields by 20–25 percent, based on simulations from African data (Alderman et al. 1995; Quisumbing 1996). Improving gender equality can also improve governance. Swamy et al. (2001) use several independent micro datasets to show that women are less involved in bribery and in bribe-taking. Cross-country data from 98 countries, both high and low income, show that corruption, measured using a "graft index," is less severe when women hold a larger share of parliamentary seats and senior positions in the government bureaucracy and comprise a larger share of the labor force.

The above evidence suggests that there are complementarities, rather than substitution, in the pursuit of distributional versus efficiency goals. Yet if governments have to make tradeoffs among distributional goals—for example, between those related to gender and those related to family background, such as poverty—gender equality may be a less pressing concern. However, if there is a strong correlation between gender and poverty, then addressing gender equity may provide additional policy levers to help in poverty reduction. Smith et al. (2003), using data on 112,970 children under three years of age from 36 developing countries, found that women's status has a significant positive effect on children's nutritional status. Women's status also has the greatest influence where it is lowest—being most important in South Asia, followed by Sub-Saharan Africa, and then Latin America and the Caribbean. In both South Asia and Sub-Saharan Africa, the developing regions with the highest poverty rates, women's status and households' economic status are fundamentally interlinked. In these regions, it makes sense to target the poorest households for improvements in women's status because it is in these households that both child nutritional status and women's status are the lowest. Indeed, some governments have made improvements in women's control of resources a central feature of their poverty-reduction strategy. For example, Mexico's National Program for Education, Health and Nutrition (PROGRESA) uses explicit gender targeting of monetary transfers to women and of higher educational subsidies to girls (Skoufias 2001).

Although returns to investment in women can be realized even if a woman does not work outside the home—in better education, health, and nutrition of her children, for example—low market returns to women's education often reduce parents' incentives to invest in their daughters' education. In many societies, low participation by women in the labor force may be the result of social and cultural constraints on women's mobility outside the home. In rural Pakistan, for example, women's education and nutrition have insignificant effects on economic productivity (Fafchamps and Quisumbing 1999). In such settings, societal restrictions may create a gap between private and social returns to investing in women. Thus, the goal of government policy is to identify those sectors or markets in which such "distortions" exist and to implement policies to eliminate or lessen them.

Land Inheritance and Schooling: A Conceptual Framework

Our empirical strategy is based on the application of a conceptual framework of intergenerational transfers to different forms of transfers in our study sites.[2] Suppose that parents can transfer either assets (land) or human capital (education) to their children. Following the wealth model of transfers (Becker 1974; Becker and Tomes 1979, 1986), we assume that parents are both altruistic and egalitarian. If parental investments in children are motivated by the goal of maximizing lifetime welfare, as suggested by the wealth model, parents may give more of one resource to the child who will derive higher returns from that resource, perhaps owing to a greater comparative advantage in using that resource. Therefore, if women have a comparative advantage in nonfarm work and returns to their schooling are higher in nonfarm jobs than in farming, daughters will receive more schooling than sons, as in the case of the Philippines. If women are subject to labor market discrimination, they will be less likely to have a comparative advantage in nonfarm work. Similarly, if women specialize in rice farming and men in commercial tree crop farming, daughters inherit paddy land and men inherit tree fields, as in Sumatra. To the extent that women are subject to social "discrimination" in the acquisition of land, as in Ghana, daughters may receive smaller land areas than sons do, even though parents have equal concerns about the welfare of daughters and sons.[3] Even under our assumption of egalitarian motives, parents may decide to transfer all of their assets to a single individual if there are increasing returns to assets or strong

---

2. For a detailed exposition of the conceptual framework and its application to different types of land, see the appendix to this chapter.

3. As will be discussed in Part III, inheritance of land is traditionally determined by the extended family, which usually consists of more than 10 nuclear families. Thus, it is not parents but the extended family, following community inheritance rules, that determines the extent of discrimination against women in intergenerational land transfers.

economies of scope or complementarity between different assets. Indeed, parents may decide to do so if they are sure that this individual could make the most profitable use of the assets and would make transfers to render the outcome egalitarian. Although such a case does not seem likely, it is theoretically possible. Therefore, it is important to examine empirically the existence of increasing returns and asset complementarities to support or disprove our central hypothesis.

The model also predicts that parents' investment strategies will change if there are changes in the relative returns to investment in children as a result of agricultural development, the expansion of nonfarm employment opportunities, or changes in the demand for male and female labor, as in the case of agroforestry.

Parents may also have different objectives motivating transfers to children. Aside from future returns that the children would bring to them (Rosenzweig 1986), parents may consider their preferences for inter-sibling equality (Behrman, Pollak, and Taubman 1982) or tradeoffs between equity and efficiency (Pitt, Rosenzweig, and Hassan 1990). The parental allocation rules may be modified by disagreement between parents and also by non-altruistic transfer motives. If parents disagree, or if they do not pool their incomes, the common preference model with a single parental utility function as discussed in the appendix to this chapter does not hold and the outcome of the allocation will be the result of bargaining between parents (see, for example, McElroy 1990). As in other household allocation outcomes (see Thomas 1990, 1994), intergenerational transfers may reflect individualistic preferences of husband and wife in decisionmaking; thus the differential bargaining power of parents may influence the allocation of land and education to children. Our empirical strategy therefore provides an opportunity to test the collective versus the unitary model of the household. A collective model of the household, which does not assume that parents share the same preferences, may be especially relevant to Ghana, where husbands and wives maintain "separate purses" and do not pool their resources (Doss 1996a). In such a case, although wife and husband have different utility functions, they are both egalitarian and give equal utility weights to daughters and sons.[4]

---

4. Empirical estimates for the United States that take into account both child earnings and marriage market outcomes provide evidence that parents either exhibit equal concern or slightly favor girls (Behrman, Pollak, and Taubman 1986). In contrast, evidence from South India suggests that during the surplus season there is significant inequality aversion and equal concern, but during the lean season unequal concern significantly favors older children over younger children and sons over daughters (Behrman 1988).

Gender Issues in Agriculture

We postulate that changes in the demand for male and female labor in farming are a driving force that induces the evolution of land inheritance rules, changing the distribution of land between daughters and sons. From this perspective, it is instructive to review changes and differences in the relative demand for male and female labor in farming systems across different regions of the world, including our three study sites.

Overview

Farming systems can be classified into three general types: (1) extensively cultivated, land-abundant systems; (2) intensively cultivated, labor-using systems with a unimodal farm size distribution; and (3) dualistic systems with different factor intensities between large and small farms (Boserup 1970; Lele 1986). These three types have usually been associated with Africa, Asia, and Latin America, respectively, although changes in relative resource endowments (for example, increasing population pressure on limited land in Africa) have caused these associations to break down gradually.

The African farming system was traditionally characterized by female farming during the era of shifting cultivation, before the plow and cash crops were introduced. Food crop production is the main task of women, who clean the burned fields and plant, weed, harvest, and carry the crop for storage or consumption. Men do little except in the felling of trees, which is mainly done by young boys of 15 to 18 years old (Boserup 1970). The female farming system is considered "traditional" because it is not based on scientific methods and does not use modern industrial inputs.

The Asian type of agriculture is characterized by numerous small and marginal farms and a large number of landless households. Extensive plow cultivation is the norm and male labor input is more dominant. Although female labor is used, it is much less compared with the African mode. There is an ample supply of labor in rural areas in Asia and hired labor is widely substituted for family labor. Women's participation in farming in the Asian mode is low partly owing to cultural norms prohibiting women from participating in farming (for example, South Asia) and the presence of the plow, which is more efficiently used by male labor. In some regions in Asia characterized by intensive cultivation of small irrigated land, both men and women must devote much time to farming to be able to meet the family's subsistence needs on a small piece of land.

The Latin American mode of farming is characterized by dualistic agriculture: a large modern plantation sector coexists with small subsistence peasant farms. The plantation sector uses a large proportion of hired labor, which is predominantly male, and a minimum of female family labor. However, female labor participation in this sector may not be minimal if we include indirect production activities (for example, cooking for hired workers). In peasant farming, women are involved in input control, such as seed selection and storage, and the disposal of output, whereas men are primarily responsible for the timely application of inputs such as fertilizer and collecting manure (Deere 1982).

An alternative typology of farming systems focuses not only on labor input by men and women, but also on access to the means of production, participation in decisionmaking, and control over the outcome of the productive process (Deere and Leon 1982). Taking these factors into account enables us to distinguish between male and female farming systems. In a patriarchal family system, for example, both men and women provide labor but men control the decisionmaking and disposal of production. In an egalitarian family system, on the other hand, both men and women participate in the production, decisionmaking, and control over the disposal of production.

In most of Sub-Saharan Africa, there is a clear sexual division of labor between crops or between farming operations. Households hold several granaries or purses, controlled by men or women depending on different but complementary responsibilities to the household (Dey 1981, 1985). Women are more heavily involved in the production of traditional food crops (such as swamp rice in The Gambia and maize in Kenya), whereas men contribute more labor to cash crops (irrigated rice in The Gambia and sugarcane in Kenya). The contributions of male and female labor based on several case studies are shown in Table 1.1. More recent evidence suggests that women in Sub-Saharan Africa are now increasingly involved in cash crop cultivation as well (Saito, Spurling, and Mekonnen 1994). The African mode is in sharp contrast to the Asian mode of a joint family farm, where men control land, labor, and other inputs but women are responsible for the disposal of output. Asian women also contribute a substantial portion of the total labor input in both food and cash crop production (maize and sugarcane in the Philippines and rice in many parts of Asia).

In Asian rice farming, much of women's labor contribution is hired labor in such activities as transplanting, harvesting, and weeding (Unnevehr and Stanford 1985: 2). Familial female labor is most importantly engaged in selecting, storing, and testing rice seeds for germination. The female labor contribution in Asia varies from about 50 percent in Nepal and India to more than 30 percent in Malaysia, Indonesia, China, Korea, and Japan; the exception is the Philippines, where women contribute less than 20 percent. As far as rice land in Asia is concerned, we expect that men inherit more land, or at least not less, than women do.

Labor Use by Gender and Crop in our Study Sites

Table 1.2 presents the average labor use by gender and crop in our study sites (see the country chapters for details). Labor in lowland rice production in the Philippines is male dominated: about three-fourths of the total labor use is accounted for by male labor, both family and hired. This implies that female

TABLE 1.1 Labor input by men, women, and children in Sub-Saharan Africa and Asia

Country and crop	Men (percent of family labor)	Women (percent of family labor)	Children (percent of children's labor)
The Gambia[a]			
Fully water-controlled rice	69	31	2
Swamp rice	17	83	6
Kenya[b]			
Maize	46	54	4
Sugarcane	90	10	. . .
Philippines			
Maize[c]	52	48	37
Sugarcane[c]	53	47	38
Rice[d]	89	11	. . .
Percent of total labor in rice production			
East Java, Indonesia[e]			
Traditional rice	35	65	. . .
Improved rice varieties	47	53	. . .
Central Java, Indonesia[e]			
Improved rice varieties	63	37	. . .
Nepal[f]	46	54	. . .
Andhra Pradesh, India[f]	52	48	. . .
Tamil Nadu, India[f]	55	45	. . .
Malaysia[f]	63	37	. . .
East Java, Indonesia[f]	65	35	. . .
Philippines[f]	81	19	. . .
China[f]	67	33	. . .
Korea[f]	64	36	. . .
Japan[f]	60	40	. . .

[a] Von Braun, Puetz, and Webb (1989).

[b] Kennedy (1989).

[c] Bouis and Haddad (1990).

[d] Res (1985).

[e] Sajogyo (1985); refers to total labor input.

[f] Unnevehr and Stanford (1985).

members of farm households work primarily at home or in the nonfarm sectors. Male labor is dominant in land preparation, crop establishment, application of chemical inputs, and threshing, whereas both male and female laborers are employed in weeding and harvesting. We conclude that rice farming in the Philippines is a predominantly male job.

TABLE 1.2 Average labor use, by gender and crop, in the study sites

Country and crop	Labor input (person-days/hectare)	Percent of family labor	
		Male	Female
Philippines			
Central Luzon			
Lowland rice	55.0	93	7
Panay			
Lowland rice	43.0	67	33
Indonesia			
Low region			
Upland rice	175.5	32	68
Young rubber	51.7	83	17
Mature rubber	94.9	91	9
Middle region			
Wet rice	221.6	57	43
Young cinnamon	67.7	55	45
Mature cinnamon	24.8	30	70
Ghana			
Young cocoa	96.8	65	35
Mature cocoa	61.0	68	32
Pure food crops	138.2	52	48

NOTE: In the Philippines the reference period is one season, whereas in Indonesia and Ghana it is one year.

In the low-lying region in Sumatra, called the Low Region, upland rice is very intensive in female family labor. Women contribute 68 percent of family labor input and men only 32 percent. However, both young and mature rubber plots utilize substantial inputs from male family members. This may at least partly explain why the matrilineal inheritance system has been gradually replaced by a patrilineal system for rubber plots, thereby providing incentives to the males who do much of the work on these plots. The dominance of the female labor for upland rice is consistent with the prevalence of ownership of upland fields by women and also conforms to social norms regarding women's role in household food security.

In the Middle Region in Sumatra, both wet rice and young cinnamon cultivation use male and female family labor relatively equally. Women are more involved in mature cinnamon cultivation, accounting for 70 percent of family labor input. The proportions are slightly different when both hired and family labor are considered. It is therefore no surprise that men and women inherit both paddy fields and cinnamon fields more or less equally in the Middle Region, even though by tradition only women can inherit land in the matrilineal societies of Sumatra (Quisumbing and Otsuka 2001).

In our Ghana sites, the family labor of women (particularly the wife) and children accounts for about one-third of total labor inputs in cocoa production. Women now own nearly one-third of cocoa fields, despite the prohibition on landownership by women under the customary land tenure rules in the Akan matrilineal society. This is because land is transferred as a gift to a wife and daughters if they help establish cocoa crop fields.[5] The production of food crops utilizes almost equal proportions of male and female labor, even though women seldom own this type of land (for reasons to be explained in Chapter 8).

In sum, the composition of male and female labor input in farming varies considerably across different regions and different types of crops. An interesting observation is that variations in labor use by gender in different types of farming are largely consistent with differences in land inheritance by daughters and sons.

Production Function Studies

Numerous studies have found that, where male and female farmers manage separate plots, as in many African farming systems, plots controlled by women have lower yields than plots farmed by men. Studies analyzing the technical efficiency of male and female farmers have suggested that this is the result of lower levels of input on women's plots, and not of inherent managerial differences between male and female farmers (Quisumbing 1996). For example, studies from Kenya, Thailand, and Korea show that, after controlling for education, age, and levels of land, labor, fertilizer, and other inputs, female farmers are as efficient as male farmers (Moock 1976; Jamison and Lau 1982; Saito, Spurling, and Mekonnen 1994).

Simulations using coefficients from the production functions estimated in these studies suggest there may be significant gains from increasing women's levels of physical and human capital. Simulations using Moock's (1976) coefficients for female farmers indicate that, if female maize farmers had the age, education, and input levels of the sample average, their yield would increase by 7 percent. If they were given men's mean input levels, age, and education, yields would increase by 9 percent. Giving all women at least a year of primary education raises yields by 24 percent, which reflects the gains from providing primary education where women have very low educational levels. Simulations with the coefficients of Saito, Spurling, and Mekonnen (1994) suggest a 22 percent increase in women's yields on maize, bean, and cowpea plots if women farmers were given the age, education, and input levels of male farmers. However, these studies do not take into account the endogenous relationships between input application and farmer characteristics. Because farmers with more education are more likely to adopt new technologies and apply mod-

---

5. The transfer of land to sons as a gift has been practiced historically (Hill 1963), but the incidence of gifts to wives and daughters seems to have increased recently.

ern inputs, the contribution of such inputs may be overstated and that of education underemphasized. The consequences of underinvesting in women's education in rural areas may therefore be underestimated.

More recent literature suggests that asymmetry in the roles and obligations within the household, particularly in African farming systems, may underlie women's lower yields. A study in Burkina Faso (Udry 1996) found that plots controlled by women have significantly lower yields than similar plots within the household planted with the same crop in the same year, but controlled by men. The yield differentials are the result of lower input intensity on female-managed plots: much less male labor per hectare is devoted to plots controlled by women than to similar plots controlled by men. Child labor and unpaid exchange labor are also applied more intensively to plots controlled by men. Moreover, virtually all fertilizer is concentrated on plots controlled by men, even though the marginal product of fertilizer diminishes. These differences in input intensity between male- and female-managed plots persist even after land quality, measurement error, or risk management behaviors are taken into account.

If the husband and wife had common objectives and preferences, reallocating resources from men's to women's plots could increase the household's aggregate output for everyone's benefit. The consistently higher input intensities on men's plots indicate a misallocation of household resources owing to stronger incentives for individuals to achieve high output on their own plots and to imperfect labor allocation processes within the household. Alderman et al. (1995) suggest that a reallocation of current factors of production across plots could increase the value of household output by 10 to 20 percent.

The lower productivity of plots managed by women may be attributed to social norms in favor of men—for example, the obligation on a woman to work in her husband's fields with no reciprocal obligation on men (Kevane and Wydick 2001). Or social discrimination against women in general may weaken the bargaining position of women within a household. In this study, we pay special attention to the role of social discrimination in land inheritance and the productivity of parcels owned by women in Ghana and Sumatra. As far as yields are concerned, however, we did not find any significant differences between men's and women's plots in our two research sites. In the Philippines, because rice farming is essentially a man's job and rice is jointly cultivated on family plots, the gender difference in farm productivity is not a major issue.

Gender Differences in Access to Land and Schooling

Data Collection Methodology

Comparisons of gender differences in land through time have hitherto been impossible because of the absence of longitudinal or historical data on men's and women's landholdings, whereas schooling data are more readily available. A major contribution of this study is the collection and analysis of gender-disaggregated data on land and schooling over three generations: the parents of our survey respondents; our respondents, their spouses, and their siblings; and the children of the respondents and their spouses.

In all three case studies, we designed a retrospective household survey of land inheritance and schooling over three generations. Although each survey was designed to take into account site-specific differences in land tenure institutions and kinship patterns, the basic structure of the survey is similar across countries. The retrospective survey on inheritance was patterned after a similar survey in the Philippines (Quisumbing 1994); it included questions on the parents, siblings, and children of the respondents, yielding information on three generations—called the parents', respondents', and children's generations.[6] The respondents were asked about pre-marriage wealth (schooling and land-ownership) of their parents and in-laws (and, where relevant, other familial sources of inheritance), the schooling and inheritance of their spouses, and the schooling and proposed land transfers to their children. Each respondent was also asked to list all of his or her siblings, their dates of birth, their educational attainment, and the areas of different types of land that they received or expected to receive from their parents or, if applicable, other relatives. In many cases, respondents received land at marriage, but stood to inherit more land after their parents' death. As will be explained in the country chapters, we collected the inheritance and schooling data from respondents (mainly husbands but often husbands and wives together). The presence of the spouse made it easier to obtain more accurate information on the spouse's parents' generation. We believe that recall error is likely to be very small, as respondents answered the questions very clearly and without hesitation. Our questions focused on the major forms of wealth in these rural communities because recall is likely to be good for large assets such as land, compared with smaller assets such as livestock and consumer durables. Moreover, most of such transfers occurred at the time of the respondents' marriage, an event of major significance in their lives, and we expect recall bias to be less than for transfers that occurred at a different time (with the exception perhaps of the parents' death).

Note, however, that, because the inheritance retrospectives were based on a random sample of respondents, our data on land and schooling will be representative of the respondent's generation, not the parents' generation. Information on parents, being obtained through respondent reports rather than self-reports, is likely to be less accurate than information on the respondents or on their children, as most children in the sample still live with their parents. Thus, it is possible that the error structure of the respondents' recall of their parents may be different from that of their own reports. Reporting bias is also likely to

---

6. The grandchild generation is called the child generation for brevity.

be greater for less educated populations (for example, Ghana) compared with better educated populations (for example, the Philippines), and for less educated households within each study site. Our estimation procedure, which takes into account unobserved family-level characteristics, deals with this possible bias in respondents' reports, because information on the parents' generation will be the same for all members of that family. Also, biases due to respondent education will be eliminated by the fixed-effects procedure, because the respondent would be the same for all observations within a particular family.[7] For respondent and spouse reports on the child generation, we are confident that there are no systematic biases that cannot be addressed with the family fixed-effects procedure, because, unlike recalls of morbidity (as in Thomas, Contreras, and Frankenberg 2002), the outcomes under study—questions on years of schooling and proposed land bequests—are easier to answer. Moreover, most of the respondents' children were still coresident at the time of the survey. We discuss the specifics of the estimation procedure in the country chapters.

Gender Differences in Land Inheritance

Although land is undoubtedly an important asset in agrarian communities of developing countries, men and women have unequal access to land in many countries, including our study sites. In Kenya, Malawi, Nigeria and Zambia, for example, the area cultivated by women ranges from one-third to two-thirds of the area cultivated by men (see Table 1.3). Land cultivated per person, however, does not differ appreciably between male- and female-headed households. Women's unfavorable access to land at present is an issue of serious concern if it has been deteriorating over time.

Our study uses retrospective data on land inheritance for the parent and respondent generations and prospective data on the child generation. In the Philippines, the fathers and mothers of the respondents owned and operated larger areas of land than their children. On the average, the fathers of the respondents owned 1.4 hectares of land and mothers owned 0.6 hectares at the time of marriage. The average size of the households' joint operational landholdings at the time of marriage was 3.5 hectares, which is larger than the sum of owned landholdings because of additional land acquired through tenancy arrangements. Share tenancy was the most common land tenure contract, particularly in Central Luzon. Landownership by females was significantly lower than that by males in the generation of the respondents' parents, even when land was relatively abundant. Owing to the practice of partible inheritance,

---

7. It is, however, possible that reports may vary by the age and birth order of siblings or of children, and in that case reporting error would be correlated with age and statistical tests would be inconsistent (Thomas, Contreras, and Frankenberg 2002). We do not deal explicitly with this type of measurement error in our study, but one option in the sibling analysis would be to include a dummy for the respondent's self-report in the analysis. This method was used in Quisumbing (1994).

TABLE 1.3 Size of cultivation area, by gender of farm manager or household head, in selected countries in Africa

Country and year	Area cultivated		Family size		Area per person	
	Male	Female	Male	Female	Male	Female
Kenya 1973[a,b]	1.8	1.2	n.a.	n.a.	n.a.	n.a.
Kenya 1989[c,d]	2.6	1.7	8.6	8.0	0.30	0.21
Malawi 1983–84[c,d]	1.3	0.9	4.9	4.0	0.26	0.22
Nigeria 1989[c,d]	2.6	0.8	7.6	4.9	0.34	0.16
Zambia 1986[a,d,e]	6.8	3.0*	3.5	1.7**	1.94	1.76

SOURCES: Kenya 1973 from Moock (1976); Kenya 1989 and Nigeria 1989 from Saito, Spurling, and Mekonnen (1994); Malawi 1983–84 from Texler Segal (1986); Zambia 1986 from Sikapande (1988).

NOTES: n.a. means not available. * indicates differences between means significant at the 5 percent level; ** at the 1 percent level.

[a] Area in acres.

[b] By gender of farm manager.

[c] Area in hectares.

[d] By gender of household head.

[e] Family size in adult-equivalents.

the respondents and their siblings inherited smaller areas of land than their parents' landholdings. On the average, male and female children in the respondents' generation received 0.6 and 0.2 hectares, respectively. The average size of landholding of the respondents' households as of the 1997 survey was only 1.5 hectares, which is much smaller than that of their parents. Despite such changes, the proportion of female inherited land has remained largely unchanged (see Figure 1.1).

Because the proportion of land inherited by females has remained consistently below 50 percent, it is clear that there has also been a persistent preference in land bequests in favor of male heirs across generations in the Philippines. The first-born son is particularly favored because it is common in the Philippines to give land to the eldest son and to provide schooling to other children to prepare them for urban jobs. Married children of either gender receive significantly more land than their single siblings do. Moreover, married males inherit more land than married females because land usually forms the main portion of the dowry given to a son upon marriage (Andersen 1962).

We hypothesize that land is preferentially given to sons because rice farming is more intensive in male labor and returns to male labor are higher than those to female labor. Among family members, the husband is more heavily involved than female members in rice production. Given the declining importance of female labor in rice farming, we expect that daughters inherit less land

FIGURE 1.1 Proportion of land inherited by females in the study sites across generations

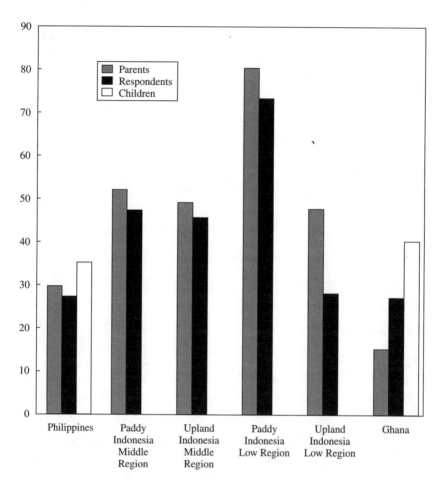

to the extent that land inheritance decisions are made in accordance with the value of land to each child.

Nonland assets passed on to the next generation include residential houses and lots, draft animals, capital equipment, vehicles, household durables, and cash. Whereas traditionally the youngest son receives the parental house and lot, it is increasingly common for the child who takes care of elderly parents to inherit the parental house and lot, regardless of birth order. We did not include nonland assets in our analysis because only 40 percent of the sample households in 1997 had decided on future bequests of nonland assets to heirs.

In the Low Region of Indonesia, mothers' inherited holdings of lowland (paddy land) tended to be larger than their husbands' in the parents' generation, reflecting the tradition of matrilineal descent. This pattern was weaker for upland (agroforestry land) and has become even weaker over generations: although daughters maintain the matrilineal custom of inheriting paddy, having larger areas than their brothers, they receive less agroforestry land and bush-fallow area. Moreover, in the Middle Region, which has traditionally been settled by matrilineal communities, daughters and sons have had approximately equal inherited areas of paddy land and agroforestry land, though there is a tendency for daughters to have inherited larger agroforestry areas and smaller bush-fallow areas. Thus, a gender-differentiated pattern of inheritance seems to have been emerging that is different from the traditional matrilineal system.[8]

An interesting feature of the Ghana survey site is the complexity of inheritance sources and potential heirs owing to the uterine matrilineal system and the practice of polygyny. Under the matrilineal system, a person can inherit from a number of matrilineal relatives, depending on the order of succession. As a result of polygyny and the practice of serial marriage, an individual may have several sets of maternal and paternal half-siblings. Land rights received from the extended family differ markedly depending on the manner of acquisition, that is, whether by inheritance, allocation, or gift.

Figure 1.1 presents information on the proportion of land inherited or to be inherited by women among the Akans over the three generations of households. At the time of marriage or independent farming, Akan fathers had 8.3 hectares of land, compared with only 1.6 hectares for mothers. This is consistent with our previous analysis of patterns of land acquisition in the parents' generations (Quisumbing et al. 2001a): men typically start farming independently by clearing forests, whereas women heads of household are less likely to acquire forestland. In the respondents' generation, land sizes at the time of marriage had declined markedly for both males and females, and proposed sizes of land to be bestowed on children had likewise declined, but not by as much as the decline between the parents' and respondents' generation. More importantly, disparities in landholding sizes between males and females are becoming smaller among Akan households. Whereas fathers had 5 to 9 times as much land as mothers in the parent generation, husbands had only 1.7 to 2.6 times as much land as their wives. In the child generation, Akan sons would stand to inherit about 40 percent more than their sisters. It seems clear that the gender gap in landownership has been narrowing through time in our sites in western Ghana.

Thus, it appears that land inheritance rules are by no means rigid institutions that are immune to change. Our country case studies clearly show changes

---

8. Because respondents' children are generally very young in the Sumatra site, the respondents had not decided to whom land would be bequeathed. Therefore, we were unable to obtain expected land inheritance data by gender in Sumatra.

in land inheritance patterns over time, indicating that inheritance rules are dynamic. The identification of factors affecting changes in the distribution of inheritance by gender is therefore an important topic in the study of gender equity.

Gender Differences in Schooling

Secondary data on literacy and schooling by gender are more widely available than those on land inheritance. According to the data compiled by the United Nations Educational, Scientific and Cultural Organization (UNESCO 1999), both female and male illiteracy rates have declined significantly over time, but the decline in the female illiteracy rate is more pronounced (see Figure 1.2). In Africa, the female illiteracy rate declined by 33 percentage points and the male illiteracy rate declined by 29 percentage points between 1970 and 2000. In Asia, female illiteracy rates dropped by 29 percentage points, while the corresponding decline in male illiteracy rates was 20 percentage points. Among the three countries where our study sites are located, the Philippines has the lowest illiteracy rates and the rates are almost the same for men and women. Ghana, which had a higher level of illiteracy in 1970 than Indonesia and the Philippines, experienced the greatest decline in illiteracy rates between 1980 and 2000. Thus, compared with the other countries, women in Ghana appear to have experienced the greatest improvement in both their share of inherited land and reduction in illiteracy, though the illiteracy rate remains high at 39 percent in 2000. In terms of our conceptual framework, these observations suggest that, in Ghana, both the demand for women's farm labor and returns to women's education have increased over time.

As is shown in Figures 1.3, 1.4, and 1.5, female school enrollment rates have generally risen over time compared with male rates at primary, secondary, and tertiary levels. Primary school enrollment rates flattened out as early as the 1970s in the Philippines, and in the 1980s in Indonesia and Ghana. By 1990, Indonesia had caught up with the Philippines in terms of primary school enrollment rate. The gender gap in primary schooling enrollment declined markedly in Ghana and Indonesia in the 1970s and 1980s. The Philippines has been characterized by minimal gender disparity in primary school enrollment since the 1970s.

The gender gap in secondary school enrollment is higher in Ghana than in the Philippines and Indonesia. The gap had been eliminated in the Philippines by 1980 and in Indonesia by the late 1990s. Although the gender gap in secondary schooling enrollment rate remained high at 14 percentage points in Ghana in 1990, it is important to note that it has also been declining over time.

School enrollment rates at the tertiary level are much lower but increasing everywhere (see Figure 1.5). It is also clear that the gender gap has been generally declining. A salient feature of the Philippines is that the female enrollment rate has surpassed the male rate for several decades. As will be shown shortly, the schooling of females exceeds that of males in the younger genera-

FIGURE 1.2 Illiteracy rates in the world, Africa, Asia, and the countries of our study sites

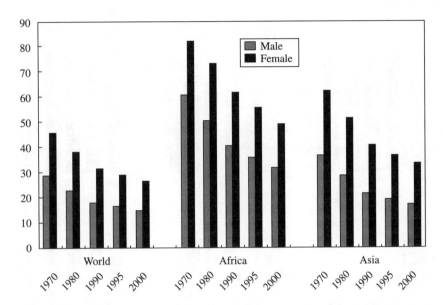

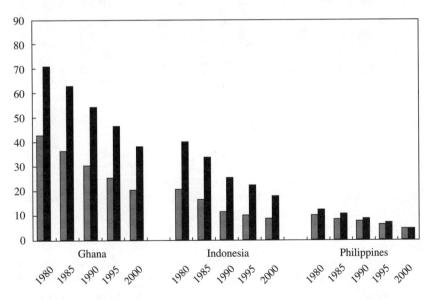

SOURCE: UNESCO database.

FIGURE 1.3 Gross primary enrollment rates in the world, Africa, Asia, and the countries of our study sites

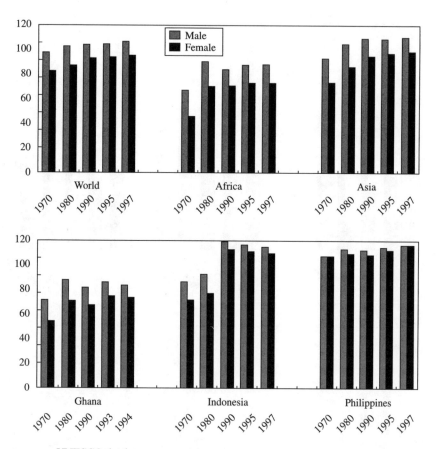

SOURCE: UNESCO database.

tion in our sample households. In contrast, the gender gap persists in Ghana and has only recently disappeared in Indonesia.

Overall, there seems to be a strong tendency for the gender gap in schooling to narrow in most countries. It may well be that widespread universal education and other global changes have contributed to the reduction in the gender gap in schooling. It is also possible that discrimination against women in rural communities and in nonfarm jobs has declined over time, which stimulates investment in women's schooling.

Table 1.4 summarizes the gender gap in schooling in three generations of our sample households by location. The schooling of respondents, their parents,

FIGURE 1.4 Gross secondary enrollment rates in the world, Africa, Asia, and the countries of our study sites

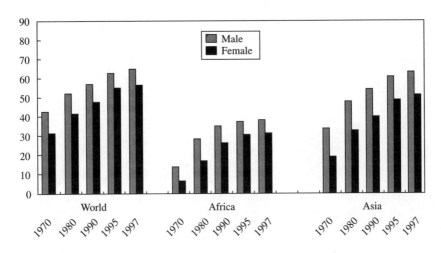

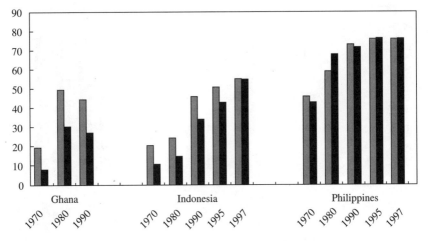

SOURCE: UNESCO database.

and their children is largely consistent with the country-level trends we have observed. In the Philippines, the parents of respondents had very little schooling: fathers obtained significantly more schooling (3.7 completed years in school) than mothers (3.2 completed years in school). Males were favored presumably because of the higher wage premium to male schooling in that generation, when relatively few outside income-earning opportunities existed for women. The respondents and their siblings completed 2.5–3.0 more years of

FIGURE 1.5 Gross tertiary enrollment rates in the world, Africa, Asia, and the countries of our study sites

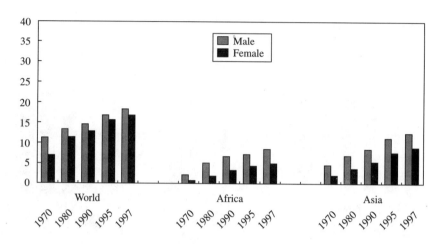

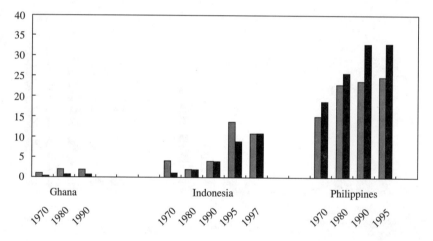

SOURCE: UNESCO database.

schooling relative to their parents. Females were favored in schooling investments, resulting in the disappearance of gender differences in schooling among respondents and their spouses. There have been marked improvements in schooling attainment between the respondents' and the children's generations. On the average, female respondents finished primary schooling (6 completed years in school), and their daughters finished secondary school (10 completed years in school). Male respondents also finished primary schooling, and their sons finished middle high school (8.5 completed years of schooling).

TABLE 1.4 Gender differences in schooling in the study sites

	Years in school (mean)	
Country and generation	Male	Female
Philippines		
Parents' generation	3.7	3.2
Respondents' and spouses' generation	6.2	6.2
Children of respondents[a]	8.5	10.0
Middle Region, Sumatra, Indonesia		
Parents' generation	3.7	2.8
Respondents' and spouses' generation	8.9	8.0
Children of respondents[b]	7.4	5.8
Low Region, Sumatra, Indonesia		
Parents' generation	2.9	1.7
Respondents' and spouses' generation	7.1	4.6
Children of respondents[b]	4.8	4.9
Ghana, Akan		
Parents' generation[c]	1.6	0.3
Respondents' and spouses' generation	7.2	3.8
Children of respondents[a]	8.6	6.9

[a] Children aged 21 years and over.

[b] Children aged 7–21 years.

[c] Refers to the parents of the head and coresident spouse.

The most remarkable finding is the clear gender gap in schooling in favor of women in the children's generation in the Philippines. This would imply that investment in women's education has become more profitable (Deolalikar 1993). Moreover, because schooling has a relatively small impact on farm income compared with nonfarm income, the increased investment by respondents in their children's education likely represents a response to the rise in returns to schooling in the nonfarm sector. It is interesting that the gender gap in schooling in favor of girls has declined among the younger children of respondents who are of school age (Estudillo, Quisumbing, and Otsuka 2001d). Moreover, we found no significant gender bias in schooling expenditures in this generation, indicating that parental preferences with respect to schooling investments have become egalitarian.

Table 1.4 also presents data on years of schooling of three generations of sample household members in the Low and Middle Region sample villages in Indonesia. In both regions, fathers obtained one more year of schooling than mothers. In the Low Region, where large areas of unexploited land were still available, schooling levels were lower than in the Middle Region. This observation may suggest that land and schooling are substitutable means of transferring parents' wealth to children, even though other factors potentially affecting schooling decisions may also be different between the two regions. Years of completed schooling increased in the respondents' generation: in contrast to their fathers, who had 3.3 years of schooling, sons have 8.0 years of schooling on the average. Daughters have lower educational attainments than sons, at 6.3 years on the average. For both generations, educational attainments are lower and the gender gap is more pronounced in the Low Region than in the Middle Region. In fact, there is no significant difference in schooling between men and women in the respondents' generation in the Middle Region. Among children aged 7–21 years in the Middle Region, we found that daughters are younger by three years than sons, and thus completed schooling is less than sons' by nearly two years. It appears that older daughters are either married or employed in nonfarm jobs outside the village.[9] In the Low Region, the average age and schooling attainment of daughters and sons aged 7–21 years are the same. Overall, we found that schooling investments in respondents' daughters and sons appear to have become equalized in our Sumatra sites.

Lastly, Table 1.4 presents summary statistics regarding the schooling of the parent, respondent, and child generations among Akan households in Ghana sites. Only households for which parental information is complete are included in the table and, for the respondent generation, only children who survived to 21 years of age are included. The general level of schooling in the parents' generation is low—84 percent of fathers and 94 percent of mothers had never been to school—and fathers had completed more years of schooling than mothers (1.6 compared with 0.3 years). Schooling attainment has increased in the respondents' generation, but it is still low. Husbands completed 7.2 years of schooling, whereas the mean for wives is 3.8 years. However, the gender gap in terms of the ratio of female to male schooling seems to have narrowed considerably over generations, reflecting the tendency for women's schooling levels to increase through time as public educational systems expand into more remote areas. The gap between males and females is much narrower in the child generation: 1.7 years for those older than 21 years of age; 1.2 years for those aged 13–21 years; and only 1.0 year for those aged 7–13 years.

It is encouraging from the viewpoint of gender equity that the gender gap in schooling has been narrowing universally in various countries and specifically in our study sites, which in Ghana and Indonesia are in poor and agriculturally marginal areas.

Schooling and Female Labor Force Participation Rates

An important question is whether schooling has a positive impact on women's labor force participation rates because returns to investments in schooling are more concretely realized in wages received in the job market. According to the

---

9. We do not notice similar age gaps in our other study sites.

World Bank (2001: 208, Table 5.2), female labor force participation rates in East Asia have risen, as indicated by an increase in the female share of the labor force. The increase is largely attributed to an increase in labor demand—rather than to the narrowing of the gender gap in schooling—that attracted large numbers of women to the job market. Entry of women into the labor force worldwide is more evident in wage employment (Schultz 1990), owing perhaps to the restructuring of production activity and employment in the formal sector that allows increased female participation.

According to Cameron, Dowling, and Worswick (2001), labor market participation by women in Korea, Thailand, Sri Lanka, Indonesia, and the Philippines is affected more significantly by schooling attainment and gender roles. Tertiary education is found to have the largest significant impact on women's labor market participation. Among the five countries, women in the Philippines have the highest labor market participation, despite the fact that the female to male ratio of GDP per capita is only 55 percent (UNDP 2000). In Korea and Sri Lanka, countries that are characterized by rigid gender roles, an increase in women's schooling attainment is less likely to increase women's labor market participation rates, perhaps because of the traditionally low bargaining position of women at home. Nor will wages received by women have a considerable impact.

Returns to Schooling by Gender

Since there is a decline in the gender gap in schooling, we would expect to observe a decline in the gender gap in economic returns to schooling or a relatively small gender gap, if schooling investments are motivated by economic returns. Note that it is possible for wage differentials to favor men even if the rate of return to an additional year of schooling is higher for women. In order to ascertain empirically whether such a conjecture is valid, we now review the literature on the returns to schooling by gender in nonfarm jobs and in agricultural production.

Table 1.5 presents estimated returns to schooling derived from wage earnings functions for men and women in rural areas. Rosenzweig (1980) tests predictions about the labor supply behavior of landless and landholding households derived from a neoclassical utility-maximizing model using Indian data from the early 1970s. The coefficient of schooling from a simple earnings function suggests that the rate of return to an additional year of schooling for men is 10 percent, whereas for women it is in the neighborhood of 2 percent. Mukhopadhyay (1991) estimates sample selection-corrected wage functions for rural men and women aged 15–65 using data from West Bengal in 1990 and finds that the private rate of return to female schooling (3.5 percent) is larger than the return to male schooling (1.6 percent). Moreover, women with larger areas of land apparently are able to command higher wages as agricultural

TABLE 1.5 Estimates of returns to schooling in rural areas

Study	Estimation method	Schooling category	Male	Female
Regression coefficients				
India				
Rosenzweig (1980)	Ordinary least squares of wage earnings function	Years of schooling	0.100	0.020
Mukhopadhyay (1991)	Wage earnings function with selectivity correction for wage earner status	Years of schooling	0.0161**	0.0352**
Sri Lanka				
Sahn and Alderman (1988)	Wage earnings function with selectivity correction for labor force participation	Primary school	0.103*	0.178*
		Grade 6–10	0.145*	0.189*
		General Certificate	0.331**	0.571**
		University/postgraduate	0.793**	1.060**
Philippines				
Behrman and Lanzona (1989)	Wage earnings function with selectivity correction for contractual and fixed wages	Years of schooling		
		Wet season	0.084**	0.067**
		Dry season	0.105**	0.070**
Lanzona (1998)	Wage earnings function with selectivity correction for wage earners staying in parental home	Years of schooling	0.0893**	0.0994**
Calculated returns worldwide (percent)				
Psacharopoulos (1994)	Returns to investment in education	Primary	20.1	12.8
		Secondary	13.9	18.4
		Higher	13.4	12.7
		Overall	11.1	12.4

NOTE: * indicates significance at the 5 percent level; ** at the 1 percent level.

workers, which suggests that returns to schooling may be higher for women from wealthier households, possibly because of their higher social status.

Sahn and Alderman's (1988) study in Sri Lanka using selectivity-corrected wage equations shows that, in rural areas, schooling has a positive effect on the wage earnings of both men and women, with gross rates of return increasing with the level of education. Estimates of internal rates of return for continuing one's education to pass the General Certificate of Exams are twice as high for women as for men in rural areas, although the returns for graduating from university are about the same for men and women.

Behrman and Lanzona (1989) find substantial returns to schooling for both men and women in five Philippine rice villages, where modern rice varieties are widely adopted. Male rates of return to an additional year of schooling are 8.4 percent and 10.5 percent in the wet and dry seasons, respectively. The rate of return to female education is about 7.0 percent in both the wet and dry seasons; however, the difference between them is not statistically significant. Similarly, Lanzona (1998) finds that the returns to schooling in the Bicol Region of the Philippines are almost the same or slightly higher for women than for men.

Khandker (1990) uses household survey data from Peru to estimate differences between men and women in returns to schooling. Rates of return to male schooling from the maximum likelihood estimates are 6 percent at the primary level (compared with 8 percent for women); 9 percent for secondary schooling (compared with 13 percent for females); and 26 percent for postsecondary (27 percent for females). The fixed-effects estimates yield an 11 percent rate of return to male schooling at the primary level (compared with 37 percent for females); 17 percent at the secondary level (compared with –2 percent for females); and 42 percent at the postsecondary level (26 percent for females). Although rates of return seem to decline for women after the secondary level using the fixed-effects estimates, in general the private rates of return to schooling in rural areas tend to be higher for women.

Psacharopoulos (1994) finds that the rates of return decline by level of schooling, with the highest return being the return to primary schooling. It seems clear that investments in primary schooling are profitable. The more important finding for our purpose is that rates of return overall to female schooling exceed those for males by more than one percentage point.

The emerging conclusion from this brief literature survey is that returns to schooling investment for women are, in general, not lower than those for men in rural areas. Where they are lower, for example in rural India prior to the Green Revolution, it is possible that the demand for women's labor is low or that women face barriers to participation in the labor market.

Let us finally review the results of farm and nonfarm income functions estimated in the three countries where our study sites are located (see Table 1.6). In the case of rice-growing villages in the Philippines studied by Otsuka, Cordova, and David (1992), it is apparent that the number of years of schooling of

TABLE 1.6 Effects of schooling on farm and nonfarm incomes in the Philippines, Indonesia, and Ghana

Study	Data	Estimation method	Schooling category	Income	
				Farm	Nonfarm
Philippines					
Otsuka, Cordova, and David (1992)	1985	Double logarithm (OLS)	Years of schooling of head	−0.05	0.34*
				(−1.11)	(1.74)
Estudillo and Otsuka (1999)	1966–67	Double logarithm (OLS)	Years of schooling of head	−0.17	0.76*
				(−1.38)	(2.07)
	1986–94	Double logarithm (OLS)	Years of schooling of head	−0.23*	0.27*
				(−2.16)	(1.76)
	1986–94	Double logarithm (OLS)	Proportion of working parents with secondary schooling	−0.56**	0.86**
				(−2.71)	(2.98)
			Tertiary schooling	−0.85**	0.87**
				(−3.16)	(2.39)
			Proportion of working children with primary schooling	−0.61	−0.22
				(−1.45)	(−0.35)

Study	Years	Method	Variable		
			Secondary schooling	−0.59 (−1.53)	0.71 (1.26)
			Tertiary schooling	−1.02** (2.37)	1.69** (2.84)
Indonesia Jatileksono (1994)	1987–88	Double logarithm (OLS)	Years of schooling of head		
			Dry season	−0.01 (−0.82)	
			Wet season	−0.004 (−0.36)	
			Dry and wet season		0.08 (0.78)
Ghana Jolliffe (1998)	1988–89	2SLS (semi log)	Household average English score	−0.011 (−1.46)	0.013 (1.22)
			Household average mathematics score	0.019* (1.97)	0.032** (2.50)

NOTES: OLS means ordinary least squares; 2SLS means two-stage least squares. Numbers in parentheses are t-values; * indicates significance at the 5 percent level; ** at the 1 percent level.

the household head has a positive impact on nonfarm income but has no significant effect on farm income. It seems that the new rice technology did not create the type of disequilibrium that increases returns to schooling. According to Estudillo and Otsuka (1999), the positive impact of schooling on nonfarm income is evident in 1966–67, indicating that schooling was important for finding lucrative nonfarm jobs even in the early years. There is also an indication that the relative importance of the schooling of household heads has declined, as shown by the decrease in the relevant coefficient in the nonfarm income regression from a value of 0.76 in 1966–67 to 0.27 in 1986–94. The schooling of the head has a negative effect on labor income from rice production, which indicates that household heads, if educated, tend to specialize in nonfarm work at the expense of work for rice production. In contrast, children with tertiary schooling appear to be the most active in nonfarm labor activities, as shown by the positive and highly significant coefficient of the proportion of children with tertiary schooling.

Jatileksono (1994) too finds no significant association between the years of schooling of household head and farm income in rice-producing villages in Lampung, Indonesia.[10] These findings are in sharp contrast to the findings in India during the Green Revolution period, in which returns to primary schooling increased during a period of rapid technical change (Foster and Rosenzweig 1996). It is apparent that more educated individuals in India were able to manage the new technology and take greater advantage of the benefits of technical change. Yang (1997: 628) found among Chinese farm households that schooling does not significantly improve labor productivity with respect to routine jobs, but the highest schooling attainment in the household improves allocative decisionmaking. This implies that work specialization at home, whereby the less educated are assigned to farm work and the better educated to nonfarm work, does not have a negative effect on farm efficiency because better educated workers continue to contribute to farm production through agricultural management decisionmaking.

Using a nationally representative dataset from Ghana, Jolliffe (1998) investigates whether measures of cognitive skills such as scores in mathematics and English have an impact on farm and nonfarm incomes. He argues that it is not years of schooling but cognitive skills obtained in school that directly increase workers' productivity and that the use of test scores can in effect control for variations in the quality of schooling. His major finding is that returns to skills are not significant in farm income, but are positive and significant for off-farm income. We may conclude that returns to schooling are higher in nonfarm jobs than in farming. If so, incentives to invest in schooling will increase with

---

10. The studies by Otsuka, Cordova, and David (1992), Estudillo and Otsuka (1999), and Jatileksono (1994) analyze the determinants of household income but do not take into account the effect of schooling on occupational choice.

increases in the availability of nonfarm jobs. We also expect that the gender gap in schooling will be smaller, to the extent that there is no discrimination against women in nonfarm jobs.

Major Hypotheses

Our maintained hypothesis is that parents are egalitarian in their bequest motives toward daughters and sons, even if husband and wife do not share the same utility function.

We postulate that the comparative advantages in farm and nonfarm work or in lowland and upland farming between men and women determine the patterns of wealth transfer to daughters and sons, in the absence of significant increasing returns to certain assets, economies of scope, and discrimination against women. In the Philippines, daughters receive more schooling than sons but sons receive more land than daughters because there is no significant discrimination against women in nonfarm jobs and women have a comparative advantage in nonfarm jobs. We hypothesize that lifetime incomes of daughters and sons are equal if there is no discrimination against women in nonfarm jobs.

In the Low Region of Sumatra, where women work on paddy fields and men work on rubber fields, daughters inherit paddy land and sons inherit rubber fields, even though the matrilineal inheritance system has traditionally been practiced. Similarly, in the Middle Region of Sumatra, where men and women work more or less equally on paddy land and upland areas growing cinnamon trees, daughters and sons inherit similar areas of both paddy land and upland areas.

In Ghana, where the demand for women's labor increased with the adoption of labor-intensive cocoa farming systems, we hypothesize that there will be an increase in the land areas transferred to women. We also postulate that the remaining difference in the inheritance of land between daughters and sons can be attributed to "social discrimination" arising from customary land tenure rules rather than "parental discrimination" against daughters.

Finally, in order to test the egalitarian hypothesis more directly, we estimate expenditure share functions, in which the age and gender composition of the household are included among the explanatory variables, to assess whether there is a significant gender bias in expenditure allocation between daughters and sons. Since household expenditures are determined by parents, the estimation of the expenditure share functions enables us to discern whether there is any parental discrimination based on the gender of household members.

Organization of the Book

Part I explores the issue of gender equity in the context of the Philippine villages. After characterizing our sample villages, households, and individuals, we analyze the determinants of land inheritance and schooling investments, using intergenerational data, and the effects of land and schooling on farm and non-farm incomes of households and individual members using regression analyses. Based on estimates of the agricultural and nonagricultural income functions, we assess the difference in lifetime income between daughters and sons using simulation methods. Finally, we inquire into intrahousehold equity by examining the difference in school attendance of young male and female children and by testing for gender bias in expenditure allocations.

Part II presents the case study of Sumatra, and Part III presents the case of Ghana. The organization of each part is essentially similar to Part I. Compared with the Philippine site, however, land tenure institutions are far more complex in these two sites. Thus, we allocate more space to the characterization of our sites. In the case of Sumatra, we do not pursue estimation of the difference in lifetime income between daughters and sons, because their current land inheritance system is egalitarian and because the gender differences in schooling are no longer significant. Rather, we investigate the potential impact of changes in land and schooling on per capita expenditures, which proxy permanent incomes. We pay special attention to "social discrimination" in Ghana, because we observe clear disadvantages for women only in Ghana study sites. In both Parts II and III, we estimate land inheritance and schooling functions, the function explaining household per capita expenditure, which includes land and schooling as explanatory variables, and expenditure share functions, in order to assess changes in intrahousehold gender equity over time as well as at present.

The summary of research findings and policy implications is discussed in Chapter 11. In particular, we advocate policies (1) to develop labor-intensive agricultural technologies, which increase the demand for female labor; (2) to extend and strengthen schooling systems in rural areas; and (3) to promote competition in nonfarm labor markets so as to eliminate discrimination against women. We are more cautious about the implementation of land titling programs to strengthen women's land rights. The ultimate goal of our study is to demonstrate that there is no conflict between policies to enhance the efficiency of investments in land and human capital and policies to promote gender equity.

Appendix: A Formal Model of Intergenerational Transfers

Following the wealth model of transfers (Becker 1974; Becker and Tomes 1979, 1986), we assume that parents are both altruistic and egalitarian.[11] Parents' egalitarian motives can be associated with different types of allocation

---

11. In the context of the Behrman, Pollak, and Taubman (1982) separable earnings–bequest model, egalitarian preferences imply that the indifference map of parents with respect to the expected earnings of children is symmetric around the 45° line. The feasible set of child earnings need not be symmetric, since children may have different genetic endowments. However, to assume extreme inequality aversion is probably too harsh, since it implies that parents value an increase in income from human capital only if it goes to the worst-off child.

rules, as suggested by the literature on fairness concepts (Farmer and Tiefenthaler 1995). The "equal outcomes" rule implies that different resources may be given to different household members, as long as the eventual outcomes (say, lifetime income) are equalized. The "equality rule" emphasizes equal split, where each person receives an equal share of the resource. The equal outcomes rule will be adopted if parents are highly averse to inequality. Both the equality rule and the equal outcomes rule will result in the same allocation if returns to assets are the same for sons and daughters, if there are decreasing returns to scale in both assets, and if there are no economies of scope between the two assets.

As will be shown in this study, the equality rule is not empirically valid in our sites, and the equal outcomes rule is supported if there is no social or market discrimination against women. The equal outcomes rule, however, will not hold in many developing countries, where women are subject to both social discrimination and discrimination in the labor market (World Bank 2001). The basic hypothesis of this study is that parents are egalitarian in the sense that they maximize a utility function with the same utility weights for sons and daughters. There is of course a possibility that parents have different utility weights for sons and daughters. As will become clearer, however, such an assumption is inconsistent with secular changes in wealth transfers in the direction of greater gender equality; nor is it consistent with the absence of significant discrimination against female members in household expenditures.

More formally, we assume that parents collectively maximize a utility function spanning generations, in which utility depends on the parents' consumption (C) and the expected future incomes of the daughter (Y_d) and son (Y_s):

$$U = U(C, Y_d, Y_s). \tag{1.1}$$

For simplicity, we assume that parents have one daughter and one son.

In our study sites in the Philippines, a major occupational choice is between rice farming and nonfarm jobs. In Ghana and Sumatra, the labor allocation between crop farming (shifting cultivation in Ghana and lowland paddy cultivation in Sumatra) and commercial tree farming (cocoa in Ghana and rubber or cinnamon in Sumatra) is a critically important issue in farm management. Thus, the theoretical frameworks are slightly different in each study site. Let us begin our exposition with the Philippine case. In this case, an income-generating function (Y_i) for each child can be specified as

$$Y_i = Y_F(S_i, E_i, g_i) + P(S_i, E_i, g_i) \, Y_N(E_i, g_i), \quad i = d, s, \tag{1.2}$$

where Y_F stands for farm income; P corresponds to the probability of work in nonfarm jobs; Y_N represents nonfarm income; S is the size of bequeathed paddy land area; E is the education level measured by years of schooling; g refers to relative gender-specific effects, such as physical strength and the extent of gender discrimination in nonfarm labor markets; and "d" and "s" index the daughter and son, respectively. Note that Y_F consists of returns to land, which can be accrued as rent income without requiring one's own cultivation, as well as returns to labor, which is realized with the probability of $(1 - P)$. Here we rule out the possibility of any economies of scope between farm work and nonfarm jobs, because major nonfarm jobs that are unrelated to farm work are available in towns and cities. Although farm enterprise may provide capital for nonfarm enterprises in a world of incomplete credit markets, such linkages are weak in the Philippine villages. Also we do not consider the case in which parents sell their land and transfer cash to their children, because land sales markets are generally inactive, owing to buyers' credit constraints (see, for example, Otsuka 2002).

We assume that S increases Y_F and consequently reduces P, whereas E increases P and Y_N, since schooling is particularly important in nonfarm jobs. The effect of E on Y_F will be positive but it may not be significant according to the results of recent empirical studies by Estudillo, Quisumbing, and Otsuka (2001a), Estudillo and Otsuka (1999), Fafchamps and Quisumbing (1999), and Jolliffe (1998), among others. In the Philippines, since rice farming is intensive in male labor and requires physical strength, we expect that men's labor has a higher production efficiency in farming than women's, whereas women's labor earnings in nonfarm jobs may be equal to or even higher than men's, depending on the extent of discrimination against women in the nonfarm labor market. Although a woman could hire all of the farm labor or rent out her land, her farm income would typically fall short of men's farm income, because the supervision of hired workers and tenants is known to be costly, and men typically provide supervision while performing farm tasks themselves (for example, Hayami and Otsuka 1993). Thus, daughters would have a comparative advantage in nonfarm jobs and the sons would have a comparative advantage in farming, even though the son may have absolute advantages in both activities.

The wealth constraint for parents is

$$W = C + \pi_S \Sigma S_i + \pi_E \Sigma E_i, \tag{1.3}$$

where the wealth of parents, W, is spent on parental consumption of goods, C (the numeraire), and on expenditures on schooling and land transfers. The unit value of land is denoted by π_S and the cost of a year of schooling by π_E.[12] In most altruistic models, a parent maximizes (1.1) subject to (1.2) and (1.3) to obtain the optimal land transfer and human capital investment to each child (Quisumbing 1994). Since transfers of land and investment in human capital occur over the life cycle, W should be interpreted as lifetime wealth.

If parents value equality of incomes between sons and daughters, in the absence of significant increasing returns and economies of scope, they will be-

---

12. If all land transfers are made from the existing stock of parental wealth, then the second term of (1.3) is implicitly included on the left-hand side of the same equation. However, we also allow for the possibility that parents purchase land to transfer to their children.

stow different amounts of physical and human assets on children depending on their comparative advantages in generating incomes from each type of transfer. Even if parents assign equal weights to daughters' and sons' incomes in their utility function, the expected future income of a son (Y_s) will be greater than or equal to that of a daughter (Y_d) if sons are better able to make use of agricultural land and if returns to sons' schooling are higher, resulting in higher incomes for sons. Otherwise, we expect that Y_s and Y_d will tend to be equalized. Because of the difference in comparative advantages in farming and nonfarm jobs between daughters and sons, we hypothesize that the wealth-maximizing allocation would result in a land bequest to the son (S_s) exceeding that to the daughter (S_d), whereas the schooling of daughters (E_d) would exceed that of sons (E_s), unless Y_s is far greater than Y_d. A major purpose of the Philippine study is to test the validity of these conflicting hypotheses by estimating the difference between Y_s and Y_d.

The hypothesis of egalitarian treatment of daughters and sons or preference for equal outcomes is refuted if the estimated Y_s and Y_d are significantly different, unless there is a gender gap in earning ability or gender discrimination in farm or nonfarm jobs. That is, preference for equal outcomes may not guarantee equal incomes if income-earning opportunities are different between sons and daughters and parents are not fully aware of differences in labor market conditions. Rosenzweig (1986), however, argues that parents may favor daughters' schooling if daughters are expected to make larger or more frequent remittances than sons. We discuss an extension of our model to deal with remittances by children below. Another possibility is that nonfarm labor income may grow faster than parents expected so that, even if parents aim to equalize incomes between sons and daughters, a daughter who has a comparative advantage in nonfarm jobs may earn more than the son. If this is the case, and if parents wish to equalize incomes among children, schooling investment in sons will increase relative to schooling investment in daughters in the next generation.[13]

Model Extensions: Different Types of Land

Since the choice between food and tree crop cultivation is particularly important in Ghana and Sumatra, we focus on the intergenerational transfer of the two types of land, i.e. food and tree crop fields, assuming that nonfarm jobs are relatively unimportant.[14] Thus, an income function is redefined as

---

13. In order to consider uncertainty over future incomes of the children, we have to model how parents form and update expectations about the returns to education. Modeling such behavior is beyond the scope of this study.

14. Although we are quite certain that nonfarm income is not as important in Ghana and Sumatra compared with the Philippines, we have to admit that we failed to collect nonfarm income data in these two sites because our primary focus was the collection of input and output data from a large number of small plots subject to intricate land transfer rules.

$$Y_i = Y_F(SF_i, E_i, g_i) + Y_T(ST_i, E_i, g_i), \quad i = d, s, \tag{1.2'}$$

where Y_F and Y_T are incomes from food and tree crop farming, respectively; and SF and ST refer to land areas for food and tree cultivation, respectively, that have been transferred through temporary allocation, inheritance, and gift in accordance with the rules of land transfer under customary land tenure systems prevailing in our Ghana and Sumatra sites.

In Ghana, land allocations for food crop farming are usually made by the extended family, which controls the allocation of bush-fallow fields, whereas cocoa land is often transferred as gifts by parents. We associate temporarily allocated land with food crop production because land rights on allocated fallow land are weak, and use rights are preserved only if the land is farmed continuously. In contrast, land with stronger rights is associated with permanent crops. Tree planting may in fact be undertaken precisely to strengthen land rights (Quisumbing, Payongayong, and Otsuka 2001; Otsuka and Place 2001).[15] In Sumatra, the distinction is between lowland paddy fields and upland tree crop fields. Compared with Ghana, individual rights on tree fields have been more clearly established, so that such land is transferred primarily from parents to their children within a single family (Quisumbing and Otsuka 2001). In contrast, however, paddy fields are often owned and inherited jointly by extended family members.

The wealth constraint corresponding to equation (1.3) is specified as

$$W = C + \pi_{SF}\Sigma SF_i + \pi_{ST}\Sigma ST_i + \pi_E\Sigma E_i. \tag{1.3'}$$

In equation (1.3'), it is assumed that parents are not concerned with the unit value of food crop or paddy area since its allocation is the purview of the extended family. Note that, since land sales markets are largely absent in Ghana and Sumatra sites, the interpretation of land prices as land unit values is especially appropriate; such land unit values may be subjectively valued and thus could be different across households. In practice, a young farmer may clear forestland to establish a farm or request an allocation of fallow land from the extended family. In either case, permission beyond one's own parents would need to be obtained—the village chief in the case of forest clearance and the extended family for the use of family land (Quisumbing, Payongayong, and Otsuka 2001; Quisumbing and Otsuka 2001). In other words, portions of SF and ST are determined exogenously and parents decide on the allocation of their owned land areas, given the exogenous land allocations. Since individual land rights are stronger for tree crop land, the allocation of ST is determined primarily by parents.

If the daughter were comparatively efficient in generating income from food crops, the extended family would allocate land for food crops to her, and

---

15. In an expanded model, the effort of wives and children to establish cocoa farms, which promotes conversion of food crop land and confers strong individual rights, should be taken into account.

parents may decide not to give her tree crop land. Conversely, if the son has a comparative advantage in using agroforestry or tree crop areas, owing to greater physical strength required for clearing forest and bushland, the extended family would not allocate a large area of food crop area to him, and parents would efficiently bequeath more tree crop land to him. Actual land transfers to the daughter and son from parents would then be unequal, depending on their comparative advantages and prior allocations of land from the extended family.

Suppose that the initial equilibrium consists of allocations of (ST_{0s}, SF_{0s}) to the son and (ST_{0d}, SF_{0d}) to the daughter, respectively, where $SF_{0d} < SF_{0s}$ and $ST_{0s} < ST_{0d}$. Suppose now that the value of land changes relative to the cost of education. Even if the comparative advantage of each child remains the same, such changes will result in a new utility-maximizing equilibrium, leading parents to change the equilibrium allocation of the two types of land and education. Alternatively, suppose that new technologies or new profitable crops are introduced, changing the comparative advantage of each child in generating income from different types of land or education. For example, if the introduction of tree crops in place of food crop cultivation under the bush-fallow system increases the demand not only for male labor but also for female labor, parents may want to reallocate a portion of land to daughters, as in the case of Ghana (or to sons as in the case of Sumatra), even if they do not traditionally inherit land. In the Ghanaian case, for example, the introduction of tree crops increases the allocation of land to daughters from ST_{0d} to ST_{1d}, where $ST_{1d} < ST_{0d}$.

As formulated above, the total amount of land transferred to children would be a result of decisions made by the extended family and parents. However, it is empirically difficult to analyze the determinants of land allocated by the extended family, which is composed of over 50 members in many cases. Thus, in this study, we focus explicitly on the analysis of parental wealth transfers and treat the transfer of wealth controlled by the extended family as exogenous in our studies of Ghana and Sumatra.

We also note that, although our exposition has been in terms of land and schooling, both physical and human capital are heterogeneous categories. For example, parents can (and do) transfer different types of nonland assets to children. Quisumbing (1994), for example, examines the determinants of intergenerational transfers of nonland assets from parents to children. Neither is human capital investment confined to schooling. In Ghana, for example, where the quality of the formal school system had been poor for at least a decade, individuals sought to develop human capital outside the schooling system by using apprenticeships or other ways of acquiring experience.

Model Extensions: Reverse Transfers from Children

Our model can also be extended to incorporate reverse transfers from children (Quisumbing 1997). Similar to the above, let us assume that parents have two children—a son and a daughter. Parents and children are altruistic and care about each other's consumption (Becker 1974; Becker and Tomes 1986; Lucas and Stark 1985).[16] We revise the exposition of the utility function in equation (1.1) so that parents care not only about their children's income but also about their consumption. Let us assume that there are two periods. The parental utility function in each period is:

$$U_{pt} = U_p[C_{pt}(Y_{pt} + r_{1t}), C_{cdt}(Y_{cdti} - r_{dt}), C_{cst}(Y_{cst} - r_{st})], \quad t = 1, 2, \quad (1.1'')$$

where parental utility, U_p, is a function of parental consumption, C_p, and children's consumption, C_{cd} and C_{cs}, in each period t. The subscripts "d" and "s" index the daughter and son, respectively, and the t subscript stands for time in periods 1 and 2. Consumption by both parents and children depends on their respective incomes, Y_p, Y_d, and Y_s, plus (net) transfers or remittances, r. Net transfers, r, are defined to be less than zero if the direction of transfer is from parent to child, and greater than zero if the transfer is from child to parent. We assume that children earn nothing in the first period and do not make transfers to parents while they are young. Children's consumption in the first period is then financed completely by parental transfers, so net transfers are negative ($r_1 > 0$).

For ease of exposition, let us talk about a typical child, c (either a daughter or a son). Y_{c2i} in the second period is given by

$$Y_{c2i} = Y_c(S_i, E_i, g_i) + l_i, \quad i = d, s, \quad (1.2'')$$

where income is derived from land, S_i, and education, E_i; g_i refers to relative gender-specific effects; and l is market luck. The parents' budget constraint is the discounted sum of the budget constraint in each period; that is:

$$W = [C_{p1} + \pi_S \Sigma S_{i1} + \pi E \Sigma E_{i1} + r1] + \delta[C_{p2}], \quad (1.3'')$$

where parental income in the first period is spent on parental consumption of goods, C_{p1}, expenditures on education and asset transfers, $\pi_S \Sigma S_{it} + \pi_E \Sigma E_{it}$, and net transfers to children, r_{ti}, and δ is the discount factor. In the second period, parents only consume and no longer make transfers to their children. Parents maximize their discounted utility in both periods (1.1″) subject to (1.2″) and (1.3″) to determine the optimal investments in human and physical capital per child. Note that, because parental consumption in period 2 will be a function of net transfers from children, parents will rationally take into account future transfers when making their consumption and investment decisions.

How are net transfers from children determined? In the second period, when children are adults, they realize earnings from human and physical capital and they choose to spend their income on own consumption or transfers to parents. Children are altruistic and also care about their parents' consumption:

---

16. For a more comprehensive review of the literature on parental motives to invest in children, see Behrman (1997).

$$U_{c2i} = U_{c2i}[C_{c2i}(Y_{c2i} - r_{2i}), C_{p2}(Y_{p2} + r_{2i})], \quad i = \text{d, s.} \qquad (1.4)$$

In the second period, children maximize their utility by choosing levels of consumption, C_c, and net transfers, r, subject to their income constraint (1.2). They make transfers to equate the marginal loss of utility from their own consumption and the marginal gain in their parents' consumption:[17]

$$(\partial U_c^i / \partial X_c^i)\,(\partial C_c^i / \partial r_i) = (\partial U_c^i / \partial C_p)\,(\partial C_p / \partial r_i). \qquad (1.5)$$

The optimal amount transferred is a function of adult income per child:

$$r^*_{i\,=\,r}(Y_c^i), \qquad (1.6)$$

which is in turn a function of parents' previous investments in the child:

$$r^*_{i\,=\,r}[(S_i,\ E_i,\ g_i) + l_i]. \qquad (1.6')$$

Under the "repayment" hypothesis, one would expect $r'_E < 0$, $r'_g < 0$, and $r'_S < 0$. That is, transfers to parents would increase with land transferred to children, education, and gender-specific effects that favor a particular child. Under altruism, transfers from children would increase, the higher is children's income and the lower is parental income. The possibility that assets may be transferred only at death, however, may induce strategic behavior by children and parents (Bernheim, Shleifer, and Summers 1985).

Following this framework, transfers from children to parents can be interpreted as a form of repayment for previous investments. One approach to testing this model empirically would be to estimate an equation for inter-child differences in parent–child transfers, and another would be to estimate inter-child differences in child–parent transfers. If particular children are favored—whether owing to gender, birth order, or parental preferences for children with these characteristics—these attributes should be significant and positive in estimates of child–parent transfers. We do not test these hypotheses statistically since we do not have remittance data for all our study sites.[18]

There is a large and growing literature on parents' differential investment in children, but evidence on differential repayment is rare and has been found mainly at the household level. Knowles and Anker (1981) argue that the positive and significant male dummy and the positive relationship between education and remittances in Kenya support the repayment hypothesis. However, their study does not examine intra-sibling differences. Karoly's (1994) study of transfers to and from origin households and migrant children in Malaysia finds that schooling investments made by the origin household are repaid through re-

---

17. Children may not observe their parents' utility directly but may have some idea about parental consumption. Note that this formulation assumes that children make independent decisions on transfers to parents. It is possible, and quite likely, that children may collude.

18. We do have remittance data from the Philippine survey. Analysis of these data is left for future work.

mittances, although this effect declines with time. In Botswana, Lucas and Stark (1985) find that the effect of education on remittances is stronger for the household head's children, who may have received more educational support. Previous work using data collected in the first Philippine survey (Quisumbing 1997) provides support for the repayment hypothesis. Better educated children, in whom parents presumably invested more, make larger transfers to parents. Within families, daughters and children with more education and experience make larger transfers to parents. However, daughters make smaller transfers to wealthier parents.

PART I

The Philippine Case

2   The Study Villages and Sample Households in Rice-Growing Areas

This chapter sets the stage for the statistical analyses to be carried out in Chapters 3 and 4. We first provide a brief description of the study villages and survey structure. In order to characterize rice-based farming systems and sources of household income in the rural Philippines, we then describe the sample households in terms of land tenure and farm size, socioeconomic characteristics, technology adoption, labor use, and sources of household income. After exploring changes in gender bias in schooling and land inheritance over generations using individual data, we set out the hypotheses to be tested in Chapters 3 and 4.

Study Villages and Survey Structure

Study Villages

Our five study villages are located in Central Luzon and Panay Island, two of the major rice-producing areas in the Philippines (Figure 2.1). These villages were randomly selected by the International Rice Research Institute (IRRI) in 1985 (David and Otsuka 1994), and have been frequently surveyed since then. They are typical rice-growing villages in the country and represent various production environments. Two villages, one in Central Luzon and another one in Panay, are fully irrigated by gravity irrigation systems, which provide a favorable rice production environment. Similarly, one village in each location is characterized by a shallow-water, favorable rainfed environment largely free from flooding and drought. The fifth village, in Panay, is located in the most unfavorable production environment, being mountainous and drought-prone.

The main crop is rice during the wet season, which extends from June to November. In the dry season, rice is planted in land with irrigation facilities, whereas in rainfed areas either cash crops are grown or the land is left fallow. Rice is sold to the markets by owner and tenant farm households, but not by landless worker households. Marketable surplus accounts for 25 percent of total rice production in the five villages. In four villages, about 30 percent of

FIGURE 2.1 Location of study villages in the Philippines

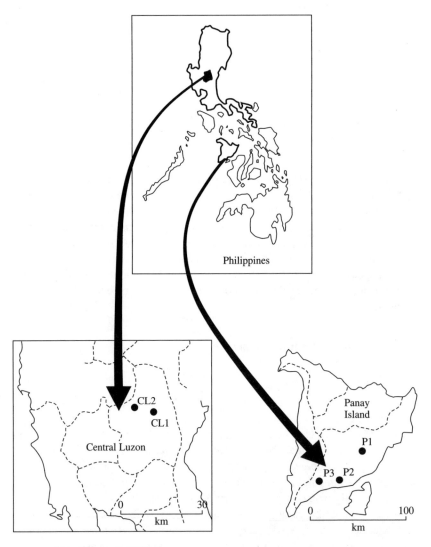

SOURCE: Estudillo et al. (2001d).

the total rice production is marketed; in Signe, the most remote study village, only 7 percent is marketed.

In sample villages in Central Luzon, the Ilocanos, an ethnolinguistic group originating in Northern Luzon, comprise the majority of the residents; in Panay, the dominant ethnic group is Ilonggo. Among the Ilocanos, land is traditionally given as a gift to a newly married son; daughters whose husbands do not inherit land may receive land rights from their parents. Both primogeniture and ultimogeniture are practiced among the Ilocanos, depending on the availability of land. Among the Ilonggos of Panay, daughters and sons may receive land rights more equally and independently, although, for land-constrained households, children who help the parents in farming receive more land than their siblings.

According to Hayami and Kikuchi (1982, 2000), the inner portion of Central Luzon began to be developed as a rice-producing region in the late 1890s and early 1900s by private *haciendas* established through royal grants and purchases of royal domain of the Spanish Crown. Our study villages in Central Luzon had big *haciendas* consisting of hundreds of hectares of land before the implementation of the land reform program in the 1970s.

Panay was presumably opened for cultivation earlier than Central Luzon because the island is easily accessible by sea. In general, our three study villages in Panay are characterized by smaller landholdings, which are predominantly owner cultivated. The original settlers in the village opened forestlands for rice cultivation, and thus the incidence of owner-cultivation was higher in Panay than in Central Luzon. Country roads in our study villages were built in the early part of the 1900s. A large-scale irrigation system in one study village in Panay was constructed during the Spanish colonial period and was modernized in 1954.

Survey Structure

The data in the Philippine study come from four rounds of surveys conducted among the same set of households in 1985, 1989, 1997, and 1998. The 1985 and 1998 surveys were income surveys and the 1989 and 1997 surveys were inheritance surveys. The original sample households were selected by stratified random sampling in accordance with the farm size groups. The sample size declined from 369 households in 1985 to 247 households in 1998 (Table 2.1), owing to outmigration, death, refusal of interview, and absence during the survey visit. Sample households that dropped out were not replaced, which means that our sample in later years is a nonrandom sample of households, given that some of the 1985 respondents have migrated.[1]

Farm households, consisting of owner-cultivator and tenant households, accounted for about three-fourths of the total sample households in each of the survey periods. There were a few farm households in 1985 that became landless households in subsequent survey years as a result of loss of land owing to pawning and outright sale, retirement from farming, and inheritance decisions

---

1. We examine the issues of attrition in Estudillo, Quisumbing, and Otsuka (2000a). In order to avoid selection bias, we employ Heckman's (1979) procedure in the estimation of the income function in Chapter 3, in which the probability that households were included in the 1998 survey is explained by their characteristics as of 1985.

TABLE 2.1 Number of sample households in Central Luzon and Panay, 1985–1998

| Survey year | Number of households | | | Farm households (percent) |
	Central Luzon	Panay	Total	
1985	183	186	369	78
1989	161	178	339	70
1997	134	141	275	75
1998	125	122	247	77

to give land to children. There were also landless households in 1985 that acquired land and became farm households in subsequent years. We define landless households as those that do not have access to farmland, which includes casual-worker households that are mainly engaged in rice farming as well as a small number of nonagricultural wage-worker households.[2]

The objective of the 1985 IRRI survey was to analyze the income distribution effects of the differential adoption of modern rice technology in favorable and unfavorable production environments.[3] The questionnaire in 1985 contained detailed information on the demographic characteristics of the members of sample households, technology adoption, input use, rice yields, prices, wages and labor contracts, tenure patterns, and income from all sources.

Quisumbing (1994) conducted the inheritance survey in 1989; we conducted the 1997 survey. The aim of the 1989 and 1997 inheritance surveys was to analyze differences in intergenerational transfers of land and investment in schooling by gender in three generations: parents of respondents; respondents and their spouses and siblings; and respondents' children.

The 1989 retrospective survey covers the transfers of wealth from the parents of respondents to the respondents and their siblings.[4] Specifically, this survey provides data on the human and physical wealth of the parents of respondents at the time of marriage, characteristics of the respondents and their siblings, and specific forms of transfers. The respondents were also asked about the transfers received by each sibling, regardless of whether the individual lived

---

2. For convenience, we lump together agricultural casual worker households and a relatively small number of nonagricultural wage-worker households. Also note that the distinction between the two is not always clear, as both types of households generally engage in both agricultural and nonagricultural jobs to varying degrees.

3. See Otsuka, Cordova, and David (1992) for a detailed discussion of the sampling procedure of the villages and households in the original survey in 1985.

4. Quisumbing (1994) included a section in the 1989 survey questionnaire on prospective inheritance by the respondents' children. However, in 1989 the fertility decisions of the respondents were not yet completed and many children were still very young. Most of the respondents had not decided on the bequest of land and on schooling investments in children.

in the survey area or had migrated. Since the respondents and their siblings had completed schooling and received land from their parents, this dataset permits an analysis of completed transfer decisions from the parents' to the respondents' generation.

The objective of the 1997 inheritance survey was to explore wealth transfers from the respondents to their children. The respondents and spouses were asked about the characteristics of their children and the actual and potential bequest of land and nonland assets to them. A large number of sample households had completed fertility decisions in 1997 and had definite ideas regarding potential bequests of land and nonland assets to their heirs, although investment in schooling was not yet completed for some of the younger children. Thus, in our analysis of the determinants of investment in schooling, we included only children aged 21 years and above. These children are no longer in school because Filipino children commonly complete tertiary education at the age of 21.

The 1998 survey, which we conducted, is an income–expenditure survey (a sequel to the 1997 inheritance survey) that collected data on individual children's earnings as well as household expenditures on consumer goods and durables. The main objective of this survey was to explore the impact of differential land inheritance and schooling investments on lifetime incomes of individual members and to examine whether gender bias in the intrahousehold allocation of expenditures exists.

The Sample Households

Farm Size and Tenure

The description of the sample households in Central Luzon and Panay refers to both the 1985 and 1998 survey periods. The average landholding of farm households was lower in Panay than in Central Luzon owing to the higher population density in Panay. However, the average size of farms in Central Luzon declined markedly from 1985 to 1998, whereas that in Panay increased slightly (Table 2.2).

Central Luzon is characterized by a lower proportion of area under owner cultivation, reflecting the history of the *hacienda* system that prevailed before the implementation of the land reform program in 1972. A major purpose of the land reform program was to transfer land to actual cultivators and to promote leasehold tenancy in place of share tenancy (Hayami, Quisumbing, and Adriano 1990). The land reform was most effectively implemented in favorable rice-growing areas, including Central Luzon (Otsuka 1991). As a result, there was a high incidence of holders of Certificates of Land Transfer (CLT) and leaseholders in this region in 1985. Most CLT holders in Central Luzon had completed the amortization payments and had become owner-cultivators by 1998. Despite the prohibition of share tenancy by land reform laws, the proportion of area under share tenancy in our sample villages in Panay was 28 percent in 1998.

TABLE 2.2 Characteristics of sample households in Central Luzon and Panay, 1985 and 1998

Characteristics	Central Luzon		Panay	
	1985	1998	1985	1998
Farm size and tenure				
Farm size (hectares)	2.0	1.6	1.2	1.4
Tenure (percent by area)				
Owner/Emancipation Patent	14.0	42.0	33.0	39.0
Certificate of Land Transfer/				
leasehold tenancy	81.0	58.0	33.0	33.0
Share tenancy	5.0	0.0	34.0	28.0
Socioeconomic characteristics				
Household size	5.5	4.7	5.8	5.1
Labor force[a]	3.4	3.4	3.8	3.9
Working members[b]	3.0	2.7	3.0	3.1
(Resident working members)	(2.7)	(2.5)	(2.5)	(2.3)
Composition of working members (percent)				
Parents	41.0	49.0	44.0	52.0
Children	21.0	27.0	28.0	31.0
Average schooling (years)				
Parents	6.0	6.9	6.6	7.2
Children	8.6	9.3	8.5	9.8

[a] Number of household members aged 15–65 years.

[b] Members of labor force who are not in school.

Socioeconomic Characteristics

The average household size in Central Luzon was slightly higher than that in Panay in 1998. We include unmarried children as household members regardless of whether they reside in the village or outside.[5] There was a reduction in the average household size in 1998 in both locations. In 1985 and 1998, respectively, about 65 percent and 75 percent of the household members belonged to the labor force, defined as those members aged 15–65 years. Among those in the labor force, about 85 percent are working members (that is, they are not in school).

Since the 1997–98 subsample is a subset of the previously surveyed households, we expect the age distribution to shift toward older age groups, with the exception of additions owing to births. In Central Luzon, the number of work-

---

5. Because we included unmarried children as members of the household, our definition of a household here is more inclusive than the usual "members of the same family sharing living and eating arrangements." It is closer to the definition of the family as "individuals related by blood or marriage."

ing members declined in 1998 because the younger household members opted to go to school. In both Central Luzon and Panay the number of resident working members declined owing to the increase in the number of educated children who were able to obtain jobs outside the village, mostly in large cities and overseas. The retirement of some of the parents from farming resulted in a decline in the proportion of working parents.

Very few working members had never attended school. However, children had attained higher levels of education than their parents. In 1998, the average educational attainment of working children was close to 10 years, whereas that of their parents was only about 7 years. The largest proportion of household members belonged to the group aged 20–64 years, who are mostly working members. The youngest members (0–5 years old) accounted for the smallest proportion. It is also noteworthy that the proportion of the elderly (65 years old and over) was only about 10 percent. About one-third of the household members belonged to the age categories of 6–19 years, consisting mainly of members who were in school.

Adoption of Modern Rice Technology

The modern rice technology package includes irrigation, modern varieties (MVs) of rice, and labor-saving technologies such as tractors, threshers, and direct seeding. The ratio of planted area with irrigation rose slightly in both Central Luzon and Panay because of increased adoption of water pumps in the favorable rainfed areas (Table 2.3). Owing to the availability of irrigation water and favorable rainfed production environments, the adoption of MVs was com-

TABLE 2.3 Changes in rice technologies, rice cropping intensity, and rice yields in Central Luzon and Panay, 1985 and 1998

Technologies	Central Luzon		Panay	
	1985	1998	1985	1998
Irrigation ratio (percent of area)	72	77	38	39
Adoption of modern varieties (percent adopters)	100	100	77	100
Adoption of labor-saving technologies (percent adopters)				
Tractor	91	98	40	80
Thresher	100	100	97	97
Direct seeding	30	56	73	97
Rice yield (tons/hectare/season)[a]	4.3	5.1	3.1	2.3
Rice cropping intensity[b]	1.8	1.8	1.5	1.5

[a] Average of wet, dry, and third cropping seasons.

[b] The number of rice crops in one year.

plete in Central Luzon as early as 1985. In Panay, 23 percent of sample farmers were still planting traditional varieties in that year. MV adoption was complete in all study villages by 1998.

Tractor adoption in Central Luzon was close to 100 percent even in 1985, whereas in Panay about 60 percent of sample farmers in 1985 and 20 percent in 1998 were using water buffalos. Thresher adoption has been close to 100 percent in both Central Luzon and Panay. Direct seeding, which is a new method of establishing rice plants by broadcasting pre-germinated or germinated rice seeds into puddled (prepared) soil, is more widely adopted in Panay. The modern rice technology package introduced in Panay in the 1970s combined early maturing MVs with direct seeding to increase cropping intensity within the rainy season.

The average rice yield rose from 4.3 to 5.1 tons per hectare per season in Central Luzon because of the adoption of newer, higher-yielding MVs and better farm management practices.[6] In contrast, the average yield in Panay declined because of the drought in the rainfed villages in 1998. Rice cropping intensity (the number of rice crops in one year) in both Central Luzon and Panay remained the same in 1985 and 1998.

Labor Use in Rice Production

Labor use in rice production by gender may affect parental decisions to bequeath land to sons or daughters. Labor use per hectare per season in rice production is shown in Table 2.4. There are three important observations from this table. First, total labor use declined significantly between 1985 and 1998 in both Central Luzon and Panay. This decline comes mainly from the reduction in labor input in crop establishment, owing to increased use of herbicides (which effectively substitute for manual weeding), and in harvesting and threshing activities, owing to improvements in threshing machinery. Second, labor use in rice production is male dominated: about three-fourths of the total labor use is accounted for by male labor, both family and hired. This implies that female members of farm households work primarily at home or in nonfarm sectors. Third, the proportion of hired labor, which is supplied mainly by landless laborer households, increased in Central Luzon and remained unchanged in Panay.

Labor input in land preparation relies solely on male labor. There was almost an equal proportion of male and female labor in crop establishment in 1985, but the proportion of female labor declined in 1998 because of the shift from transplanting, which is traditionally a female task (IRRI 1985), to direct seeding, which is commonly performed by males. Male labor is more impor-

---

6. Newly released MVs have greater tolerance to pests and diseases, higher adaptability to environmental stresses such as drought, floods, and saline soil conditions, shorter maturity period, and superior grain quality that commands higher market prices (IRRI 1997).

TABLE 2.4 Labor use per hectare in rice production during the wet season in Central Luzon and Panay, 1985 and 1998

	Central Luzon		Panay	
	1985[a]	1998	1985[a]	1998
Rice farming activities (person-days/hectare/season)[b]				
Land preparation	15	14	11	8
Crop establishment	27	13	8	3
Crop care	5	3	10	13
Harvesting and threshing	32	25	25	19
Total	79	55	54	43
Composition of labor input (percent)				
Family male	36	26	29	24
Family female[c]	4	2	6	12
Hired male	38	52	50	62
Hired female	22	20	15	2

[a] Refers to the sample households in 1998.

[b] One person-day is assumed to be 8 hours.

[c] Female labor includes a small amount of children's labor.

tant in crop care activities because chemical input application is a task designated for males, although weeding is performed by both males and females. Harvesting and threshing activities are done by both males and females, but male labor is more dominant. Thus, we conclude that rice farming is a predominantly male job.

Factor Shares in Rice Production

Factor shares analysis in rice production is of particular interest in the analysis of land bequests and schooling investments because returns to land and labor are closely related to values of inherited land and acquired schooling. Following convention (Barker and Herdt 1985), we disaggregate the gross value of rice production into payments to four major categories of inputs: (1) current inputs, (2) capital inputs including family-owned and hired capital, (3) labor inputs of family and hired workers, and (4) land. For owned factor inputs, imputations are made using prevailing wage and rental rates. The return to land is computed as the residual after deducting the sum of payments to current inputs, capital, and labor from the gross value of output.

Factor shares per hectare per season, estimated as the average of wet, dry, and third cropping seasons, are shown in Table 2.5. The factor share of current inputs in Central Luzon declined, partly as a result of the adoption of integrated pest management, which minimizes the use of chemical inputs; in contrast, the

TABLE 2.5 Factor shares per hectare per season in rice production in Central Luzon and Panay, 1985 and 1998 (percent)

	Central Luzon		Panay	
Factors	1985	1998	1985	1998
Gross output[a]	100	100	100	100
Current inputs	29	17	21	27
Capital	15	6	11	11
Owned	4	1	2	1
Hired	11	5	9	10
Labor	26	26	29	40
Family	12	5	10	9
Hired	14	21	19	31
Land	30	51	39	22

[a] Average of wet, dry, and third cropping seasons.

factor share of current inputs in Panay increased, owing to greater use of chemical inputs, partly as a result of increased MV adoption. The factor share of capital in Central Luzon declined owing to a decrease in the rental price of hired capital, whereas in Panay the factor share of capital remained the same.

Although the total labor use in rice production per hectare per season declined, the factor share of labor increased in Panay and remained the same in Central Luzon. Such changes can be explained by the increase in the wage rate. We found that real daily wage rates deflated by a nominal paddy price index in land preparation and transplanting rose 1.5 to 2.0 times over the 13-year period from 1985 to 1998. The increase in real wage rates can be explained primarily by the increase in labor demand in the nonfarm sector as the Philippine economy experienced relatively rapid growth during the mid-1990s. During the same period, farm technology, rice prices, and other factor prices did not change favorably to increase labor demand in agriculture. The factor share of family labor declined as a result of substitution of hired labor for family labor. As will be shown, despite such substitution, landless households' share of income from agriculture declined because of the rapid expansion of nonfarm employment opportunities. There is hardly any doubt that it was the development of nonfarm sectors, and not agricultural technology, that triggered structural changes in the rural rice economy in the Philippines in the period after the Green Revolution.

The factor share of land increased from 30 percent to 51 percent in Central Luzon but decreased in Panay. The former can be explained by increased yields resulting from improved technologies; the latter can be attributed to the decline in yields owing to drought in our survey year. The increased factor share of land and decreased share of family labor indicate that rice farming provides sizable land income to farm households but no longer offers major employment opportunities. Note that land income is computed as a residual return and, as such, may include returns to human capital.

Household Income Sources

Farm income consists of rice income and income from nonrice crop and live-stock production. For farm households, rice income represents the returns to owned capital, family labor, and land, whereas for landless households rice income is derived from earnings from hired employment. Nonfarm income consists of income from formal wage employment and informal employment in retail, rural transport, and domestic services earned by resident working family members, and of remittances from family members working outside the village.[7]

Table 2.6 shows the breakdown of total household income into different components for farm and landless households. In 1985 farm income was the most important income source of farm households, comprising 83 percent of total household income in Central Luzon and 64 percent in Panay. The major contributor to farm income was rice production. Landless households in Central Luzon derived 66 percent of their total income from farm jobs in 1985, of which wage earnings from rice production were a major component. In Panay the proportion of nonfarm income of the landless households was substantially higher because some households depended mostly on nonfarm employment.

It is remarkable that the share of farm income, particularly rice income, of the farm households declined considerably between 1985 and 1998. This decline was brought about primarily by the reduction in the share of family labor income in rice production. Family members devoted less time to farm production activities and increased their involvement in nonfarm employment. As a result, the share of nonfarm income rose markedly among farm households in both locations. We also found that the share of land income remained fairly constant in Central Luzon but decreased in Panay because of poor harvests. Recall that the factor share of land in rice production rose considerably in Central Luzon. Yet the fact that the share of land in total income did not rise indicates that land is no longer the decisive factor determining rural household income.

The landless households' share of nonfarm income increased at the expense of farm income. Moreover, their wage earnings from rice production activities became of secondary importance in 1998. The dependence of the landless on nonfarm income was already high in Panay in 1985, partly because there were nonagricultural wage-worker households and partly because children in this region have historically migrated, either temporarily or permanently, to urban areas owing to the scarcity of farm land. The shift of the income structure

---

7. None of our sample households explicitly obtained substantial income from income-earning assets other than those used in rice farming. The importance of farm assets is comparatively low, as can be ascertained from the small factor share of owned capital.

TABLE 2.6 Annual income of farm and landless households in Central Luzon and Panay, 1985 and 1998

	Central Luzon		Panay	
	1985	1998	1985	1998
Income sources (percent)				
Farm households				
Farm	83	60	64	24
Rice	69	54	40	11
Nonrice crop and livestock	14	6	24	13
Nonfarm	17	40	36	76
Nonfarm employment	8	34	17	41
Remittances	9	6	19	35
Total	100	100	100	100
Total income (thousand pesos/year)	23.2	111.1	16.8	83.8
Landless households				
Farm	66	31	24	16
Rice	51	24	16	5
Nonrice crop and livestock	15	7	8	11
Nonfarm	34	69	76	84
Nonfarm employment	28	58	50	64
Remittances	6	11	26	20
Total	100	100	100	100
Total income (thousand pesos/year)	9.4	48.0	13.1	58.4
Income ratio of farm to landless households				
Farm	3.1	4.4	3.5	2.2
Nonfarm	1.2	1.4	0.6	1.3
Total income	2.4	2.3	1.3	1.4

NOTE: Exchange rates were US$1 = 20 pesos in 1985 and US$1 = 38 pesos in 1998.

in favor of nonfarm income among the landless households has been more remarkable in Central Luzon presumably because of its proximity to Metropolitan Manila, which has been the center of recent economic development accompanying increased nonfarm employment opportunities.

The disparity between the farm and landless households in terms of total income remained fairly constant, whereas the nonfarm income gap increased (see the bottom panel of Table 2.6). In Panay the landless households received more income from nonfarm sources than the farm households in 1985, but this trend was reversed in 1998 when the farm households reaped more benefits from employment outside the village. If the farm households continue to receive greater incomes from the integration of the urban and overseas labor markets, there will be increasing inequality in the distribution of income between the landed and landless households.[8] Given that the share of farm income declined, the contribution of disparity in farm incomes to the total income gap must have decreased.[9]

Overall there has been a clear shift of household income away from land toward nonfarm labor income. According to our descriptive statistics, the increased availability of nonfarm employment tends to distribute income unequally between farm and landless households. Hayami and Kikuchi (2000) argue, however, that the expansion of nonfarm employment has acted to equalize the distribution of income in another rice village in the Philippines because it enables the landless farm households to increase their income. In contrast, Adams (1996) finds in rural Pakistan that remittances from abroad have a negative effect on equity. Thus, the effect of increased nonfarm income on income distribution needs to be examined carefully. Before that, we would like to identify statistically the factors affecting the amounts of farm and nonfarm income.

The Sample Individuals

Distribution of Sample Individuals by Generation

Our survey respondents are all heads of households. In 1989, we had 339 respondents (of whom 37 were female) with 900 male and 932 female siblings. In 1997, we had 275 respondents (8 females) who were the parents of 767 male and 715 female children aged 21 years and older and of 133 male and 108 female children aged 13–20 years (Table 2.7). All the male respondents were married, while 6 female respondents in 1989 and 2 in 1998 were single female heads of households.[10] Male respondents are overrepresented because in farming villages the head of a farming household is typically the husband.

The respondents' parents were born around 1910, got married in the 1930s, and completed childbearing by the 1950s (Table 2.8). When the parents of the respondents formed their own households and started farming independently, the land frontier was still being opened for new cultivation. Un-

---

8. The income gap in nonfarm income in favor of farm households will likely continue in the future. We found that, among working children aged 15–65 years who were no longer in school in 1997, the children from landless workers' households were less frequently engaged in nonfarm jobs. These children, on the average, obtained only 8 years of schooling, whereas the children from the farmers' households obtained 10 years. Sons of landless households were particularly disadvantaged because they obtained only 6 years of schooling, whereas farmers' sons obtained 10 years.

9. Moreover, there was a decline in the income gap across the five villages, indicating that the production environment has less impact in determining household income.

10. The female respondents fall into the following categories: (1) a widow living with her young children; (2) a woman whose husband is alive but sick or incapable of making major decisions at home; (3) a single woman living with aging parents; and (4) a single woman living alone.

TABLE 2.7 Number of individuals belonging to the sample households in the Philippine villages, 1989 and 1997

Individual members	Male	Female
1989[a]		
Parents of respondents	339	339
Respondents and spouses	333	339
Siblings of respondents	900	932
1997[b]		
Respondents and spouses	273	275
Older children of respondents[c]	767	715
Younger children of respondents[d]	133	108

[a] Sample size was 339 households.

[b] Sample size was 275 households.

[c] Children aged 21 years and over.

[d] Children aged 13–20 years.

cultivated forestland was abundant but cleared fields were considered to be the most important form of wealth. Nonfarm employment opportunities were very limited; the majority of the parents of the respondents were farmers, and land-less agricultural laborers were rare.

The respondents and their siblings were born mostly in the 1930s and 1940s, established their own households in the 1960s, and completed fertility

TABLE 2.8 Demographic characteristics of household members, by generation, in the Philippine villages, 1989 and 1997

Individual members	Year of birth		Completed years in school		Difference in schooling between males and females
	Male	Female	Male	Female	
1989					
Parents of respondents	1906	1911	3.7	3.2	0.5*
Respondents and spouses	1938	1941	6.2	6.2	0.0
Siblings of respondents	1939	1940	6.7	7.2	−0.5**
1997					
Respondents and spouses	1938	1941	6.3	6.3	0.0
Older children of respondents[a]	1967	1967	8.5	10.0	−1.5**
Younger children of respondents[b]	1981	1981	8.0	8.8	−0.8**

NOTE: * indicates significance at the 5 percent level; ** at the 1 percent level.

[a] Children aged 21 years and over.

[b] Children aged 13–20 years.

decisions by the late 1980s to the early 1990s. Almost all the respondents and their siblings are married. The land frontier had closed well before the respondents and their siblings were ready to become independent farmers in the 1960s. Given peasants' financial difficulty in purchasing land, the only practical way by which the respondents and their siblings could obtain access to additional land (other than through land inheritance) was to enter into tenancy contracts with landowners (Binswanger and Rosenzweig 1984). However, because of the suppression of tenancy arrangements by land reform law, obtaining access to cultivable land through tenancy agreements became more difficult over time (Hayami and Otsuka 1993). It is no surprise that the number of landless households increased in the respondents' generation, accounting for 25 percent of our sample households in 1997.

On the average, in 1997 there were 6.3 children per family, the older children of the respondents having been born in 1967. At the time of the 1997 survey, one-half of the children were married and living separately from their household of origin. Most of the unmarried children were living with their parents, but each family usually had at least one nonresident working member. In the late 1970s and early 1980s, when the children were in school, the demand for labor increased sharply as a result of the development of the nonfarm sector and the integration of domestic and international labor markets. Because of the increasing returns to human capital for nonfarm jobs, the respondents had stronger motivation to invest in children's schooling. The cost of schooling also decreased further in 1986, when, in addition to primary education, secondary education in public schools was mandated to be free. To our knowledge, the quality of schooling did not change much with the greater entry of children, partly because of the children's enhanced motivation to study and increased governmental support for secondary education.

Whereas the respondents are mainly engaged in farm work, the children are engaged in various types of occupations. Among the sons, about 55 percent work as farmers or farm laborers, 30 percent hold informal nonfarm jobs such as peddling, carpentry, driving, and handicraft, and 15 percent are professionals, including government and public offices employees, medical practitioners, accountants, teachers, and overseas workers. Among the daughters, about 50 percent are involved in their own housekeeping, 6 percent work as farmers or farm laborers, 24 percent work in informal nonfarm work, and 20 percent are professionals.

Schooling Attainment

The parents of the respondents had very little schooling (see Table 2.8). Fathers obtained significantly more schooling (3.7 completed years in school) than mothers (3.2 completed years). Males were favored presumably because of the higher wage premium to male schooling in that generation, when relatively few outside income-earning opportunities existed for women.

The respondents and their siblings completed 2.5 to 4.0 more years of schooling relative to their parents. Females were particularly favored in schooling investments, resulting in the disappearance of gender differences in schooling among respondents and their spouses. Sisters of the respondents obtained significantly more schooling than their brothers—in contrast to their mothers, who completed fewer years in school than their fathers did. Some of the sisters of the respondents reside in the cities and work in nonfarm jobs, where returns to female schooling are comparatively high. There have been marked improvements in schooling attainment between the respondents' and the children's generations. On the average, female respondents finished primary schooling (6.0 completed years in school), whereas their daughters finished secondary school (10.0 completed years in school). Male respondents also finished primary schooling, but their sons finished middle high school (8.5 completed years of schooling).[11]

The most remarkable finding is that the gender gap in schooling in favor of women has widened in the children's generation. This would imply that investment in women's education has become more profitable (Deolalikar 1993; Psacharopoulos 1994). Moreover, because schooling has a small impact on farm income relative to nonfarm income (Jolliffe 1998; Estudillo and Otsuka 1999; Fafchamps and Quisumbing 1999; Estudillo, Quisumbing, and Otsuka 2001a), the increased investment by respondents in their children's education likely represents a response to the rise in returns to education in the nonfarm sector.

Land Inheritance

Fathers and mothers of the respondents owned and operated larger areas of land than their children. On the average, the fathers of the respondents owned 1.4 hectares of land and mothers owned 0.6 hectares at the time of marriage (Table 2.9). The average size of households' joint operational landholdings at the time of marriage was 3.5 hectares, which is larger than the sum of owned landholdings because of additional land acquired through tenancy arrangements. Share tenancy was the most common land tenure contract, particularly in Central Luzon. Landownership by females was significantly lower than that by males in the parents' generation, even when land was relatively abundant.

Owing to the practice of partible inheritance, the respondents and their siblings inherited smaller areas of land than their parents' landholdings.[12] On the

---

11. The *t*-test of the difference in means of completed years in schooling across generations for the same gender group showed a significant increase in educational attainment over time.

12. In Panay, where the population density is higher than in Central Luzon, we observe "joint ownership" for small plots of land that cannot be divided into smaller units without sacrificing efficiency. A piece of land is cultivated on rotation by children (including females) over an agreed period of time, normally one year. Rotation, which is also found in our Sumatra sites, may be a way to avoid excessive land fragmentation.

TABLE 2.9 Landholdings, by gender and generation, in the Philippine villages (hectares)

Individual members	Male	Female	Male minus female
Parents' owned landholdings	1.40	0.60	0.80**
Inherited landholdings[a] by:			
Respondents and spouses	0.58	0.22	0.36**
Siblings of respondents	0.44	0.25	0.19**
First born	0.61	0.32	0.29**
Married	0.50	0.27	0.23**
Older children of respondents[b]	0.33	0.18	0.15**
First born	0.39	0.22	0.17**
Married	0.45	0.23	0.22**
Younger children of respondents[c]	0.26	0.10	0.16**

NOTE: ** indicates significance at the 1 percent level.

[a] Includes actual and prospective bequests.

[b] Children aged 21 years and over.

[c] Children aged 13–20 years.

average, male and female children in the respondents' generation received 0.6 and 0.2 hectares, respectively. The average size of landholdings of respondents' households as of the 1997 survey was only 1.5 hectares, which is much smaller than their parents' landholdings. Older and younger children of the respondents, on the average, receive about 0.25 hectares.

There has also been a persistent preference in land bequests in favor of male heirs. The first-born son is particularly favored because it is common in the Philippines to give land to the eldest son and to provide schooling to other children to prepare them for urban jobs. Married children of either gender received significantly more land than their single siblings do. Moreover, married males inherited more land than married females because land usually forms the main portion of the male dowry given to a son upon marriage (Andersen 1962).

We hypothesize that land is preferentially given to sons because rice farming is more intensive in male labor and returns to male labor are higher than those to female labor. Among the family members, the husband is more heavily involved than female members in rice production.[13] Given the declining importance of female labor in rice farming, we expect that daughters inherit less land, to the extent that land inheritance decisions are made in accordance with the value of land to each child.

13. Female family members are observed to be more actively engaged in post-production activities such as rice milling, winnowing and gathering of grains, and processing of milled rice as native delicacies (Diaz et al. 1994).

Nonland assets, which are passed on to the next generation, include residential houses and lots, draft animals, capital equipment, vehicles, household durables, and cash. Whereas traditionally the youngest son receives the parental house and lot, it is increasingly common for the child who takes care of elderly parents to inherit the parental house and lot, regardless of birth order. We did not include nonland assets in our analysis because only 40 percent of the sample households in 1997 had decided on future bequests of nonland assets to heirs.

The Scope of the Philippine Study

As we have just seen, there have been considerable changes in land inheritance and schooling between men and women over generations. We hypothesize that parents are concerned with both efficiency and the gender equity of wealth transfers to their heirs. The fact that the importance of male labor has increased in rice farming over time indicates that sons have greater comparative advantage than daughters in farming. Consequently, parents tend to bequeath larger areas of land to sons than to daughters. For both efficiency and equity considerations, parents invest more in the schooling of daughters than of sons, because daughters have a comparative advantage in nonfarm jobs where returns to human capital investments tend to be higher.

In order to substantiate these hypotheses, we will perform various regression analyses in the following two chapters. First, we will explore the determinants of land inheritance and schooling decisions made by parents for respondents and by respondents for children, in order to demonstrate that land inheritance and schooling are the two major alternative ways of transferring wealth from one generation to another. Second, we will estimate an agricultural income function to confirm, among other things, the weak effect of human capital on the efficiency of farm management. Third, we will identify the critical importance of human capital, represented by schooling, in nonfarm jobs through the estimation of functions explaining both participation in nonfarm employment and wage earnings. Fourth, based on the estimation of the agricultural income and nonfarm income functions, we will assess the implications of differential land inheritance and schooling between sons and daughters on their lifetime incomes. Fifth, we will examine the importance of land and human capital in the income distribution of rural households by performing the decomposition analysis of income distribution. After conducting these analyses in Chapter 3, we will proceed in Chapter 4 to analyze patterns of expenditures and schooling of younger children in order to shed light on gender equity among current household members including younger children.

3 Gender Equity in Land Inheritance and Schooling

The major purposes of this chapter are to examine parents' preferences with respect to the allocation of land bequests and investments in schooling between sons and daughters, and to assess the effects of differential land inheritance and schooling on lifetime income. For these purposes, we estimate land inheritance and schooling determination functions, farm and nonfarm income determination functions, and wage earnings function.

We demonstrate that the gender bias against daughters in schooling investment disappeared in the respondents' generation and that, in the children's generation, daughters' schooling attainment is significantly higher than sons'. On the other hand, we find that sons consistently inherit larger areas of farmland than daughters. We also provide statistical evidence that the gender bias associated with parents' schooling and landholding gradually disappeared, indicating that parents have egalitarian bequest motives for sons and daughters. Consistent with such findings, estimated lifetime incomes of sons and daughters tend to be equal, which supports the central thesis of this study that parents follow the "equal outcomes" rule as they care equally for sons and daughters.

Analyses of Land Inheritance and Schooling

Readers who are not interested in the technical details of statistical estimation can proceed directly to the "Summary of Findings" at the end of this section on page 73.[1]

Specification of Estimated Functions

Let us assume that both years of schooling and the amount of land bequeathed to children are jointly determined by parents. Since land is typically bestowed as part of the marriage gift, and since children usually finish schooling prior to marriage, we can assume that schooling is predetermined at the time that

---

1. This section draws on Estudillo, Quisumbing, and Otsuka (2001b).

parental land bequest decisions are made. Moreover, whereas it is rare for children never to have attended school in the Philippines, it is not unusual for some children not to receive any land from their parents.

This suggests that an appropriate estimation model would be a recursive simultaneous system of equations, in which the schooling investment function is estimated first, followed by the estimation of the second-stage land inheritance function, using the predicted values of schooling as one of the regressors in the land inheritance function. Since not all children receive land, the land inheritance function is estimated as a Tobit. Estimating both functions simultaneously allows us to exploit the correlation between error terms in the two equations and provides additional evidence on whether or not schooling and land are viewed as substitutes by parents.

Denoting inherited land in hectares by S and completed years in school by E, we specify the system of equations as follows:

$$S^* = \Sigma a_i \text{ (child characteristics)} + \Sigma b_j \text{ (parents' characteristics)}$$
$$+ \Sigma c_k \text{ (daughter dummy)} \times \text{(parents' characteristics)}$$
$$+ d \text{ (predicted years of schooling)} + \text{intercept} + e_1,$$
$$S = S^* \text{ if } S^* > 0$$
$$S = 0 \text{ otherwise}, \tag{3.1}$$

where a_i, b_j, c_k, and d are regression parameters and e_1 is an error term.

$$E = \Sigma \alpha_i \text{ (child characteristics)} + \Sigma \beta_j \text{ (parents' characteristics)}$$
$$+ \Sigma \gamma_k \text{ (daughter dummy)} \times \text{(parents' characteristics)}$$
$$+ \text{intercept} + e_2, \tag{3.2}$$

where α_i, β_j, and γ_k are regression parameters and e_2 is an error term and Corr $[e_1, e_2] = e_{12}$. The system of equations is estimated using full information maximum likelihood (Greene 1997). We estimate equations (3.1) and (3.2) separately for the wealth transfers from the generation of parents of respondents to respondents and siblings, and from respondents to children.

Child characteristics include birth year and its squared term, and eldest son, other son, and eldest daughter dummies. From the estimated coefficients of the last three dummies, we can test whether there is autonomous discrimination against daughters and younger children within a household. If a_i and α_i, related to gender and birth order effects, are found to have opposite signs, they are consistent with the hypothesis that land inheritance and schooling are alternative ways of transferring wealth. In other words, we expect that if sons are favored in land inheritance they are disfavored in schooling. We use three additional child characteristics as identifiers for the schooling equation: a dummy for being born after 1955, a dummy for the death of one's father before age 15, and a similar dummy for the death of one's mother. The dummy for being born after 1955 attempts to capture the impact of changes in landownership through land reform—which was implemented around 1975 in our survey villages (Otsuka 1991)—on the schooling of children who would have been in their early twenties or younger. If land reform increased parental wealth significantly, children would have had more opportunities to proceed to higher education rather than join the labor force. The death of either parent before age 15 is hypothesized to decrease completed years of schooling, owing to the loss of an income earner.

Parents' characteristics include father's and mother's education in terms of schooling years, and father's and mother's inherited land in hectares.[2] Since the interaction terms between parents' characteristics and daughter dummy are also included, b_j and β_j are expected to measure the effects of parental characteristics on son's land inheritance and schooling, whereas c_k and γ_k capture the gender bias associated with parental characteristics. Thus, for example, if an educated mother particularly favors her daughter's schooling, the coefficient of the interaction term between the daughter dummy and mother's education is positive. For the transfer from the respondents' to the children's generation, we also included dummies for the tenure status of respondents' inherited land as one of the parental characteristics. Tenure information on land held by the respondent's parents is not available in the 1989 data. All living children, as well as deceased children who were at least age 21 at death, are included in the estimation.[3]

Land Inheritance and Schooling in the Respondents' Generation

Table 3.1 presents regression results for the recursive simultaneous equation system with completed years of schooling and land bequests for the respondent generation. In the schooling equation, the coefficient on birth year is positive and that on its square is negative, suggesting a secular increase in education through time, albeit at a diminishing rate. Neither sons nor eldest daughters are favored relative to other daughters, although the coefficient on the eldest son dummy is negative (though only significant at 10 percent). Thus, in general, schooling investments are gender neutral in the respondent generation. Father's education has a strong positive effect on schooling, probably owing to increased income earned by those with more schooling. There are no indications that better educated fathers and mothers treat children of either gender preferentially in schooling investments. In contrast, gender preference seems to be associated with parental landownership. Mothers with more land invest preferentially in their daughters' schooling. As expected, the death of the father before the child

---

2. For the respondents' generation we used the size of parents' owned land at the time of marriage as the variable representing parents' physical resources, and for the children's generation we used the respondents' inherited landholdings.

3. Children commonly begin farming independently at the age of about 21, or earlier if they get married.

TABLE 3.1 Determinants of schooling and land bequests in the respondents' generation: Simultaneous equations, Tobit estimates

Variables	Schooling	Land
Constant	−3,230.23**	−617.02
	(−3.54)	(−0.70)
Birth year	3.26**	0.65
	(3.45)	(0.72)
Birth year squared	−0.82**	−0.17
	(−3.36)	(−0.74)
Eldest son	−0.49	1.07**
	(−1.65)	(4.76)
Other sons	−0.36	0.73**
	(−1.51)	(3.86)
Eldest daughter	−0.28	0.42*
	(−1.18)	(2.42)
Father's schooling	0.11**	0.06*
	(3.05)	(1.99)
Mother's schooling	0.09*	−0.05
	(1.80)	(−1.73)
Daughter × father's schooling	−0.05	−0.08*
	(−1.01)	(−2.38)
Daughter × mother's schooling	0.03	0.02
	(0.47)	(0.55)
Father's land	0.05	0.10**
	(1.34)	(5.02)
Mother's land	0.07	0.07**
	(1.76)	(3.33)
Daughter × father's land	0.04	0.01
	(0.86)	(0.24)
Daughter × mother's land	0.12*	0.13**
	(2.50)	(3.00)
Village dummies[a]		
CL1	−0.33	−0.49*
	(−1.21)	(−2.39)
CL2	−0.18	−0.32
	(−0.75)	(−1.74)
P1	0.65*	−1.23**
	(2.52)	(−4.83)
P2	0.94**	−0.30
	(3.38)	(−1.14)
Dummy for birth year after 1955	0.20	
	(0.62)	
Dummy for death of father before age 15	−0.80**	
	(−3.53)	

(continued)

TABLE 3.1 *Continued*

Variables	Schooling	Land
Dummy for death of mother before age 15	−0.43	
	(−1.63)	
Years of schooling (endogenous)		0.15
		(0.86)
Number of observations	1,934	1,934
Log-likelihood ratio		−3,410.32
Variance estimates		
σ^2	9.23	2.81
ρ		−0.16
s_{12}/s_{22}		−0.09
		(−0.49)
$s[e_1 \mid e_2]$		1.66**
		(45.99)
F-test of the equality of coefficients		
Father's schooling = mother's schooling	0.13	11.96**
Father's land = mother's land	0.14	0.22
Schooling interaction terms equal	0.75	3.05*
Land interaction terms equal	0.96	17.26**
Schooling plus interaction terms equal	4.50*	6.05**
Land plus interaction terms equal	0.21	7.98**

NOTES: Numbers in parentheses are *t*-values; * indicates significance at the 5 percent level; ** at the 1 percent level.

[a] CL1 and CL2 refer to Central Luzon Villages 1 and 2, and P1 and P2 refer to Panay Villages 1 and 2, respectively.

reached 15 years of age has a detrimental effect on schooling—an effect greater than that of the mother's death, possibly because fathers were the main bread-winners in the older generation. The dummy for being born after 1955—a proxy for the potential impact of land reform—has no significant effect on schooling for the members of the older generation, who were born in the 1940s. By the time land reform was implemented, most of the children in this generation would already have left school.

Turning to the land equation, we find that birth year and its squared term do not significantly affect land inheritance in the respondents' generation, which means that earlier-born children do not receive significantly more land than later-born children. Dummy variables for gender and birth order show that the eldest son, other sons, and the eldest daughter receive more land than do other daughters (the control category).[4] Eldest sons have the largest share of the

---

4. One possible reason land is unequally distributed among heirs is to maintain economies of scale in rice production. There are indivisibilities in rice farming such as those associated with

parents' bequeathed land, significantly exceeding the bequest to eldest daughters. Sons of better educated fathers receive more land, whereas their daughters are disfavored, as shown by the positive and significant coefficients of father's education and the negative and significant coefficient of its interaction term with the daughter dummy. Note that the father's education might be a proxy for household nonland wealth, which might have been used to expand the size of landholdings eventually bequeathed to sons. The correlation between father's schooling and age is only −.42, indicating that his schooling is not intimately related to his farming experience.

There are clear wealth effects on land inheritance in the respondents' generation. The coefficients of parents' landholdings are positive and significant, indicating that children whose parents had larger landholdings inherited larger areas of land. It is also interesting to note that, among the respondents and their siblings, mothers' owned land has a far greater effect on daughters' than on sons' inherited land. In contrast, fathers' owned land has a significant effect on sons' inherited land, but the interaction with the daughter dummy is not significant, which fails to support the presence of gender bias associated with fathers' landholdings.

To assess whether parents with more physical and human capital treat children of different sexes differently, we perform an F-test of the equality of coefficients of the following cases (see the bottom panel of Table 3.1): (1) father's and mother's landholdings and schooling; (2) interaction terms of the daughter dummy with father's and mother's landholdings and schooling; and (3) the sum of the coefficient of father's and mother's landholdings and schooling and the relevant interaction term with the daughter dummy. If the coefficients of the relevant variables are significantly different from each other, gender preference exists with respect to the influence of parental resources. In the schooling function in the respondents' generation, we found significant inequality of coefficients in case (3) with respect to the schooling attainment of parents, which indicates the presence of gender bias; that is, better educated fathers prefer to invest in sons' schooling. In the land inheritance function, we found significant differences in coefficients in cases (2) and (3) with respect to landholdings of parents, which means that there exists gender bias in relation to parental landholdings; that is, land-owning mothers preferentially bestow land on daughters. Thus, we cannot rule out discrimination by the parents: mothers favor girls and fathers favor boys.

Interestingly enough, years of schooling is not significant in the land regression, indicating that parents do not compensate children who complete fewer years in school with larger land bequests, holding all other child char-

---

capital equipment, marketing, and even farming knowledge. As will be shown later, however, the estimated rice income function does not provide evidence to support the existence of significant scale economies in rice production.

acteristics constant. This result is consistent with bequest patterns in the United States, which show that parents tend to divide their estates equally among heirs, regardless of the size of the estate or earnings differentials among heirs (Menchik 1980).

Land Inheritance and Schooling in the Child Generation

Table 3.2 presents the estimation results for the child generation. Comparing the results in Table 3.1 with those in Table 3.2 enables us to ascertain whether or not intergenerational transfer patterns have shifted over time. It is immediately apparent that the gender-specific pattern of investment in schooling and land bestowals is more pronounced in the child generation.

Eldest daughters tend to receive more schooling than other daughters do.[5] There is also a strong indication that both the eldest son and other sons receive less schooling than other daughters in the children's generation. Thus, a clear gender preference has emerged for schooling investments in the children's generation.[6] In this generation, better educated mothers favor sons, contrary to the hypothesis that mothers prefer to invest in daughters' human capital because they benefit more from investment in daughters, whereas fathers benefit more from sons.[7] Although it is difficult to explain this result, one possible reason could be that educated mothers, who have some decisionmaking power within households, express reluctance to invest in daughters' schooling because educated daughters tend to leave home.

The secular increase in schooling continues to benefit later-born children, as shown by the significantly positive coefficient on birth year, and the implementation of land reform seems to have conferred additional benefits on this generation of children, who would have been nine years old, on average, at the time of implementation. None of the parental death dummies is significant, probably because very few of the parents were deceased.[8]

Similarly to the respondents' generation, both eldest sons and other sons are favored with respect to land inheritance, which is in sharp contrast to school-

---

5. Butcher and Case (1994) report that daughters' schooling in the United States has been affected negatively by the presence of other daughters. Note, however, that these findings are challenged by Hauser and Kuo (1998) and Kaestner (1997). Using more extensive datasets and younger birth cohorts, these authors offer no strong support for the effects of the gender composition of siblings on daughters' (and sons') education. They unanimously agree that an additional sibling reduces significantly the schooling investments in each child.

6. The effect of birth order on children's schooling appears to differ by culture. Although we find that birth order is more important in the case of sons in the Philippines, Binder (1998) finds that among Mexican households girls' schooling depends relatively more on birth order, whereas boys' schooling is more sensitive to the number of children and parental wealth.

7. According to Thomas (1990, 1994), parents tend to devote more resources to improve the health outcomes and survival rates of children of the same sex. Couch and Dunn (1997) find that intergenerational correlations of schooling, earnings, and hours of work are stronger across pairs of parents and child of the same gender than parents and child of different gender.

8. If a parent was deceased at the time of our survey, we interviewed the surviving spouse.

TABLE 3.2 Determinants of schooling and land bequests in the children's generation: Simultaneous equations, Tobit estimates

Variables	Schooling	Land
Constant	−33,876.11**	−555.63
	(−24.06)	(−0.12)
Birth year	34.54**	0.58
	(24.12)	(0.12)
Birth year squared	−8.80**	−0.15
	(−24.19)	(−0.12)
Eldest son	−1.21**	0.61**
	(−2.96)	(2.85)
Other sons	−1.72**	0.54*
	(−4.69)	(2.05)
Eldest daughter	0.46*	0.16
	(2.06)	(1.68)
Father's schooling	0.12*	0.02
	(2.39)	(0.79)
Mother's schooling	0.13*	0.01
	(2.42)	(0.36)
Daughter × father's schooling	0.09	0.03
	(1.34)	(1.02)
Daughter × mother's schooling	−0.21**	−0.01
	(−2.78)	(−0.17)
Father's land	0.34	0.19**
	(1.68)	(2.58)
Mother's land	0.25	0.06
	(0.63)	(0.45)
Daughter × father's land	−0.02	−0.02
	(−0.08)	(−0.28)
Daughter × mother's land	−0.03	0.13
	(−0.54)	(0.89)
Tenure dummies		
Owned	−0.17	0.06
	(−0.76)	(0.72)
Leasehold	0.16	−0.04
	(−0.39)	(−0.24)
Share tenant	0.06	0.05
	(0.06)	(0.19)
Village dummies[a]		
CL1	−0.73*	0.42**
	(−2.45)	(2.90)
CL2	0.14	0.57**
	(0.54)	(5.86)
P1	1.02**	0.06
	(3.51)	(0.31)

(continued)

TABLE 3.2 *Continued*

Variables	Schooling	Land
P2	0.34	0.18
	(1.25)	(1.61)
Dummy for birth year after 1955	0.67*	
	(2.30)	
Dummy for death of father before age 15	0.16	(0.12)
Dummy for death of mother before age 15	0.50	(1.52)
Years of schooling (endogenous)		−0.02
		(−0.17)
Number of observations	1,471	1,471
Log-likelihood ratio		−2,083.17
Variance estimates		
σ^2	7.36	0.59
ρ		0.10
s_{12}/s_{22}		0.03
		(0.21)
$s[e_1 \mid e_2]$		0.76**
		(36.49)
F-test of the equality of coefficients		
Father's schooling = mother's schooling	0.05	0.11
Father's land = mother's land	0.10	2.19
Schooling interaction terms equal	6.55**	0.05
Land interaction terms equal	0.40	0.89
Schooling plus interaction terms equal	8.75**	3.25*
Land plus interaction terms equal	0.93	12.64**

NOTES: Numbers in parentheses are *t*-values; * indicates significance at the 5 percent level; ** at the 1 percent level.

[a] CL1 and CL2 refer to Central Luzon Villages 1 and 2, and P1 and P2 refer to Panay Villages 1 and 2, respectively.

ing investment. Wealth effects—particularly in father's land—continue to persist. However, there is no indication that parents exhibit preferential treatment by gender based on the resources they control. Although the coefficient on predicted schooling is negative—indicating that children who complete more years in school receive less land—it is not significantly different from zero. From this result, we cannot say that parents trade schooling for land sequentially. However, judging from the coefficients of the dummies for eldest son and other sons, which are positive in the land inheritance regression and negative in the schooling regression, the hypothesis that schooling and land inheritance are alternative means of intergenerational wealth transfer cannot be denied.

The *F*-tests of the equality of coefficients (see the bottom panel of Table 3.2) show a much less pronounced gender bias in schooling investments associated with parental wealth and land inheritance in the child generation, indicating that parental wealth transfers to the younger generation have become more egalitarian. However, the gender-differentiated pattern of wealth transfers, in which sons are preferred with respect to land inheritance whereas daughters are treated more favorably in schooling investments, persists even in the child generation.

Family fixed-effects results (not reported here) allow us to control effectively for family-level unobservables, which may affect the intrahousehold distribution of schooling and land, although they are single-equation estimates that do not take into account correlation between the two types of transfers.[9] The results are qualitatively similar to the simultaneous equation Tobit results. Fixed-effects estimates on schooling show that sons tend to have less schooling relative to younger daughters, which is diametrically different from the case of land inheritance. With regard to land bequests, none of the interaction terms of parental education with child gender is significant in the fixed-effects results, suggesting that better educated parents do not necessarily favor children of the same gender in land bequests. Nor do fathers with larger landholdings exhibit gender preference in land bequests in either the respondents' or the children's generation. However, the interaction term of mother's land with the daughter dummy is significant and positive in both generations, suggesting that mothers tend to favor daughters, relative to sons, in land inheritance. The coefficient of this interaction term has a higher value in the fixed-effects Tobit model in the children's generation, which means that mothers tend to favor daughters even more in the younger generation. Since daughters are favored in schooling whereas sons are favored in land inheritance, the question immediately arises as to the net effects of such differential treatment on daughters' and sons' lifetime incomes.

---

9. Land and schooling regressions were also estimated with family fixed effects for the subset of households that intend to bestow land on at least two children. Using family fixed-effects methods allows us to control for the possible correlation between the explanatory variables and error terms resulting from the omission of unobservable household characteristics. Because of this procedure, we lost 23 percent of children above 21 years of age in the respondents' generation but only 1 percent in the children's generation. In terms of households excluded from estimation, we excluded 22 percent of households in 1989 and 9 percent of households in 1998. The restriction to children aged 21 years or older excluded more households in 1989 because most of the sample children were still young. Note, however, that, since selection into the sample is a family-specific unobservable, sample selection does not bias the estimated coefficients. For the land equation, because the dependent variable is censored, we applied Honoré's (1992) fixed-effects estimation method, that is, a least-absolute deviations method, which is preferred to an ordinary Tobit with dummy variables. Since years of schooling is a continuous variable, we also applied random-effects and household fixed-effects models.

Summary of Findings

1. In the respondent generation, schooling is neutral with respect to gender and birth order. In the child generation, the eldest daughter tends to receive more schooling than other daughters, and both the eldest son and other sons receive less.
2. In both the respondent and child generations, the eldest son and other sons are favored with respect to land inheritance, which is in sharp contrast to schooling investments. This is consistent with the substitutability of land inheritance and schooling investments in wealth transfers in the rural Philippines.
3. In the respondent generation, better educated fathers prefer to invest in sons' schooling, whereas landowning mothers preferentially bestow land on daughters. This gender bias associated with parents' schooling and landholdings seems to have been weakened in the child generation, indicating that parental wealth transfers have become more egalitarian.
4. Predicted years of schooling has a negative but nonsignificant coefficient in the land inheritance function, which suggests that parents do not compensate children who complete fewer years in school with larger land bequests.

Determinants of Household Incomes

This section identifies the determinants of households' farm and nonfarm incomes, with a particular focus on the effects of farm size and human capital variables in two income functions.[10] Our hypothesis is that parents have egalitarian bequest motives. They tend to give more land to sons and provide more schooling to daughters because such a bequest pattern maximizes the amount of aggregate family wealth by exploiting the comparative advantage of sons in farming and daughters in nonfarm employment.

Specification of Regression Functions

We estimate separate income functions for the 1985 and 1998 survey years, for which income data are available, because changes in nonfarm employment opportunities, among other things, led to structural changes in income determination functions over time. The explanatory variables included are the following: (1) new rice technology, represented by the interaction term between the adoption of modern varieties (MV) of rice and the presence of irrigation; (2) farm size; (3) land tenure dummies for owner-cultivators, holders of a Certificate of Land Transfer (CLT) or leaseholders, and share tenants, with landless workers being the default category; (4) the number of working mem-

---

10. This section draws on Estudillo, Quisumbing, and Otsuka (2001a).

bers; (5) proxies for the human capital of working members represented byratios of female working members and working members in certain age and schooling categories; and (6) village dummies. We interacted both MV–irrigation and farm size with a farm household dummy (denoted by FHD), because there are landless households in the sample. Thus, the coefficients of these variables pertain to the behavior of farm households. Since MV adoption was completed in 1998, the MV–irrigation variable measures the impact of irrigation.

We estimated an ordinary least squares (OLS) regression model for the full sample in 1985 ($N = 369$), whereas for 1998, for which we have 247 households, we used the two-stage Heckman (1979) procedure to correct for the selectivity bias potentially caused by migration of some of the 1985 respondents.[11]

The dependent variable in the first-stage regression, which is a probit function, is equal to 1 if the household is present in both years and to 0 if it is present only in 1985. Independent variables are identical to those in the 1985 income determination functions, since the determinants of income in 1985 would affect a household's decision to remain in the village but not income earned in 1998.[12] The predicted inverse Mills ratio, or selectivity correction, is then used as a regressor in the second-stage equation, with income as the dependent variable. A double-log specification is used for continuous variables, so that the estimated coefficients are elasticities. On the other hand, if the explanatory variables are expressed in proportions, logarithms are not computed, so the coefficient shows the percentage changes in income when the proportion changes from zero to unity.

Estimation Results

Table 3.3 shows the estimation results of the function explaining the probability that the households were present in both 1985 and 1998. Significant coefficients of owner, CLT/leasehold, and share tenancy dummies imply that landless households are more likely to migrate. Those households with more female members have a higher propensity to leave the village because females more commonly seek nonfarm jobs than males (Lanzona 1998). In contrast, households with a higher ratio of working members with tertiary education and households located in irrigated and favorable villages are more likely to stay. The former result does not imply that educated members work in the village. It

---

11. In addition to the two-stage Heckman (1979) procedure, we also estimated an OLS model for the income functions in 1998. We found that the results of the OLS model in terms of the magnitude and standard errors of the coefficients of the explanatory variables are fairly similar to the results of the two-stage Heckman procedure, indicating that the selectivity bias is not significantly large.

12. It is important to mention that the two-stage Heckman procedure can be theoretically applied only in the 1998 income determination functions because of the identification problem. It is difficult to think of a single identifying instrument that affects the probability of the household being present in 1985 that does not affect household income in the same year.

is more likely that educated members go outside to engage in nonfarm jobs and other members stay in the village, as will be demonstrated in subsequent sections of this chapter.

The other four columns of Table 3.3 demonstrate the estimation results of the reduced farm income determination functions. The coefficient of the MV– irrigation variable is significant in the farm income functions and the value of the coefficient rose from 0.16 in 1985 to 0.42 in 1998. These coefficients indicate that the availability of irrigation combined with the adoption of higher-yielding modern varieties increased farm income by 17 percent in 1985 and 52 percent in 1998.

Since land income is the major contributor to farm income, it is not surprising to find that farm size has a highly significant coefficient in the farm income function. The coefficients of 0.63 in 1985 and 0.45 in 1998 are significantly less than unity, which indicates that farm income increases less than proportionally with farm size. Such findings suggest the absence of scale economies in rice farming in the Philippines, which precludes the possibility of transferring land to a single heir to benefit from scale advantages. Compared with the landless households, owner cultivators, CLT holders and leaseholders, and share tenants have increasingly captured the increased returns to land and entrepreneurship.[13] None of the tenure status dummies, however, is significant in the nonfarm income functions; thus, landless households do not appear to have inherent constraints in getting nonfarm jobs.

Human capital variables (age, schooling, and gender) do not seem to exert any significant impact on farm incomes. The absence of significant effects of schooling in rice farming indicates that land and schooling are not close complements. We obtain the same qualitative result when schooling of the household head is used as a schooling variable in the estimation of the income function (Otsuka, Cordova, and David 1992). This is also consistent with the general observation that schooling does not affect the pace of MV adoption in the Philippines (for example, Otsuka, Gascon, and Asano 1994). The coefficient of the ratio of female working members is not significant in either farm or nonfarm income functions, which would imply that women tend to contribute to farm and nonfarm incomes as much as men. As we have seen in Chapter 2, however, women do not work much in rice farming. Therefore, the absence of a gender effect on farm income is surprising. It may well be that the marginal gender effect, which can be estimated by regression techniques, is nil even though the overall effect of gender is substantial. That is to say, women do not work much on the farm because the marginal product of their labor input declines significantly if they allocate more labor to farming.

---

13. According to Estudillo, Fujimura, and Hossain (1999), private profitability for farm households in rice production has risen over the past 30 years partly owing to higher domestic rice prices relative to the world rice price, improvement in yields, and the shift of tenure relations in favor of leasehold tenancy and owner cultivation.

TABLE 3.3 Income determination functions in Central Luzon and Panay, 1985 and 1998

Variables	Probability of being present in 1985 and 1998 (probit)[a]	Farm income		Nonfarm income	
		1985	1998	1985	1998
Constant	-0.38	7.34**	8.84**	6.01**	8.49**
	(-0.75)	(22.73)	(12.06)	(9.11)	(7.91)
FHD × MV × irrigation[b]	-0.13	0.16*	0.42*	0.11	-0.52
	(-0.89)	(1.95)	(1.84)	(0.69)	(-1.51)
FHD × log farm size[b]	0.06	0.63**	0.45**	0.14	0.07
	(0.60)	(9.26)	(4.96)	(1.06)	(0.51)
Owner	0.65**	1.11**	1.21**	-0.20	0.01
	(2.53)	(7.00)	(5.05)	(-0.63)	(0.04)
Certificate of Land Transfer/leasehold tenancy	0.69**	0.72**	0.97**	-0.23	0.00
	(3.17)	(5.33)	(4.28)	(-0.90)	(0.00)
Share tenancy	0.48*	0.27	0.76**	-0.42	0.60
	(1.69)	(1.50)	(2.60)	(-1.22)	(1.43)
Number of working members	0.06	0.21*	0.15	0.58*	0.87**
	(0.35)	(1.73)	(0.97)	(2.29)	(3.73)
Ratio of female working members	-0.89*	0.08	-0.12	0.21	-0.23
	(-2.21)	(0.34)	(-0.45)	(0.43)	(-0.58)
Ratio of working members					
Aged 56–65	-0.21	-0.48*	0.13	1.58**	0.67
	(-0.49)	(-1.71)	(0.33)	(2.52)	(1.10)
Aged 46–55	-0.57	0.33	-0.23	1.45**	0.24
	(-1.29)	(1.14)	(-0.58)	(2.38)	(0.40)

Aged 36–45	0.19	0.04	0.11	0.91*	1.08*
	(0.56)	(0.21)	(0.31)	(1.94)	(2.10)
Aged 26–35	0.02	0.04	0.08	0.81*	1.14*
	(0.08)	(0.21)	(0.26)	(1.81)	(2.33)
Ratio of working members with secondary schooling	0.29	0.25	–0.06	0.86**	0.02
	(1.15)	(1.60)	(–0.30)	(2.58)	(0.05)
College education	0.88**	0.17	–0.14	1.09**	1.19**
	(2.48)	(0.84)	(–0.54)	(2.74)	(3.22)
Village dummies					
CL1[b]	0.99**	0.85**	0.73*	–0.37	0.77
	(3.33)	(4.55)	(1.88)	(–1.03)	(1.32)
CL2[b]	0.07	0.23	0.90**	–0.33	0.70
	(0.24)	(1.24)	(3.01)	(–0.89)	(1.56)
P1[c]	0.66*	0.41*	0.10	0.62*	0.79
	(2.20)	(2.13)	(0.29)	(1.69)	(1.52)
P2[c]	0.99**	0.46**	–0.45	0.17	0.46
	(3.55)	(2.62)	(–1.31)	(0.50)	(0.92)
Selection control			–0.72*		–0.72
			(–1.67)		(–1.15)
Number of observations		361	220	298	186
Log-likelihood ratio	–201.68				
R^2		.50	.54	.16	.24

NOTES: FHD refers to the farm household dummy; MV refers to modern rice varieties. Numbers in parentheses are t-values; * indicates significance at the 5 percent level; ** at the 1 percent level

[a] Explanatory variables in the probit are the 1985 values of the regressors in the 1985 income determination functions.

[b] CL1 and CL2 refer to irrigated and rainfed villages in Central Luzon, respectively.

[c] P1 and P2 refer to irrigated and rainfed villages in Panay, respectively.

Both the relatively old and young members were engaged in nonfarm work in 1985, which would reflect the fact that the predominant nonfarm employment opportunities in 1985 were those in which almost all age groups can participate, such as informal trade, carpentry, and small manufacturing. In 1998, in contrast, formal employment in the nonfarm sector became more dominant and, hence, the better educated members of the younger generation were engaged in nonfarm jobs. This interpretation is further supported by a positive and highly significant coefficient of college education in the nonfarm income function in 1998.[14] In contrast, in 1985 there is no significant difference in the nonfarm income between secondary school and college graduates.[15] Highly remunerative nonfarm jobs in recent years seem to require college education. The coefficients of the selection control variable are negative and weakly significant in the farm income function. It appears that the selection bias is not too large partly because of the weak effect of locational selection and partly because of the large variance of the selection variable.[16]

It is important to emphasize that our regression results provide evidence that schooling has a significant impact on nonfarm income but not on farm income. Thus, daughters are sent to school because women experience increased returns in human capital in the nonfarm sector (Psacharopoulos 1985, 1994). In contrast, sons, who have less schooling, receive land because they have a comparative advantage in rice farming. This would imply that schooling investment increases one's comparative advantage in nonfarm jobs.

Determinants of Nonfarm Income

Since farm income is earned by the collective labor input of family members, incomes cannot be assigned to individual members. In contrast, it is feasible to identify earners of nonfarm incomes. In this section, in order to identify more precisely the effects of schooling on nonfarm incomes, we estimate the func-

---

14. We estimated an income determination function using average age and schooling of working members in the household as human capital variables instead of ratios of working members falling into different age and schooling groups. Again, we found that schooling has a positive and significant effect on nonfarm income in 1998. Moreover, we found that schooling squared has a positive and significant coefficient in the nonfarm income function, indicating that nonfarm income increases more than proportionately with schooling.

15. Initially we tried to include schooling variables such as the ratio of working parents and children falling into different schooling categories. However, we found serious multicollinearity between parents' and children's education, indicating that parents' schooling is an important determinant of children's schooling (Couch and Dunn 1997).

16. We did a regression run of total income using the same right-hand-side variables as in Table 3.3. The results of the regression function of total income in 1985 are fairly similar to farm income and in 1998 are fairly similar to nonfarm income. These results are reasonable considering that farm income comprised a major portion of total household income in 1985, whereas nonfarm income was the more dominant income source in 1998.

tion explaining individual household members' decisions to participate in non-farm jobs as well as the wage earnings function.

Participation in Nonfarm Employment

We would like to determine whether daughters are indeed more involved than sons in nonfarm jobs.[17] Table 3.4 shows the characteristics and extent of participation in nonfarm employment by 352 single working children in our sample households in 1998. In our analysis of the determinants of nonfarm income, we consider only the 1998 sample because income data for individual household members were not available in 1985. Income data were available for all children regardless of their civil status and place of residence. We consider only unmarried working children, whether they reside in the village or have migrated. We excluded married working children because we do not have enough information on their household characteristics, which could potentially affect their labor market behavior.

Participation in nonfarm employment is defined as receiving income from paid nonfarm employment, which includes salaried employment, whether in the government or private sector, and any informal self-employment (for example, running a local variety store, vending, carpentry and masonry, sewing, and driving). In general, participants in nonfarm employment are full-time non-farm workers deriving a substantial portion of their monthly earnings from non-farm jobs.[18] Remittances sent by sons and daughters are about the same—455 pesos per month for daughters and 438 pesos per month for sons—which precludes the possibility that parents favor daughters' schooling, if they are expected to make larger remittances than sons (Rosenzweig 1986). Irrespective of gender, the amount of remittances is affected by the schooling attainment of children. On the average, a college graduate sends 1,146 pesos per month, a high school graduate 62 pesos, and an elementary school graduate 38 pesos. On the other hand, daily wage-workers and permanent laborers in rice farming, as well as unpaid family workers in their own rice farming activities and the unemployed, are considered to be nonparticipants in nonfarm activities.

Of the females, 60 percent participate in nonfarm employment, whereas among males the figure is only 42 percent. Female participants are about the same age as the male participants but have 1.6 more years of schooling. Non-participants of either gender complete fewer years of schooling and earn considerably less than the participants. A number of the nonparticipants work as unpaid family labor in rice farming. Male nonparticipants inherit larger areas of land, and female nonparticipants receive the smallest.

---

17. This section draws on Estudillo, Quisumbing, and Otsuka (2001c).

18. Only seven individuals participating in nonfarm employment reported having participated in farm employment.

TABLE 3.4 Participation in nonfarm employment and earnings of single working children in Central Luzon and Panay, 1998

Characteristics	Participants		Nonparticipants	
	Male	Female	Male	Female
Number of individuals	83	92	115	62
Average age	27	29	28	33
Average schooling (years)	9.6	11.2	8.0	10.1
Average inherited landholdings				
(hectares)	0.19	0.15	0.26	0.12
Average labor earnings				
(thousand pesos/year)	65.4	69.7	1.3	0.3
Nonfarm	64.9	69.7	0.0	0.0
Farm	0.5	0.0	1.3	0.3

NOTE: The exchange rate was US$1 = 38 pesos.

Estimation of Wage Earnings Function

We estimated the wage earnings function using a two-stage Heckman (1979) procedure to avoid the sample selection bias caused by a large number of non-participants who do not have nonfarm income. The first-stage estimation is a probit function in which the dependent variable is the probability that the individual participates in nonfarm employment. The dependent variable takes the value of 1 if the individual is a participant in nonfarm activities, and 0 if not.

The independent variables include individual characteristics such as age, age squared, schooling, daughter dummy, and size and tenure status of inherited land, as well as household characteristics such as number of working members, age and schooling of parents, value of house in 1989, adoption of modern rice technology represented by MV–irrigation interacted with the farm household dummy; and village dummies.[19] Village dummies capture regional differences in rates of participation in nonfarm employment.

We expect that nonfarm labor market participation increases with schooling, because it would positively affect expected labor earnings. It will also increase with age for a certain range and then decline gradually, so that age is expected to have a positive coefficient, whereas its squared term would have a negative coefficient. To the extent that female children have a comparative advantage in nonfarm work over male children, the daughter dummy is expected to have a positive coefficient. Dummies for tenure status, the area of inherited land, and rice technology variables are used to capture the possible effects of labor de-

---

19. We also included an interaction term between gender and schooling but it was insignificant.

mand for farm work on the decision to work in the nonfarm sector. We also presume that the individual job choice is affected not only by individual characteristics but also by the characteristics of other household members, particularly those of parents, because job choice may be determined jointly by household members. Thus, we include the number of working members in the household aged 15–65 years, regardless of type of job and parents' characteristics.

The second stage is an OLS regression, with yearly nonagricultural income as the dependent variable. The independent variables are those pertaining to individual characteristics, including a dummy variable for gender. It is assumed that nonfarm earnings are affected solely by individuals' characteristics because these are the attributes that are relevant in the labor market.

Table 3.5 shows the estimation results of the nonagricultural earnings function. Schooling and the daughter dummy have positive and highly significant effects on the probability of participating in nonfarm employment. These results are consistent with our hypothesis that daughters have a comparative advantage in nonfarm jobs. Participation in nonfarm employment increases with age, albeit at a diminishing rate. Controlling for their own age, children with older parents tend to participate less in nonfarm employment.

Our probit function estimates are transformed into probabilities by using the probability distribution function and inserting average values of the explanatory variables. We found that college graduates have a 74 percent probability of participating in nonfarm employment, in contrast to only 64 percent for secondary school graduates. On the average, daughters have a 70 percent probability of participating in nonfarm employment, compared with only 56 percent for sons.

TABLE 3.5 Nonfarm wage earnings function of single working children in Central Luzon and Panay, 1998

Variables	Probability of participating in nonfarm activities (probit)	Nonfarm income
Constant	−3.41**	−220,822.50
	(−3.04)	(−0.96)
Age	0.25**	9,509.56
	(3.75)	(0.50)
Age squared	−0.00**	−152.12
	(−3.81)	(−0.48)
Schooling	0.07**	11,555.73*
	(2.68)	(2.17)
Daughter dummy	0.42*	−5,248.74
	(2.44)	(0.80)

(continued)

TABLE 3.5 *Continued*

Variables	Probability of participating in nonfarm activities (probit)	Nonfarm income
Size of inherited land	−0.26	
	(−0.78)	
Dummies for tenure status of inherited land		
Owned	0.17	
	(0.61)	
Certificate of Land Transfer/leasehold tenancy	0.32	
	(1.21)	
Share tenancy	−0.44	
	(−1.00)	
Number of working members	−0.01	
	(−0.15)	
Parents' age[a]	−0.02	
	(−1.89)	
Parents' education[a]	0.01	
	(0.31)	
Value of house in 1989	−0.00	
	(−1.14)	
FHD × MV × irrigation[b]	0.21	
	(0.94)	
CL1[c]	−0.13	
	(−0.43)	
CL2[c]	0.10	
	(0.30)	
P1[d]	−0.25	
	(−0.74)	
P2[d]	0.39	
	(1.43)	
Number of observations	352	175
Selection control		44,133.83
		(0.42)
Wald χ^2		48.41
p-value		.00

NOTES: Numbers in parentheses are z-statistics; * indicates significance at the 5 percent level; ** at the 1 percent level.

[a] Average of mother and father.

[b] FHD refers to the farm household dummy; MV refers to modern varieties of rice.

[c] CL1 and CL2 refer to irrigated and rainfed villages, respectively, in Central Luzon.

[d] P1 and P2 refer to irrigated and rainfed villages, respectively, in Panay.

As expected, schooling is significant in the second-stage wage regression function. The estimated coefficient implies that an additional year of schooling increases nonfarm income significantly by 11,555 pesos per year, which is equivalent to about 15 percent of the yearly salary of a regular government employee in 1998. It is likely that returns to college education are quite high. Among our sample individuals, those who finished college have an average income three times higher than that for individuals who finished secondary schooling. Since the daughter dummy is insignificant, daughters earn as much as sons (the control), which means that gender discrimination in nonfarm jobs in the Philippines is nil. The selection control variable is not significant, indicating that the selection bias associated with not including nonparticipants in the nonagricultural wage earnings function is not too large.

Estimated Effects of Wealth Transfers on Lifetime Income

Readers who are not interested in the technical details of statistical estimation can proceed directly to the "Summary of Findings" at the end of this section on page 87.

Recall that the current distribution of land and education between sons and daughters is such that sons inherit 0.15 hectares more (Table 2.9), whereas daughters stay in school for 1.5 years longer than sons (Table 2.8). An important question is how much an additional hectare of land bequeathed to sons or an additional year of schooling invested in daughters contributes to their lifetime incomes. For this purpose, we make hypothetical computations based on the estimation results of the agricultural income function and the nonfarm wage earnings function.

The total income of the individual (Y_i) is specified as

$$Y_i = Y_F(S_i, A_i, g_i) + P(E_i, A_i, g_i)Y_N(E_i, A_i)$$
$$= R(S_i) + [1 - P(E_i, A_i, g_i)] Y_1(S_i)$$
$$+ P(E_i, A_i, g_i)Y_N(E_i, A_i), \quad i = \text{d, s}, \tag{3.3}$$

where Y_F stands for farm income; P corresponds to the probability of working in nonfarm jobs; Y_N represents nonfarm income; S is size of bequeathed land area; E is education level measured by schooling; A is age; g refers to gender-specific effects, such as physical strength and the extent of gender discrimination in nonfarm labor market; and "d" and "s" index the daughter and son, respectively.

We assume that Y_F is divided into returns to land (R) and labor (Y_1), both of which are functions of farm size (S). $Y_1(S)$ refers to labor income from farming when a family member works full time on-farm. Component farm incomes (that is, R and Y_1) are assumed to be independent of schooling (E), gender (g), and age (A). In accordance with the estimation results of the nonfarm labor earnings function, P is a positive function of E, A, and g, whereas Y_N is a function of E and A.

In our assessment of the value of land, we consider two important roles of land: as an input for income generation and as a collateral asset. Land serves as an insurance against major income shocks because it can be used as collateral for credit. Thus, the market price of land would reflect not only the discounted present value of expected incomes accrued to land but also its collateral value (Binswanger and Rosenzweig 1986). In the Philippines, the land market is severely restricted owing to the prohibition on transactions in land received through the land reform. However, an informal market in usufruct rights has emerged—the phenomenon known as usufruct mortgage or land pawning (Nagarajan, Quisumbing, and Otsuka 1991). Under pawning transactions, the cultivation right is pawned to the creditor in return for cash. Thus, we use the average value of pawned land in the sample villages, which is 138,000 pesos per hectare, with a standard error of 43,000, as a proxy for land values. This value corresponds to the cost to parents of bequeathing land to heirs. This value may underestimate the free market value of land for heirs, to the extent that the land market distortion decreases its value.[20]

Another method of assessing the value of land to heirs is to compute the annual increase in income associated with an increase in farm size of 0.15 hectares using the estimated coefficients from the agricultural income function. However, this method underestimates the potential market value of land because it does not include the collateral value. In our estimate of $R(S_i)$, we therefore use the pawning value of land, which is a stock value, multiplied by the prevailing annual interest rate of 0.12 to convert it to a flow value. The more difficult task is the estimation of average labor income from farming ($Y_1(S)$), because family labor is unpaid and detailed time allocation data for each family member were hard to collect. We estimated $Y_1(S)$ by multiplying the average daily agricultural wage rate of 120 pesos by the assumed number of full-time working days of 240. Income from farming is then multiplied by the probability of participation in farming, or $1 - P(E, A, g)$, as calculated from the probit function of participation in nonfarm activities.[21] Finally, predicted values of nonfarm income were obtained by using the estimated coefficients of the probit and the second-stage regression reported in Table 3.5.

---

20. Returns to specific experience acquired by heirs who have previously farmed family land also increase the value to the heir of land bequests, which would not be realized by outsiders acquiring the same plot through land market transactions (Rosenzweig and Wolpin 1985).

21. The probit used for the bootstrapping procedure, to be reported below, is slightly different from that reported in Table 3.5. For bootstrapping, we combined share tenants with landless workers, so that the excluded category consists of those who did not benefit from the land reform. The proportion of share tenants in the sample is very small (4 percent), so that repeated sampling for the bootstrap procedure often did not include enough observations on share tenants to be able to estimate a coefficient for the share tenancy variable.

As can be seen from equation (3.3), the effects of land and schooling on farm and nonfarm incomes are different between daughters and sons, as P is affected by gender (g_i). To explore the implications for sons and daughters of a differential pattern of intergenerational transfers, we conducted three counterfactual experiments: (1) give both sons and daughters the same educational level as the sample average; (2) give both sons and daughters the same land inheritance as the sample average; and (3) give both sons and daughters the same land and education as the sample average. For each counterfactual scenario, we used the estimated coefficients of Table 3.5 and equation (3.3) to predict annual income separately for sons and daughters.

Because annual income is predicted from estimated coefficients, it is subject to forecast or prediction error. It is difficult to come up with an analytical form for the standard error of predicted annual income, so we employed a bootstrapping procedure to estimate standard errors for sons' and daughters' incomes under the baseline (actual) situation as well as for the counterfactual scenarios (Efron 1979; StataCorp 2001).[22] Baseline annual incomes and the changes in incomes under the different scenarios, together with their (bootstrapped) standard errors, are presented in Table 3.6.

Examination of Table 3.6 shows that the current situation—where daughters have 1.5 years more schooling than sons, whereas sons inherit 0.15 hectares more—is inherently egalitarian. Although sons' annual income is greater than daughters', the difference ($Y_D - Y_S$) is not statistically significant. We use the counterfactual scenarios to examine the implications of this pattern of transfers: are parents sacrificing the family's income in the interests of equity?

The last two columns of Table 3.6, which show the changes in daughters' and sons' incomes, respectively, enable us to answer this question. For purposes of discussion, suppose that family income is defined as the sum of sons' and daughters' incomes, and that each family has one son and one daughter. We find that giving sons and daughters the same level of schooling or giving them the same land and schooling results in a large decrease in daughters' income that cannot be compensated for by the increase in sons' income, resulting in a net decline in family income. Equalizing transfers of land increases daughters' income and only slightly decreases sons' income, but the increase in daughters' income is much less than the decrease that would result if schooling were to be equalized among sons and daughters. These results suggest that the existing distribution of land and schooling among sons and daughters is not only egalitarian but also efficient in terms of maximizing family income.

---

22. Essentially, the bootstrapping procedure involves drawing, with replacement, N observations from the N observation dataset, over several replications, and estimating the statistics of interest. After building a dataset of estimated statistics over k replications, one can calculate the standard deviation from the bootstrap distribution. In our case, $N = 352$, and the number of replications k equals 1,000.

TABLE 3.6 Estimates of changes in daughters' and sons' incomes under different scenarios of land and schooling (thousand pesos)

Simulation	Daughters' income Y_D	Sons' income Y_S	Difference $Y_D - Y_S$	Change in daughters' income ΔY_D	Change in sons' income ΔY_S
Baseline	78.30	86.14	−7.85		
	(5.88)	(8.38)	(8.58)		
Give sons and daughters	67.57	90.60	−23.03*	−10.73**	4.46*
same schooling	(5.69)	(9.14)	(10.44)	(3.88)	(2.25)
Give sons and daughters	81.59	85.35	−3.76	3.29**	−0.80
same land	(5.97)	(8.26)	(8.39)	(0.99)	(0.97)
Give sons and daughters	68.85	89.42	−20.58*	−9.45*	3.28
same land and schooling	(5.76)	(8.98)	(10.27)	(3.93)	(2.26)

NOTES: Numbers in parentheses are bootstrapped standard errors, 1,000 replications; * indicates significance at the 5 percent level; ** at the 1 percent level.

We now proceed to investigate whether the short-term egalitarian distribution of investments in children with respect to current earnings is translated into equal lifetime incomes for sons and daughters. One method for estimating lifetime incomes is to obtain the present value of annual income separately for sons and daughters, assuming a certain discount rate and a specified duration of employment. Another is to estimate the incomes of daughters and sons at different ages, to yield an age–income profile over the life cycle. We employ the latter method because our estimation procedure enables us to calculate the probability of participation in nonfarm work at different ages, without making assumptions about the duration of employment. We thus used equation (3.3) and the estimated coefficients in Table 3.5 to predict annual incomes of sons and daughters at different ages between 20 and 50 years. These results are presented in Table 3.7.[23]

At all age ranges, daughters have a higher probability than do sons of participating in nonfarm employment. As a result, daughters earn more nonfarm incomes, but sons earn more farm income using larger areas of inherited land. A test of the differences between sons' and daughters' incomes, using bootstrapped standard errors, reveals that the differences are not significant at all ages, which is consistent with our earlier results. Thus, we conclude that Fili-

---

23. We also computed the income estimates for the younger (15–20) and oldest (60 years) age ranges. However, we found that the estimates are more unreliable than those in the middle ranges. The age–income profile for the 15–20 age range is counter to conventional wisdom, probably because in this generation children aged 15–20 years are still in school.

TABLE 3.7 Estimated incomes of daughters and sons at different ages (thousand pesos)

Age	Probability of daughters' participation in nonfarm work	Probability of sons' participation in nonfarm work	Daughters' income Y_D	Sons' income Y_S	Difference $Y_D - Y_S$
20	0.31	0.16	72.45	76.32	−3.87
			(8.85)	(8.97)	(8.06)
30	0.70	0.51	49.44	52.97	−3.53
			(16.26)	(17.08)	(8.05)
40	0.62	0.43	50.85	55.86	−5.01
			(16.96)	(17.97)	(8.17)
50	0.27	0.14	76.68	82.39	−5.71
			(27.25)	(29.18)	(8.55)

NOTES: Numbers in parentheses are bootstrapped standard errors, 1,000 replications; * indicates significance at the 5 percent level; ** at the 1 percent level.

pino parents are motivated by "equal outcomes" rules in investing in their children's schooling and in land bequests.

Summary of Findings

1. The current pattern of intergenerational transfers in the child generation, whereby sons inherited 0.15 hectares of additional land and daughters received 1.5 more years of schooling, is egalitarian. Average predicted annual incomes of sons are not significantly greater than the average predicted annual incomes of daughters.
2. At all age ranges in the life cycle, daughters earn more nonfarm income, whereas sons earn more farm income using larger areas of inherited land. Yet income differences between sons and daughters at all ages are not statistically significant.
3. Thus, parents bequeath more land to sons and favor daughters in schooling investments in order to equalize incomes between sons and daughters, while exploiting the comparative advantage of sons in farming and of daughters in nonfarm work.

Summary and Conclusions

The major purpose of this chapter was to examine the preferences of parents with respect to the allocation of land and investments in schooling between sons and daughters in two generations of households. First, we found an increasing trend in completed years of schooling over generations. Second, there was a declining trend in the amount of land inherited by children owing to increasing scarcity of cultivated land. Third, in the older generation, the "same gender" principle holds with respect to some parental transfers: better educated fathers prefer to improve the educational achievement of sons; and landowning mothers preferentially bestow land on daughters. In the children's generation, however, gender preference associated with parental characteristics has largely disappeared. Yet the gender-differentiated pattern of investment is clearer in the child generation: sons continue to be preferred with respect to land inheritance, whereas daughters are now treated more favorably with respect to schooling investments.

The last finding may be explained by the fact that rice farming is intensive in male labor where returns to specific experience are higher for males, whereas women tend to receive higher returns on their education in the nonfarm sector. That is, parents transfer land and invest in schooling in accordance with sons' and daughters' comparative advantage in farming and nonfarm activities, respectively. This implies that intergenerational transfers aim to equalize overall lifetime wealth among children.

Our statistical analyses show that the differential pattern of investment in sons and daughters results in annual incomes and life-cycle incomes that are not significantly different between sons and daughters. Indeed, equalizing the distribution of schooling and land among sons and daughters would likely decrease the family's combined income, owing to the significant and large decrease in daughters' income, which would not be compensated for by an equal increase in sons' incomes. It is clear that, even though bequest decisions may be motivated by egalitarian concerns, this pattern has its efficiency advantages as well.

We conjecture that the development of a competitive nonfarm labor market is likely to reduce discrimination against women by stimulating investments in daughters' education. In a competitive nonfarm labor market, the rates of return to human capital are equalized across individuals regardless of their sex. In many developing countries, however, the nonfarm labor market is not yet well developed, and schooling investments in men and the rates of return to male labor are typically higher. As the nonfarm labor market develops and the demand for labor increases, there will be competitive pressure to employ female labor. Thus, female wages will increase and the gender gap in wage rates will be reduced, which will induce parents to invest more in daughters' schooling. How far this experience in the Philippines can be generalized is an important empirical question to be explored in other settings.

4   Inter- and Intrahousehold Equity in the Philippines

In Chapter 3 we found that in our sites in the Philippines schooling is now more important as a determinant of nonfarm income, which had increased more rapidly than farm income. We also found that parents tend to invest more in the schooling of daughters than of sons. In this chapter, we first analyze the consequences of the increased importance of nonfarm income and human capital for the interhousehold distribution of income by applying the Gini decomposition analysis. Second, we explore whether parents continue to favor daughters in schooling among younger children of school age by estimating a schooling attainment function. If a significant gender gap in favor of daughters persists, the intrahousehold distribution of income may become skewed in daughters' favor given increasing returns to schooling in nonfarm jobs. We therefore hypothesize that, if parents have egalitarian bequest motives, they tend to invest equally in the schooling of younger daughters and sons. Finally, in order to obtain corroborative evidence for the egalitarian behavior of parents, we estimate expenditure share functions in which gender and age characteristics of children are included as explanatory variables.

Sources of Household Income Inequality

We want to examine whether the increased importance of nonfarm income and the decreased importance of farm income have resulted in an inequitable distribution of overall household income. For this purpose, we apply a decomposition analysis of the Gini measure of inequality as developed by Fei, Ranis, and Kuo (1978), Pyatt, Chen, and Fei (1980), and Shorrocks (1983). This decomposition formula is designed to assess the inequality of distribution of a particular source of income relative to the distribution of overall income.

The Gini decomposition formula is as follows:

$$G(Y) = \Sigma s_i\, R(Y,\, Y_i) G(Y_i) = \Sigma s_i PG(Y_i), \qquad (4.1)$$

where $G(Y)$ equals the Gini ratio of total household income; Y_i equals the income of the ith source; s_i equals the share of the ith type of income; $R(Y,\, Y_i)$

equals the rank correlation ratio; $G(Y_i)$ equals the Gini ratio of ith income; and $PG(Y_i)$ equals the pseudo-Gini ratio of income inequality. The rank correlation ratio is defined as

$$R(Y, Y_i) = \text{Cov}\{Y_i, r(Y)\}/\text{Cov}\{Y_i, r(Y_i)\}, \qquad (4.2)$$

where $r(Y)$ and $r(Y_i)$ denote the ranking of households in terms of Y and Y_i, respectively. It is clear that R is unity if $r(Y) = r(Y_i)$. Otherwise, R is shown to be less than unity. In general, the larger the correlation between Y and Y_i, the larger is R.

In the computation of $G(Y)$, households are ranked in accordance with Y, but in the case of $G(Y_i)$ they are ranked in accordance with Y_i. In order to adjust this difference, the rank correlation appears in the formula. In fact, $R(Y, Y_i)G(Y_i)$ is equal to the pseudo-Gini ratio, $PG(Y_i)$, which can be obtained if we use the ranking of households in accordance with total income Y in the computation of the component Gini ratio for Y_i. If $PG(Y_i)$ is greater than $G(Y)$, the distribution of the ith type of income is less equal than other types of income. Thus, by making a comparison between $PG(Y_i)$ and $G(Y)$, we can assess whether the ith type of income is inequality increasing or inequality decreasing. The importance of $PG(Y_i)$ in overall inequality is weighted by its share in the overall household income.

In Table 4.1 we show the Gini coefficients of total household income inequality for the full set of sample households in 1985 and for a subset of the 1985 sample that took part in the 1998 survey. In the case of the subsamples, the contribution of farm income to total income inequality in Central Luzon declined absolutely from 0.40 to 0.21 and relatively from 87 percent to 46 percent and in Panay declined absolutely from 0.23 to 0.04 and relatively from 57 percent to 9 percent. This is the result of the increased demand for hired farm labor and the increase in farm wage rates, which enabled the landless households to improve their income position relative to the farm households.

Conversely, the contribution of nonfarm income to the inequality of income distribution increased appreciably, not only because the importance of nonfarm income increased with the development of the nonfarm sector but also because the income gap between more and less educated workers widened. The inequality contribution rose much more in Panay than in Central Luzon, primarily because working household members in Panay are more actively involved in employment outside the village, as reflected in a larger nonfarm income share. The presence of a large number of nonresident working members is likely to contribute to the rise in income inequality because the returns to labor in urban and overseas labor markets are considerably higher than labor returns in village employment.[1] The pseudo-Gini coefficients of nonfarm income exceed the overall

---

1. Similarly, Leones and Feldman (1998) found that remittance income in a less developed village in Leyte Province in the Philippines was a major contributor to household income inequality. They report that, when the remittance income is excluded, nonfarm income did not contribute much to total household income inequality. This implies that the returns to labor in overseas employment are substantially higher than the returns to labor in local jobs.

TABLE 4.1 Contributions of income components to total household income inequality in Central Luzon and Panay, 1985 and 1998

Inequality components	Central Luzon			Panay		
	1985		1998	1985		1998
	Full sample	Subsample[a]	Subsample[a]	Full sample	Subsample[a]	Subsample[a]
Gini coefficient	0.49	0.46	0.45	0.46	0.40	0.47
	(100)	(100)	(100)	(100)	(100)	(100)
Contribution of income components						
Farm income	0.40	0.40	0.21	0.25	0.23	0.04
	(81)	(87)	(46)	(55)	(57)	(9)
Income share	0.81	0.85	0.56	0.58	0.59	0.22
Pseudo-Gini	0.49	0.47	0.36	0.43	0.39	0.19
Nonfarm income	0.09	0.06	0.24	0.21	0.17	0.43
	(19)	(13)	(54)	(45)	(43)	(91)
Income share	0.19	0.15	0.44	0.42	0.41	0.78
Pseudo-Gini	0.50	0.41	0.56	0.49	0.43	0.55

NOTE: Numbers in parentheses are percentage contributions to the total Gini coefficient.

[a] The subsample refers to the households that were present in both the 1985 and 1998 surveys.

Gini coefficients considerably in 1998, which implies that nonfarm income has replaced farm income as a major source of income inequality.

The decreasing contribution of farm income and the increasing contribution of nonfarm income to total household inequality attest that the inequality associated with land distribution has exerted a smaller influence on the distribution of household income in recent years. In contrast, the inequality in the distribution of human capital has assumed much greater importance in the determination of household income inequality. It is difficult or practically infeasible to compare directly the inequality of income distribution associated with unequal human capital distribution with that of land distribution. However, we can examine changes in the distribution of schooling and operational landholdings from 1985 to 1998. The coefficient of variation in schooling is 11.6 in 1985 and 10.3 in 1998, suggesting that inequality in schooling among working members of subsample households remained largely the same. Similarly, there has been no substantial change in the inequality of land distribution in the subsample of households in terms of the Gini coefficient of land distribution, which is 0.49 in 1985 and 0.54 in 1998. Therefore, the inequality of nonfarm income distribution seems to have widened not because the distribution of human capital has worsened but because returns to human capital have widened considerably.

Summary of Findings

1. There was a shift in household income structure away from farm to non-farm income sources between 1985 and 1998. This shift has resulted in an increase in household income inequality owing to the increased contribution of nonfarm income to total household income inequality.
2. If the importance of human capital relative to land continues to increase, the current inheritance patterns—whereby parents give more land to sons and invest more in the schooling of daughters—may result in serious income inequality in favor of daughters in the future.
3. If parents are egalitarian, we expect them to compensate by adjusting schooling investments in the younger generation, such that the gender gap in schooling will become smaller for younger children of school age.

School Attendance of Younger Children

Readers who are not interested in the technical details of statistical estimation can proceed directly to the "Summary of Findings" at the end of this section on page 97.

Parents will invest in a child's schooling if the expected payoff is equal to or higher than the costs.[2] Parents may give more schooling to women if invest-

---

2. An ethnographic study by Bouis et al. (1998), however, indicates that parental decisions regarding schooling depend not on differential expected payoffs from the schooling of boys and girls but on the inherent ability of the child.

ment in women's schooling is more profitable than that for men. In the Philippines, the opportunity cost of studying in colleges seems particularly low for women; unlike for men, there are relatively few decent employment opportunities (such as factory work) for female high-school graduates, compared with other high-performing East Asian countries.

In this section we examine whether parental gender preference continues to affect the schooling attainment of younger children aged 13–20 years in favor of daughters. In the Philippines, primary school children are commonly aged 7–12 years, high school students are aged 13–16 years, and college students are aged 17–20 years. In our sample households, almost all children aged 7–12 years are in school because primary education is free in the Philippines and primary schools are numerous even in rural areas.

High school education has been mandated to be free since 1986. Although there are relatively few high schools in rural areas compared with urban areas, 82 percent of sons and 95 percent of daughters aged 13–16 years are in high school (Table 4.2). The proportion is much lower for college education because this is not publicly supported and its cost can be prohibitively high for some rural families. Among sons aged 17–20 years, 60 percent are in college; among daughters, the corresponding percentage is 72 percent. The question is whether such differences in school attainment between daughters and sons are statistically significant.

We estimated a model of schooling attainment to determine whether there is significant gender bias in investments in the schooling of children aged 13–20 years. The dependent variable is completed years in school and the independent variables are seven age dummies, three gender/birth order dummies, parents' characteristics and the interaction term between the daughter dummy and parents' characteristics, and village dummies. The estimated function is specified as:

$$\text{Years in school} = \alpha_0 + \sum_{i=1}^{7} \alpha_i \, (\text{age dummies})$$

$$+ \sum_{i=8}^{10} \alpha_i \, (\text{gender/birth order dummies})$$

$$+ \sum_{i=11}^{14} \alpha_i \, (\text{parents' characteristics})$$

$$+ \sum_{i=15}^{18} \alpha_i \, (\text{daughter dummy}) \times (\text{parents' characteristics})$$

$$+ \sum_{i=19}^{22} \alpha_i \, (\text{village dummies}) + \varepsilon_i. \tag{4.3}$$

TABLE 4.2 Proportion of children in school, by age and sex, in Central Luzon and Panay, 1998

| | Male | | Female | |
Age	Number	Percent	Number	Percent
13	10	100	6	83
14	20	85	15	93
15	19	68	22	100
16	20	85	14	93
17	15	67	17	82
18	22	60	14	71
19	11	45	11	54
20	16	62	9	78
All	133	72	108	84

Age dummies are included to account for incomplete schooling decisions at younger years, with age 20 as the excluded category. Gender/birth order dummies consist of the eldest son, eldest daughter, and other son dummies (other daughter is the control). Parents' characteristics include inherited land and completed years of schooling. The coefficients on parents' characteristics measure the effect of parents' characteristics on sons' schooling attainment, whereas the interaction terms between parents' characteristics and the daughter dummy are expected to measure the gender bias associated with parental characteristics. On the other hand, the coefficients on gender/birth order dummies are expected to capture the extent of gender bias that is independent of parental characteristics.

Equation (4.3) is estimated using ordinary least squares (OLS) for all the 241 sample children in 1998 who were aged 13–20 years and the household fixed-effects (FE) model for 191 children belonging to a subsample of households that had at least two children.[3] We use a subsample of households with at least two children so that the gender/birth order dummies become relevant in the FE model. The FE procedure eliminates selectivity bias since selection into the sample is a family-specific variable. It is also appropriate because it controls for unobserved household-specific variables, which may be correlated with variables included in the model. If such correlation exists, the estimated coefficients on the variables may be biased. According to the estimation results in Table 4.3, however, this is not the case; the results of the FE and OLS models are fairly similar with respect to the magnitude of the coefficients and their

---

3. We also estimated a probit function on school attendance where the dependent variable is unity if the child is in school, and zero otherwise. The probit regression results are fairly similar to the OLS results.

TABLE 4.3 Determinants of schooling attainment of children aged 13–20 in Central Luzon and Panay, 1998

Variables	Fixed effects	Ordinary least squares
Constant		10.03**
		(15.06)
Age dummies[a]		
13	−5.10**	−4.61**
	(−8.12)	(−7.86)
14	−4.33**	−3.74**
	(−7.98)	(−7.78)
15	−3.90**	−3.15**
	(−7.48)	(−6.75)
16	−2.50**	−1.92**
	(−4.73)	(−3.96)
17	−2.81**	−2.34**
	(−5.11)	(−4.72)
18	−1.39**	−0.75
	(−2.72)	(−1.56)
19	−1.77**	−0.73
	(−2.94)	(−1.38)
Gender/birth order dummies		
Eldest son	−0.78	−1.10
	(−0.81)	(−1.33)
Other son	−0.94	−1.60*
	(−0.98)	(2.05)
Eldest daughter	0.09	−0.34
	(0.22)	(−0.90)
Father's schooling		−0.004
		(−0.75)
Mother's schooling		0.19**
		(2.57)
Daughter × father's schooling	0.03	0.05
	(0.38)	(0.55)
Daughter × mother's schooling	−0.01	−0.10
	(−0.11)	(−0.91)
Father's land		0.24
		(1.04)
Mother's' land		0.35
		(0.73)
Daughter × father's land	−0.63*	−0.36
	(−1.84)	(−1.09)
Daughter × mother's land	0.57	−0.62
	(0.43)	(−0.57)

(continued)

TABLE 4.3 *Continued*

Variables	Fixed effects	Ordinary least squares
Village dummies[b]		
CL1		0.76*
		(1.99)
CL2		−1.12**
		(−2.43)
P1		0.66
		(1.46)
P2		−0.41
		(−1.05)
Breusch–Pagan Lagrange multiplier test (*p*-value)	19.16 (.00)	
Hausman test, fixed effects versus random effects (*p*-value)	9.37 (.80)	
Number of observations	191	241
F-test of the equality of coefficients		
Father's schooling = mother's schooling		2.94
Father's land = mother's land		0.05
Schooling interaction terms equal	0.11	0.00
Land interaction terms equal	0.81	0.06
Schooling plus interaction terms equal		3.13*
Land plus interaction terms equal		1.68

NOTES: Numbers in parentheses are *t*-values; * indicates significance at the 5 percent level; ** at the 1 percent level.

[a] Excluded category is 20 years of age.

[b] CL1 and CL2 refer to Central Luzon Villages 1 and 2; P1 and P2 refer to Panay Villages 1 and 2.

respective standard errors. Note that the estimation of the FE model precludes direct estimation of the coefficients on the parents' characteristics and village dummies. Thus, the effects of parental characteristics are captured through the interaction terms, if they affect children differently depending on their gender.

Even though the results of the OLS and FE models are fairly similar, the Breusch–Pagan Lagrange multiplier test attests to the significance of family-specific random effects (Table 4.3). However, the Hausman test suggests that the subset of coefficients estimated using fixed-effects and random-effects methods do not differ statistically. As expected, children aged 19 years and below have lower levels of schooling than children aged 20 years. In the OLS estimates, other sons appear to receive less schooling than other daughters do. However, when we take into account family-level unobservables, the advantage held by daughters disappears—gender/birth order effects are no longer significant. Recall that daughters are favored in schooling investments in the older generation of children. Once family-level unobservables are taken into account, there is no longer any evidence for a pro-daughter bias among younger children.

Parents' characteristics do not seem to have significant effects on children's schooling. The OLS estimates suggest, however, that mother's completed years in school, but not father's completed years in school, has a highly significant coefficient. This result is consistent with the common findings in the literature that mother's education has a positive effect on child well-being such as nutrition, health, and education (Thomas 1990, 1994; Strauss and Thomas 1995). In the FE estimates, the negative and significant coefficient of the interaction term between the daughter dummy and father's land indicates that fathers who inherited more land tend to give less schooling to daughters. Although the significance level is not high, it may well be that fathers who are endowed with more land, and hence stronger bargaining power, attempt to invest more in the schooling of sons to prevent income inequality arising from differential investments in the schooling of sons and daughters.

The *F*-test of the equality of coefficients (see the bottom panel of Table 4.3) shows that parents are largely egalitarian with respect to schooling investments in younger children, as demonstrated by the equality of most of the coefficients on father- and mother-specific asset ownership as well as the interaction terms of the daughter dummy with parental wealth variables.

Summary of Findings

1. We found that schooling investments among younger children of school age (13–20 years) are largely void of gender bias. Parents tend to invest equally in the schooling of younger children regardless of gender and birth order.
2. The effects of parental schooling and landholdings on the schooling attainment of younger children are in most cases not significant, indicating the absence of a gender bias in schooling investments associated with parental wealth. There is, however, some indication that fathers who inherited more land tend to give less schooling to daughters.

Determinants of Consumption Expenditure Shares

In this section, we further explore whether parents are egalitarian with respect to the gender of their children by estimating expenditure share functions in which the proportions of male and female children are explanatory variables.[4]

---

4. This section draws on Estudillo, Quisumbing, and Otsuka (2001c).

If these age/sex composition variables are insignificant, the evidence support-ing the hypothesis of egalitarian parental preference will be strengthened.

Data on Expenditure Shares

We divide the household expenditure items into food, housing, clothing, schooling, health, and cigarettes and alcohol.[5] Food is the most important ex-penditure item, comprising 58 percent and 55 percent of the total monthly household expenditure in 1998 in Central Luzon and Panay, respectively (Table 4.4).[6] Housing expenditure comprises about 30 percent. Expenditure on school-ing is only about 5 percent because many of the respondents' children are no longer in school and only direct expenses for schooling are included. Though unreported, we observe that the expenditure shares of clothing for male and fe-male adults and children are almost equal, indicating a relatively equitable intrahousehold distribution of spending on clothing.

We consider per capita expenditure (PCE) to be an appropriate indicator of household wealth per household member, which is expected to affect the ex-penditure shares. In terms of PCE, the difference between Central Luzon and Panay is relatively small. We did not compute expenditures per adult equiva-lent, because adult-equivalent scales are typically constructed using calorie re-quirements by age and sex, and would not necessarily apply to other expendi-ture categories.

Engel's law is observed to hold in our sample villages: the proportion of expenditure on food declines with an increase in income. In the poorest (in terms of household income) sample village, food expenditure accounts for 70 percent of the total expenditure, whereas in the richest village it accounts for only about 56 percent. The total per capita expenditure of the poorest village is only 60 percent of that of the richest village. The proportion of housing expen-diture is generally higher in higher-income villages and in villages where there is a high proportion of working members overseas. The total monthly expen-diture in Central Luzon is 78 percent of total monthly income, whereas it is 81 percent in Panay. The PCE is higher in Central Luzon than in Panay, although the average household size in the two locations is roughly the same.

---

5. Food expenditure items include cereals, root crops, fish and meat, eggs and milk, vegeta-bles, fruits, beverages, and oil, herbs, and spices bought outside and produced at home. Housing expenditure items include utilities, housing repairs, and purchases of durable goods. Clothing refers to clothing and footwear of male and female adults and children. School expenditure items include tuition, books, supplies, and others for primary, secondary, college, and vocational schools. Health expenditures include government and private hospital expenses, doctors' fees and medicines, pre-natal care, and immunizations. Cigarette and alcohol expenditures are grouped separately because they are commonly considered to be "adult goods" in expenditure analyses.

6. Data on expenditures are based on a one-week recall for food; a one-month recall for hous-ing; a six-month recall for clothing, schooling, and health; and a one-week recall for cigarettes and alcohol. All expenditure items were adjusted to a monthly basis.

TABLE 4.4 Household consumption expenditures in Central Luzon and Panay, 1998

Expenditure items	Central Luzon (percent)	Panay (percent)
Food[a]	58	55
Housing[b]	26	31
Clothing	4	1
Schooling	5	4
Health	4	7
Cigarettes and alcohol	3	2
Total	100	100
Total expenditure (pesos/month)	6,116	5,311
Per capita expenditure (pesos/month)	1,390	1,207

NOTE: The exchange rate was US$1 = 38 pesos.

[a] Includes foods bought outside the home and consumption of own production.

[b] Includes utilities, housing repairs, and purchases of durables.

Specification of Estimated Functions

Readers who are not interested in the technical details of statistical estimation can proceed directly to the "Summary of Findings" at the end of this section on page 107.

We estimate a system of household expenditure functions to examine the manner in which parents allocate household resources to broad expenditure categories. We focus on identifying whether some expenditure items are geared toward certain demographic categories in terms of gender and age.

We estimate the expenditure share functions in two stages. The first stage is an ordinary least squares (OLS) regression of the natural logarithm of per capita household expenditure ($\ln PCE$); the second stage is a Tobit regression of the expenditure shares, which incorporates the predicted values of the natural logarithm of PCE ($\ln PCE^*$) as one of the regressors. To the extent that households smooth consumption over their lifetime, PCE can effectively represent household permanent income that is a measure of long-run household resource availability. Because PCE is considered to be a choice variable, we calculate its predicted value using instrumental variables that affect PCE but not the expenditure shares. The instruments are the interaction term between the farm household dummy and farm size, and dummies for the tenure status of current landholdings. Farm size and land tenure status are expected to affect wealth but not expenditures directly. Our first-stage regression function is specified as

$$\ln PCE = \beta_0 + \beta_1 \text{ (farm household dummy} \times \ln \text{ farm size)}$$
$$+ \beta_2 \ln \text{ father's schooling} + \beta_3 \ln \text{ mother's schooling}$$
$$+ \beta_4 \ln \text{ household size} + \sum_{i=5}^{7} \beta_i \text{ (tenure dummies)}$$
$$+ \sum_{j=8}^{16} \beta_j \text{ (gender/age group proportions)}$$
$$+ \sum_{k=17}^{20} \beta_k \text{ (village dummies)} + \mu. \tag{4.4}$$

The interaction term of the farm household dummy and the natural logarithm of farm size is included in equation (4.4) in order to compare the expenditure patterns of farmer households with those of landless households. We define landless households as those that do not have access to farmland, including households headed by casual workers, who are mainly employed in rice farming, and by nonagricultural wage-workers. Landless households, which have generally lower incomes, comprise about one-third of our sample. Following convention, we include the logarithm of schooling of fathers and mothers as explanatory variables in the ln *PCE* function.[7] According to Estudillo, Quisumbing, and Otsuka (2001a), college education is a significant factor affecting household nonagricultural income. Finally, μ represents an error term.

Household size represents the amount of available labor resources in the household as well as the size of the consumption unit, and tenure variables represent access to land resources. For household gender/age groups, we use the proportion of male and female members in age brackets 0–5, 6–9, 10–19, 20–64, and 65 and over. We did not apply a finer age classification because of the small number of households in our sample. Because of these limitations, the gender bias in the schooling of teenagers may not be revealed by the household expenditure share analysis as sharply as in the analysis of schooling attainment for individuals. The excluded category is the proportion of male members aged 20–64 years.

In the second-stage regression we estimate a series of reduced form expenditure share functions, specified as

$$W = \gamma_0 + \gamma_1 \ln PCE^* + \gamma_2 \ln \text{ household size} + \gamma_3 \ln \text{ father's schooling}$$
$$+ \gamma_4 \ln \text{ mother's schooling} + \gamma_5 \text{ (father's land)}^{\frac{1}{2}} + \gamma_6 \text{ (mother's land)}^{\frac{1}{2}}$$
$$+ \sum_{i=7}^{15} \gamma_i \text{ (proportion in each gender/age group category)}$$
$$+ \sum_{i=16}^{19} \gamma_i \text{ (village dummies)} + \theta, \tag{4.5}$$

---

7. We do not include the schooling of children as an explanatory variable because it is endogenous.

where **W** is a vector of expenditure shares, γ are parameters, and θ is an error term. These could be considered as a system of equations, but, because of the censoring of the dependent variable and the endogeneity of per capita expenditure, we estimate the expenditure share for each category as a recursive simultaneous equations Tobit regression.

Household size is expected to capture the effect of the strength of size economies or diseconomies in household consumption expenditures. We use fathers' and mothers' inherited landholdings and schooling as indicators of the exogenously determined bargaining power of spouses—both human and physical asset ownership critically determine spouses' potential income earnings. We do not use the logarithm of fathers' and mothers' inherited landholdings because some respondents and their spouses do not inherit any land.[8] Instead, owing to the possible declining marginal effects of inherited land, we use the square root of the level of fathers' and mothers' inherited land. Using the *F*-test, we examine whether the coefficients on the husband's and the wife's human and physical capital are significantly different from each other, after controlling for household expenditures.

Estimation Results

According to our regression results, the elasticity of PCE with respect to farm size among the farming households is 0.12 (Table 4.5). PCE declines significantly with an increase in household size, which implies that total household expenditure increases less than proportionally with an increase in the number of household members. As will be discussed shortly, this result may be related to scale economies in consumption within a household. Mother's schooling, but not father's schooling, affects PCE significantly. This may be because males primarily work in the rice sector, in which schooling has no significant impact on incomes, whereas some of their spouses work in the nonagricultural sector, in which wages are relatively higher for better educated workers (see Chapter 3). Thus, it is not unreasonable to observe that only the wife's schooling affects PCE significantly. Households of owner-cultivators and leaseholders/CLT holders have a PCE significantly higher than that of the landless households, whereas the share-tenant households seem to have roughly the same PCE as the landless households after controlling for the effect of farm size. A household's demographic characteristics in terms of the sex and age grouping of its members do not have a significant impact on PCE. This may suggest the absence of

---

8. Initially we tried including the predicted logarithm of PCE squared in the second-stage regression using both Tobit and OLS procedures. Instruments for the predicted logarithm of PCE squared were obtained by squaring some of the variables used as instruments in the first-stage regression. The coefficients on many variables in the second-stage regression are similar in the specifications with and without the predicted logarithm of PCE squared in both Tobit and OLS regressions. This indicates that the presence of nonlinearity in the data is not considerable.

TABLE 4.5 Determinants of per capita expenditures in Central Luzon and Panay, 1998

Variables	Natural logarithm of per capita expenditures
Constant	7.08**
	(24.00)
FHD × ln farm size[a]	0.12*
	(2.15)
Ln household size	−0.63**
	(−6.06)
Ln father's schooling	−0.04
	(−0.58)
Ln mother's schooling	0.24**
	(3.02)
Ratio of landholdings	
Owned	0.25*
	(2.24)
Leasehold/Certificate of Land Transfer	0.32**
	(3.08)
Share tenancy	0.17
	(1.03)
Proportion of household members	
Males aged 0–5	0.44
	(0.50)
Males aged 6–9	−0.10
	(−0.14)
Males aged 10–19	−0.42
	(−1.48)
Males aged 65+	−0.26
	(−0.99)
Females aged 0–5	−0.04
	(−0.07)
Females aged 6–9	−0.12
	(−0.18)
Females aged 10–19	0.14
	(0.45)
Females aged 20–64	0.09
	(0.33)
Females aged 65+	0.60
	(1.73)
Village dummies[b]	
CL1	0.35*
	(2.21)
CL2	0.30*
	(1.67)

(continued)

TABLE 4.5 *Continued*

Variables	Natural logarithm of per capita expenditures
P1	0.46**
	(2.71)
P2	0.04
	(0.26)
Number of observations	250
R^2	.34

NOTES: Numbers in parentheses are *t*-values; * indicates significance at the 5 percent level; ** at the 1 percent level.

[a] FHD refers to farm household dummy.

[b] CL1 and CL2 refer to Central Luzon Villages 1 and 2; P1 and P2 refer to Panay Villages 1 and 2.

gender and age biases in the generation of household income and its allocation to current expenditures, which is consistent with the findings of Medina (1991) that the household structure in the Philippines is relatively egalitarian.

Table 4.6 shows the estimation results of the expenditure share functions. We include food, housing, clothing, schooling, and health but exclude cigarettes and alcohol because they comprise only a small proportion of total household budgets. Moreover, only 60 percent of the households reported having any expenditure on cigarettes and alcohol.[9] According to the estimation results, the share of food in total expenditure tends to decline with an increase in PCE, whereas the housing share increases significantly. These findings indicate that increased availability of resources allows households to shift their consumption pattern away from food toward housing.

Larger households have a lower food share but a significantly larger expenditure share on housing and schooling. An increase in household size may bring about economies of scale in food consumption but diseconomies in the consumption of housing and schooling. The former finding conforms to the finding of Deaton and Paxson (1998) that per capita demand for food decreases with household size in the United States, Great Britain, France, South Africa, Taiwan, Thailand, and Pakistan. Larger households may benefit from economies of scale with respect to food expenditures, probably owing to increasing returns to activities with large fixed costs, such as cooking (Fafchamps and Quisumbing 1999). However, we cannot confirm this directly because our data pertain to food purchases, not the combination of expenditure on food and time spent by households in food preparation. Larger households may also benefit from direct economies of scale in expenditure through bulk buying, thus paying less

---

9. This may reflect underreporting of alcohol and tobacco consumption, a common occurrence in household surveys.

TABLE 4.6 Determinants of expenditure shares in Central Luzon and Panay, 1998

Variables	Food	Housing	Clothing	Schooling	Health
Constant	1.86**	−0.97*	0.07	−0.70*	−0.08
	(3.13)	(−1.79)	(0.39)	(−2.04)	(−0.11)
Ln *PCE*[*a]	−0.13*	0.14*	−0.01	0.07	−0.002
	(−1.67)	(2.01)	(−0.57)	(1.59)	(−0.02)
Ln household size	−0.09*	0.09*	−0.01	0.09**	0.001
	(−1.72)	(1.82)	(−0.57)	(2.85)	(0.01)
Ln father's schooling	0.02	−0.02	0.01	0.02*	−0.02
	(0.95)	(−1.21)	(0.44)	(1.79)	(−0.87)
Ln mother's schooling	−0.04	0.02	0.01	−0.01	0.01
	(−1.44)	(0.82)	(1.05)	(−0.56)	(0.50)
SQRT father's land[b]	0.02	−0.04*	0.01*	0.003	−0.02
	(1.12)	(−1.80)	(1.85)	(0.28)	(−0.97)
SQRT mother's land[b]	−0.006	−0.04	−0.00	0.001	0.02
	(−0.19)	(−1.23)	(−0.30)	(0.02)	(0.58)
Proportion of household members					
Males aged 0–5	0.05	−0.13	−0.02	−0.12	0.49
	(0.20)	(−0.56)	(−0.32)	(−0.83)	(1.60)
Males aged 6–9	0.15	0.10	−0.03	0.003	−0.14
	(0.73)	(0.53)	(−0.47)	(0.03)	(−0.57)
Males aged 10–19	−0.14	0.10	0.04	0.17**	−0.20*
	(−1.51)	(1.21)	(1.39)	(3.22)	(1.76)
Males aged 65+	0.10	−0.06	−0.04	−0.06	−0.01
	(1.23)	(−0.85)	(−1.61)	(−1.11)	(−0.18)
Females aged 0–5	−0.19	0.30	−0.07	−0.11	0.18
	(−0.95)	(1.64)	(−1.19)	(−0.94)	(0.83)
Females aged 6–9	0.05	−0.06	−0.10	0.15	−0.16
	(0.29)	(−0.36)	(−1.44)	(1.37)	(−0.62)
Females aged 10–19	−0.05	−0.06	0.01	0.14**	0.03
	(−0.58)	(−0.78)	(0.61)	(2.86)	(0.34)
Females aged 20–64	−0.61	0.01	0.001	0.009	0.11
	(−0.75)	(0.20)	(0.01)	(0.17)	(1.24)
Females aged 65+	−0.12	0.09	0.01	−0.002	0.09
	(−1.10)	(0.95)	(0.41)	(−0.03)	(0.74)
Village dummies[c]					
CL1	−0.05	−0.01	0.04**	0.007	−0.04
	(−1.14)	(−0.40)	(2.80)	(0.26)	(−0.69)
CL2	−0.01	−0.04	0.03*	−0.007	−0.06
	(−0.17)	(−0.87)	(1.83)	(−0.26)	(−1.06)
P1	−0.06	−0.004	0.01	−0.002	−0.005
	(−1.10)	(−0.07)	(0.67)	(−0.07)	(−0.07)

(continued)

TABLE 4.6 *Continued*

Variables	Food	Housing	Clothing	Schooling	Health
P2	−0.09*	0.06	−0.00	−0.01	−0.01
	(−2.10)	(1.61)	(−0.06)	(−0.74)	(−0.27)
Number of observations	250	250	250	250	250
Log-likelihood ratio	82.24	104.15	172.25	107.36	−40.94
F-test of the equality of coefficients					
Males 10–19 =					
females 10–19	0.90	1.08	1.95	0.00	1.71
Father's land =					
mother's land	0.03	0.00	1.96	0.00	2.27
Father's schooling =					
mother's schooling	1.27	1.44	0.65	1.29	0.31

NOTES: Numbers in parentheses are *t*-values; * indicates significance at the 5 percent level; ** at the 1 percent level.

[a] *PCE** refers to the predicted values of per capita expenditure.

[b] SQRT refers to the square root of the levels of mothers' and fathers' inherited landholdings.

[c] CL1 and CL2 refer to Central Luzon Villages 1 and 2; P1 and P2 refer to Panay Villages 1 and 2.

per unit, and from minimizing wastage through better management of refrigerators and storage facilities at home.

The significantly higher expenditure shares of larger households on housing may be the result of our use of the cost of housing repairs and construction rather than the imputed rental value of housing services, because of the absence of house rental markets. This may overstate the housing expenditures of larger households. Finally, schooling budget shares also increase with household size, most probably because of the increase in the number of members of school age in large families. Its coefficient is 0.09, implying that a 1 percent increase in household size is associated with a 0.09 percentage point increase in schooling budget shares, which is not unreasonable.

The effects of father's and mother's schooling and inherited landholdings on expenditure shares are not significant except in a few cases.[10] A father's

---

10. Father's and mother's schooling and inherited landholdings are proxies for the relative income contributions of spouses. We do not use the income shares of each spouse because they may be endogenous to expenditure share functions. Nonetheless, there is ample evidence in the literature that women's increased income contribution is associated with expenditure patterns that are more child oriented and income enhancing, such as health and education of children (Kennedy and Peters 1992; Hoddinott and Haddad 1995; Haddad et al. 1996). On the other hand, fathers' higher income shares tend to be associated with increased expenditures on "adult" goods such as cigarettes and alcohol, partly because these goods are consumed mostly by adult males.

schooling has a positive and significant effect on the expenditure share of schooling, whereas a father's inherited landholdings decrease the housing share and increase the clothing share. The significance levels are low in all three cases. The insignificance of the effect of mother's schooling on the expenditure share of children's schooling is unexpected because evidence from other developing countries shows that mother's schooling is associated with higher education budget shares (Quisumbing and Maluccio 2003). We speculate that this is because of the relatively high mean and low variance of women's schooling. In our sample, for example, the mean of mother's schooling is relatively high (6.46 years) and its standard deviation is relatively low (2.93 years).

The insignificance of the coefficients on parental characteristics suggests that, once per capita expenditures are controlled for, parental characteristics do not have any additional explanatory power. One possible reason the effect of inherited landholdings on expenditure shares is minimal is the declining importance of land income among rice-farming households (Estudillo and Otsuka 1999). The share of land income among our sample households declined from 34 percent in 1985 to 24 percent in 1998, which means that households finance a major portion of their expenditures from other sources of income. The major factor behind the shift of household income structure away from land is the recent development of nonfarm labor markets and improved access of households to such markets. A recent long-term study of the Philippine village by Hayami and Kikuchi (2000) provides ample support for our interpretation.

Using the *F*-test, we examine whether the coefficients on father's and mother's schooling and the coefficients on father's and mother's inherited landholdings are the same after controlling for per capita expenditures (a proxy for permanent income).[11] The computed *F*-values shown in the bottom panel of Table 4.6 are all below the critical *F*-values at the 5 percent level of significance. Equality of coefficients suggests that human and physical assets brought into marriage by mothers and fathers have equal effects on consumption expenditures, which is consistent with the hypothesis that the consumption expenditure patterns desired by fathers and mothers do not differ substantially.

It is possible that the allocation of resources among household members depends upon their contribution to household income. In some countries, the distribution of food may be skewed in favor of adult males because they are potential labor market participants whose productivity is sensitive to health status (Pitt, Rosenzweig, and Hassan 1990). Boys may be favored relative to girls (Pitti-

---

11. This procedure cannot accurately test whether a common preference model of the household is more appropriate than the collective model, because we included human capital, a variable that affects not only the extent of spouses' bargaining powers but also their wage rates. The common preference model assumes that all individuals within the household share the same preference or that there is a single decisionmaker who decides for all, whereas the collective model views the household as a collective entity made up of individuals who have different preference orderings (Doss 1996b).

grew 1986; Levine 1987; Behrman 1988) if males enjoy higher wage rates, making investments in the health outcomes of boys more profitable. In rural Pakistan, medical expenditures on elderly males are lower compared with younger male working members, reflecting each group's contribution to household income (Kochar 1999).[12]

In general, the shares of household members in different age/sex categories do not significantly affect the budget shares devoted to food, housing, and clothing.[13] However, the share of health expenditures of males aged 10–19 years is significantly less. This is different from the finding by Bouis et al. (1998) that adolescent boys, who spend more time away from home and agricultural labor, may be more prone to serious accidents than adolescent girls, which may explain why health expenditures were higher for adolescent boys than adolescent girls in their Bukidnon study sample. It is also important to point out that a significant share of expenditures on schooling is allocated to males and females aged 10–19 years. These are the household members who are most likely in secondary or tertiary education, which is substantially more expensive than primary education partly because children must commute to or board in towns and partly because tuition fees are much higher in college. The coefficients on the proportions of males and females in this age group are not significantly different, confirming once again the absence of a gender bias with respect to schooling investments among younger children.[14]

To recapitulate, we have found that household expenditure allocation in our Philippine study sites may well be characterized as egalitarian. As far as consumption expenditure allocation is concerned, we found no evidence that girls are disfavored.

Summary of Findings

1. In general, the shares of household members in different age/sex categories do not significantly affect the shares of expenditures on food, housing, clothing, schooling, and health. This indicates that rural household expenditure allocation tends to be egalitarian in the Philippines.

---

12. It is also interesting that coresidence of fathers and sons in Pakistan may benefit the fathers, although not in terms of wealth but in increases in consumption of goods and leisure. Increases in sons' incomes are accompanied by decreases in fathers' days of work and such increases in income are used to finance expenditures on household public goods such as consumer durables and ceremonies (Kochar 2000).

13. Past studies on intrahousehold allocation of food using actual food intake show that food distribution among household members in Filipino households is generally egalitarian (Bouis 1991; Bouis and Peña 1997).

14. In Vietnam, there is a strong association between household income and child schooling and this association is stronger for girls, indicating that schooling of girls is treated like a luxury good (Behrman and Knowles 1999).

2. We have evidence that father's and mother's schooling and landholdings generally do not have significantly different effects on schooling expenditures for younger children, indicating the absence of parental discrimination.

Explanations for Gender Equity in the Philippines

Overall, we have found that intergenerational transfers of land and schooling investments and the intrahousehold allocation of expenditures are not biased against women or girls in the Philippines. This section examines four possible explanations for relative gender equality in the Philippine context: (1) historical and social aspects of gender relations; (2) a policy of universal education; (3) the value of Filipino women at home; and (4) market returns to schooling.

Historical and Social Aspects of Gender Relations

Filipino women historically enjoyed an honored position equal to their male counterparts. The recent practice of bequeathing more land to sons in the Philippines was uncommon in the distant past. During pre-Hispanic times, "Filipino women own and manage their garden plots and pass them on to the next generation" (Weir 2001). A division of labor along sexual lines existed: women had full control of decisions regarding food crop production, whereas men were engaged in hunting and fishing. As in other countries, women's participation in food crop production declined substantially with the intensification of agriculture and the introduction of the plow (Boserup 1970). It had become a common practice to give land to sons because of the larger contribution of male labor to farming.

Whereas pre-Hispanic culture was generally egalitarian, Spanish colonial culture, with its traditions of *machismo,* was more discriminatory against women. The Spanish colonial period, which began in 1521 and lasted for about 350 years, contributed to the practice of giving land to sons. Spanish clergy preached the dominance of men over women in the control of household resources; landownership became confined to the elite male. The traditional Filipino woman's control over landownership and decisionmaking in food crop production as well as rights to land inheritance was undermined (Alcantara 1994).

Although many women professionals were found in the teaching profession during the Spanish era, there were many more who would have wanted to pursue a university education but were unable to do so because few schools were open to women. Nevertheless, a historian writes that, in the late Hispanic colonial period in the late 1800s, "mentally, socially, and in almost all the relations of life, Filipino women were regarded as equals of men" (Lopez 1902).

Even in more recent times, Filipino women's performance in the social and political arena is comparable to that in Japan and the United States. According to the Human Development Report (UNDP 2000), the value of the gender empowerment measure is 0.479 for the Philippines, 0.490 for Japan, and 0.707 for the United States. The lower value for the Philippines is explained solely by the low value of women's GDP per capita, which is the result of the country's lower per capita GDP. In terms of political and professional representations, Filipino women perform comparably well or even better. The proportion of female professional and technical workers in the Philippines is the highest among the three countries—65 percent in the Philippines, 44 percent in Japan, and 53 percent in the United States—and the proportion of female administrators and managers is comparable to that in the United States—34 percent in the Philippines, 9 percent in Japan, and 44 percent in the United States.

A Policy of Universal Education

One of the most important legacies of the American colonization, which began in 1898 and lasted for about 50 years, was its policy of universal education introduced before the Second World War. The Philippines saw a spectacular increase in school enrollment rates in the 1960s, particularly of girls, who were disfavored in schooling in the Spanish period. The universal education policy contributed to eliminating gender differences in schooling. As we have shown in Table 2.8, the gender gap in schooling was eliminated in the respondents' generation, who were of primary school age during the implementation of the universal education policy.

Secondary schooling was mandated free in 1986 during the Aquino administration. This policy has contributed significantly to improving the schooling attainment of respondents' children, who completed three to four more years of schooling than their parents (Table 2.8). In June 2001, the Arroyo administration implemented a "zero collection" policy, which completely exempts parents from paying school fees, and even voluntary contributions such as funds for local school maintenance and projects. Since the main aim of the policy is to make primary and secondary schooling accessible to all, we expect a further increase in the average schooling attainment of the younger generation.

Overall, it is evident that the secular improvement in schooling facilities in the country has had a far-reaching impact on increases in the schooling attainment of female children and the elimination of gender differences in schooling.

The Value of Filipino Women at Home

Many social scientists believe that Filipino families are more egalitarian and much less patriarchal in comparison with countries in South Asia.[15] Gender

---

15. A typical Filipino has many relatives, comprising the core family members and extended members including in-laws. Members maintain close relationships centered mainly upon reciprocal obligations. The bilateral kinship system (descent is traced bilaterally on both the father's and mother's side) and relatives are reckoned both on consanguineal principles and in affinal terms (Kikuchi 1989; Miralao 1997).

equality is evidenced in the distribution of food. During mealtime, food is laid on the table for everyone to partake of, regardless of gender or age; this indicates that there is no discrimination between boys and girls or between children and adults (Bouis et al. 1998). This is in contrast to Bangladesh, where adult males are served first, and working males are more likely to receive more calories because their productivity depends on their health status (Pitt, Rosenzweig, and Hassan 1990). Since Filipino children and adults have equal access to food, it appears that intrahousehold food distribution in households in the Philippines is not dependent on members' contribution to household income.

Husband and wife carry out household decisionmaking jointly in a Filipino home, which suggests that spouses' bargaining power may not be critically affected by their contribution to household income. According to David (1994) and Alcantara (1994), however, the husband's preference emerges more dominantly in fertility decisions, presumably because the husband is financially responsible for supporting the household.

Parents consider schooling and land to be alternative forms of intergenerational transfers to equalize the lifetime incomes of children. In a detailed account of the history of a *barrio* in Central Luzon, Fegan (1982: 119) described that, after the land frontier had closed in the *barrio* in the 1940s, schooling became the substitute for a farmland as a form of inheritance. Parental investments in schooling and the extent to which such investments improve the lifetime income of a child are major considerations in the calculation of the division of property (mainly farmland) for bequest to children.

Market Returns to Schooling

According to Psacharopoulos (1985, 1994), the worldwide estimates of the rate of return to female education exceeded those for males by more than one percentage point in the 1970s and 1980s. In Indonesia, women are acquiring secondary and tertiary education in relatively larger numbers than men in response to greater relative returns to female higher education (Deolalikar 1993). Wage rates remain lower for females than for males, but the percentage increase in wages associated with post-primary schooling is greater for females (Behrman and Deolalikar 1995). Although the rate of return to the schooling of females is increasing, the gender gap in absolute earnings of men and women remains high at 23 percent for developed countries and 27 percent for developing countries (World Bank 2001: 55, Table 1.2).

Using data from the Bicol region in the rural Philippines, Lanzona (1998) finds that there is a 17 percent wage gap in nonfarm sector jobs in favor of males after controlling for education and experience, even though the women in his sample receive more schooling than the men. Lanzona's findings are supported by the wage function estimates of Maluccio (1998: Tables 1, 3, 4, and 5) using data from the same study area. These two authors do not give a clear explanation of why the wage gap exists when women are more educated than men. They point out, however, that the wage gap is one of the major reasons females surpass men in outmigration from the village. Moreover, the findings of these two authors are inconsistent with the results of our own studies reported in Chapter 3, which show no significant gender disparity in nonfarm income. We speculate that Lanzona's (1998) and Maluccio's (1998) findings reflect the relative poverty and backwardness of the Bicol region compared with our study areas. We must also emphasize that additional studies need to be undertaken to examine which case is more typical in the Philippines.

Summary and Conclusions

The first objective of this chapter was to assess the contribution of farm and nonfarm incomes to total household income inequality. The contribution of farm income to total household income inequality declined, primarily as a result of increased demand for hired labor and the increase in farm wages. On the other hand, the contribution of nonfarm income to total household income inequality has increased, owing importantly to increased inequality in returns to human capital in the nonfarm sector. This implies that parents' choices about who will receive land and who is to be sent to school are likely to result in serious income inequality between sons and daughters in a dynamic context. However, we found that schooling investments between younger sons and daughters no longer exhibit the pro-female bias that we found among older children, indicating that parents have adjusted their investment strategies through time to equalize incomes of heirs.

The second aim was to determine whether there is a gender bias in the intrahousehold allocation of expenditures. We did not find any strong evidence that daughters and wives are particularly disfavored in expenditure allocations compared with sons and husbands. Thus, intrahousehold allocations of expenditures and schooling investments may well both be described as egalitarian in the case of the rural Philippines.

The third objective of this chapter was to test whether a unitary or a collective model characterized decisionmaking within rural Philippine households. Our evidence is mixed. Using the expenditure shares regressions, we cannot reject the null hypothesis of a unitary model of the household. However, when we examine individual schooling outcomes, we find that parents do not have identical preferences with respect to investments in their younger children's schooling: for example, fathers who inherited more land tend to give less schooling to daughters. Such a finding may appear to support a collective model of the household.

Although parents exhibit preferential treatment toward children of a specific gender, the overall results for the younger generation suggest that gender or birth order do not affect schooling decisions for the younger generation of children. Thus, in comparison with other countries (for example, Bangladesh), where discrimination against girls is clear in both the expenditure regressions and the individual regressions (Quisumbing and Maluccio 2003), the Philippines emerges as relatively egalitarian.

It is expected that returns to human capital will increase as a result of the rapid development of the nonfarm sector. If, at the same time, labor markets become competitive, the gender–wage gap will be reduced. Parents will then increase their investments in the schooling of both daughters and sons in response to the increasing returns to human capital. In the longer run this trend will strengthen the wife's bargaining position vis-à-vis her husband's, which may further increase the advantages of making joint decisions within the household. In this situation, concerns for intrahousehold equity do not conflict with efficiency objectives.

PART II

The Sumatra Case

5   The Study Villages and Sample Households in Agroforestry Areas

This chapter sets the stage for a comprehensive analysis of gender, schooling, and land inheritance in Sumatra, a traditional matrilineal area. We first describe the major characteristics of the study villages and the survey design in our Sumatra sites. Customary land tenure institutions prevail in our sites and, as in the Ghana sites, have undergone substantial changes. Moreover, the prevailing land tenure institutions are markedly different across locations and between lowland paddy and upland fields. We provide explanations for these land tenure institutions and their structure, and characterize the sample households in terms of farm size, family size, schooling, changing land use, labor use in agricultural activities, and sources of household income. In the third section, we explore dynamic changes and cross-sectional differences in schooling and land inheritance by gender using individual survey data gathered from a large sample of communities. Lastly, we set out the hypotheses to be tested statistically in Chapters 6 and 7.

Study Villages and Survey Structure

Study Villages

According to a community-level study of land tenure institutions conducted in the Kerinci Seblat National Park in West Sumatra and Jambi Provinces by Otsuka et al. (2001), the traditional matrilineal inheritance system in this region has undergone substantial changes that are specific to particular geographic settings (see Figure 5.1 for the locations of the survey sites). Although similar studies have not been attempted in other regions of Indonesia, the transformation of the matrilineal system would probably be unique to Sumatra, because patrilineal inheritance seems to dominate in Java and other regions. Solok district is located at the highest altitude—more than 1,000 meters above sea level—where coffee is a major tree crop. In this region, where the traditional matrilineal inheritance system is strongest, daughters alone tend to inherit both lowland and upland fields, even though collective family ownership has been replaced by more in-

115

FIGURE 5.1 Location of study areas in Indonesia

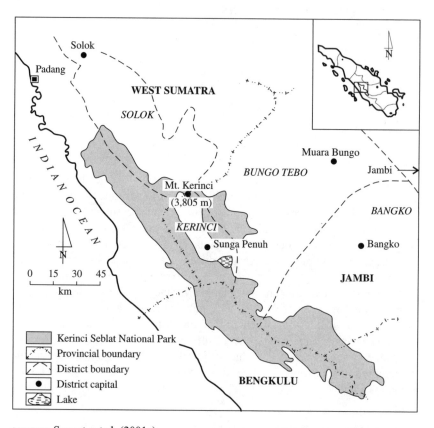

SOURCE: Suyanto et al. (2001c).

dividualized ownership systems. Kerinci district, where cinnamon is a major tree crop, is located in the Middle Region at altitudes approximately 500–1,000 meters above sea level. In this region, the most common inheritance practice is for daughters and sons to inherit land equally. Bungo Tebo is located in the lowest region, where rubber is a major tree crop. Sons commonly inherit upland fields and daughters inherit lowland paddy fields in this region.

The major ethnic groups are the Minangkabau in Solok, the Kerinci ethnic group in Kerinci, and the Melayu Jambi in Bungo Tebo. These people have historically relied on wet rice cultivation and, hence, areas along streams and rivers have been devoted largely to paddy fields. A more collective and matrilineal type of family ownership is common for lowland paddy fields. Paddy fields are surrounded by agroforestry plots or commercial tree plots, including both mature trees and newly planted trees, intercropped with annual crops, and by bush-fallow plots under shifting cultivation. Natural forests are typically located in the mountainous terrain further away from village centers. The bush-fallow area was originally converted from primary forests.

In order to explore the implications for gender equity of different patterns of evolution of the matrilineal inheritance system, we selected two contiguous villages in Kerinci district (henceforth called the Kerinci villages), in which lowland paddy cultivation and upland cinnamon agroforestry are the two most important farming systems, and another two contiguous villages in Bungo Tebo district (henceforth called the Bungo Tebo villages), in which lowland paddy and upland rubber agroforestry coexist. The two selected villages in each region are similar in terms of topographical, ecological, and socioeconomic environments. Almost all inhabitants belong to the Kerinci ethnic group in Kerinci, whereas the Melayu Jambi account for the majority of population in Bungo Tebo. In our observation, both ethnic groups have traditionally practiced matrilineal inheritance and matrilocal residence systems akin to the Minangkabau in Solok, who have been intensively studied by ethnographers and anthropologists (Kato 1982; Errington 1984).[1]

Survey Structure

In each site, we conducted two types of surveys: (1) a household survey to collect household-level data on land tenure, land use, and agricultural and agroforestry production and (2) an intensive inheritance/expenditure survey administered in a subsample of households selected from the first survey to collect detailed data on land inheritance, schooling, household income, and expenditures by individual household members. In Kerinci, a random survey of 50 households in each of the two villages was conducted first. The three survey rounds took place in August to September 1996, February to March 1997, and August 1997. In Bungo Tebo, the sample initially consisted of all the households in one village (128 households). After the survey, it became clear that the number of upland plots was inadequate for the estimation of the age profile of the profitability of rubber production. Thus, we added another 40 households, which were randomly chosen from a contiguous village. We interviewed both husband and wife in the household survey. To investigate whether evolutionary changes in land tenure institutions have affected the distribution of land rights by gender, as well as schooling investments between daughters and sons, a retrospective survey of inheritance and schooling was implemented for a subsample of 60 households, each randomly drawn from the original household

---

1. Although the Solok villages were not included in the inheritance retrospective, they were part of a broader study of land tenure and agroforestry management, which examined the evolution of land tenure institutions in response to population pressure using data from a large number of communities (Suyanto, Tomich, and Otsuka 2001c). It was from this larger study that we discerned that the practice of matrilineal inheritance in Solok was very similar to that in Kerinci and Bungo Tebo.

samples in the Kerinci and Bungo Tebo sites. The inheritance survey included questions on the parents, siblings, spouses, and children of the respondents, yielding information on three generations—called the parents', respondents', and children's generations. To obtain equal representation in terms of male and female respondents, half of the sample consisted of husbands and the other half of wives. Spouses were present during most of the interviews, so we interviewed both husband and wife together.

As shown in Table 5.1, we found that 140 lowland paddy fields in Kerinci were either owned by our sample households or cultivated by the sample households under tenancy or borrowing arrangements.[2] Of the 140 paddy fields, 82 percent were irrigated by traditional simple gravity systems using streams flowing from nearby mountains, and the rest were rainfed. The average size of paddy field was less than a half-hectare and a typical household owned two to three plots. Upland fields were divided into 155 young cinnamon fields with trees aged 1–3 years, 264 productive cinnamon fields with trees aged 4–13 years, and 37 bush-fallow fields. A considerable number of cinnamon fields were intercropped with coffee, even though cinnamon trees predominate. To simplify the analysis of agricultural income, we chose 63 young and 175 productive fields planted exclusively to cinnamon for a detailed survey of production, input use, and cost.[3]

The main cinnamon harvest (when trees are felled) occurs after 8–10 years of growth. Coppices regrow after harvesting and, in most cases, this process can be repeated three times. Because of the declining rate of regrowth, old trees are cut and usually new ones are planted after four harvests. Minor output is "produced" when certain branches are pruned, beginning four years after planting or regrowth. Young fields were intercropped with annual crops, mostly with chili; in our sample fields, 62 percent were intercropped in the first year, 21 percent in the second year, and 5 percent in the third year. Intercropping intensity declines primarily because of the increasing competition with growing trees for sunlight.

Bush-fallow fields accounted for only a small proportion of area in Kerinci because this area was an early settlement and is densely populated. Bush-fallow fields were generally located in areas far from village centers and were planted to food crops in the distant past. Only one-third of our sample households owned such land, which reflects the near exhaustion of easily accessible

---

2. Note that a rotation system of cultivating lowland paddy fields is common under the joint family ownership system, in which only qualified households cultivate the land in a particular year. There were 99 paddy fields that were jointly owned but happened to be cultivated by other joint family members who were not among the sample households during the 1996/97 wet season. Therefore, we focus only on 140 paddy fields that are exclusively cultivated by our sample households.

3. Since coffee is a minor crop, the choice between cinnamon alone and cinnamon intercropped with coffee seems to be of secondary importance.

TABLE 5.1 Number of sample households and sample plots, by land use, in Kerinci and Bungo Tebo, 1996–1997

Types of field	Kerinci		Bungo Tebo	
	Households	Plots	Households	Plots
Total	100	415	162	564
Lowland rice fields	88	140	112	228
Young cinnamon fields[a]	46	63 (155)[b]		
Productive cinnamon fields[c]	79	175 (264)[b]		
Upland rice fields			27	27
Young rubber fields[d]			20	33 (177)[e]
Mature rubber fields[f]			95	128 (198)[e]
Bush-fallow	33	37	102	148

[a] Fields with trees aged 1–3.

[b] Total number of cinnamon fields including those intercropped with coffee.

[c] Fields with trees aged 4 and over.

[d] Fields with a dominant tree age of 0–7.

[e] Total number of rubber fields including those intercropped with cinnamon.

[f] Fields with a dominant tree age of 8 and over.

cultivable land in the Kerinci valley. At present, some of the bush-fallow fields are secondary forests.

The sample households in Bungo Tebo operated 228 plots of lowland rice fields and 27 upland rice plots in the wet season of 1995/96. Of the 228 lowland rice fields, 53 percent are under joint family ownership operated on rotation among family members. The rest of the upland plots comprise 177 young rubber fields (with a dominant tree age of 1–7 years), 198 mature rubber fields (with a dominant tree age of 8 years and above), and 148 bush-fallow fields. The rubber farming system under investigation is called "jungle rubber" because wild woody species are allowed to grow among rubber trees, which may help protect rubber trees from grass weeds (Gouyon, de Foresta, and Levang 1993).[4] The production technologies have changed little since rubber was introduced a century ago, despite the availability of seemingly profitable alternative technologies (Barlow and Jayasuriya 1984). Because of the increase in cinnamon prices relative to rubber prices in recent years, some farmers have

---

4. The plant biodiversity of jungle rubber is one-half to two-thirds that of a natural forest (Michon and de Foresta 1995).

experimented with intercropping cinnamon with young rubber fields. Thus, only 33 of the young rubber fields were pure rubber fields, whereas 128 of the mature rubber fields were pure stands. By and large, cinnamon occupies only small areas, because the altitudes of our study sites are too low for commercial cinnamon production. For the survey of production costs and revenue, we chose fields that are exclusively planted with rubber and conducted interviews during the wet and dry seasons of 1996–97 (December 1996 and June–July 1997). We do not believe, however, that this procedure causes serious selection bias.

As in Kerinci, bush-fallow areas in Bungo Tebo are generally located in areas far away from village centers. Bush-fallow areas occupy larger areas in Bungo Tebo than in Kerinci, because Bungo Tebo is more recently settled and less densely populated. Bungo Tebo is endowed with meager areas of productive lowland paddy fields, which explains why this region is sparsely populated.

Land Tenure and the Sample Households

Concepts of Property in Matrilineal Sumatra

Traditionally, descent and inheritance in matrilineal Sumatra, as exemplified by the Minangkabau, occur through the female line. Although the Minangkabau are not found in our study sites, our informal interviews with elders and knowledgeable members in our study villages strongly suggest that, historically, villages in our sites were subject to the same matrilineal inheritance system. Except for the special case of adoption, individuals take after the sublineage (*paruik*), lineage (*payung*), and clan (*suku*) of their mother, and remain with these groups throughout their lives (Kato 1982: 51). Unmarried men typically work as farm laborers or emigrate to other areas to accumulate funds or establish a trade (Errington 1984), and upon marriage they cultivate their wives' land.[5] Residential patterns are also extended and uxorilocal, although Kato (1982) argues that they are, strictly speaking, duolocal. Sons-in-law, who belong to a different matrilineal line, have rights only to visit their wives, and traditionally do not live in the wives' natal home, or *rumah gadang*.[6] Major decisions are vested in the lineage head (*mamak*), a maternal uncle. Traditionally, the tie between a maternal uncle and his nieces or nephews (children of his sister) was stronger than the tie between a man and his children.

Classification of property and its transmission across generations occur along gender-differentiated lines. Minangkabau society classifies property into two types: *harto pusako,* or "ancestral property," and *harto pancarian* or "earned

---

5. Indeed, emigration of single men to work abroad—sending them on a *rantau*—is a long-standing practice among the Minang of West Sumatra, and is considered part of the coming of age process of young men (Errington 1984).

6. Also called an *adat* house, the *rumah gadang* is supposed to house one sublineage or *saparuik,* which literally means "people of one womb."

property" (Kahn 1980: 26).[7] Ancestral property belongs to the lineage, whereas earned property can be obtained or purchased with one's own efforts. For example, irrigated rice land (*sawah*), the ancestral homestead, gold, and water buffaloes are classified as ancestral property, whereas tools and workshops are "earned property." These two forms of property are subject to different systems of inheritance. Ancestral property is always inherited by women, and almost always passes from mother to daughters. In contrast, the rules of inheritance for earned or acquired property are relatively flexible. The owner is free to sell, mortgage, or give away acquired property. Earned property can also be passed on to either sex, but reverts to ancestral property in the next generation.[8]

Although it is difficult to quantify the growing importance of earned property, there is no question that it is becoming more prevalent, because expanding tree crop fields are basically considered to be earned property. The growing importance of earned property has had major implications for the individualization of property systems in Sumatra. Aside from its association with commercial and artisanal activities, earned property also pertains to newly opened agricultural land, particularly shifting cultivation area (Kato 1982: 169). Newly opened land that becomes wet rice fields has the potential of becoming ancestral land in the next generation, particularly if it requires sizable investments of labor and material from the developer's lineage. Newly opened land for shifting cultivation was, prior to the advent of commercial agroforestry, of a rather impermanent nature. The clearing of upland fields was not a major operation like creating new *sawah,* and its impermanent nature made the lineage of its developer less likely to control it. Since shifting cultivation area was considered earned property, its rules of disposal were relatively flexible (Kato 1982: 169). The anthropological studies, however, do not indicate whether shifting cultivation area remains earned property, even if it is under fallow for many years, probably because this type of earned property did not have much economic significance until the growth of the cash economy and the advent of commercial tree crops, namely coffee, in the nineteenth century.

Population pressure also made it increasingly difficult for entire lineages to be housed in a single *adat* house; new residences tended to be nuclear rather than extended dwellings. As earned property became more important, and as population pressure increased, so the nuclear family gained importance in relation to the extended family.

The rise in significance of the nuclear family was accompanied by the growing prevalence of *hibah* (gift), a specific type of transfer of earned property that generally takes place between a father and his children. If a man wishes

---

7. This discussion of the inheritance of different types of property is from Kahn (1980) and Kato (1982).

8. In some villages, earned property owned by women is passed on to their daughters; that owned by men is passed on to sons.

to make sure that his individually earned property goes to his children rather than to the children of his sisters, he may arrange a transfer through *hibah* while he is alive.[9] Moreover, education offers another way for a father to invest his earned property: investment in his children produces fruits of earned property, which could not be contested by his matrilineal relatives after his death (Kato 1982: 183).

This summary of the anthropological and ethnographic evidence strongly suggests that inheritance regimes are not static.[10] The inheritance system appears to have evolved in parallel with the changes in communal land tenure institutions in the direction of individualized ownership in response to population pressure.

Prevailing Land Tenure Institutions

Table 5.2 describes the land tenure institutions that prevail in our study sites as well as in other villages in West Sumatra and Jambi provinces (Suyanto, Tomich, and Otsuka 2001a, 2001b). Cultivated land, particularly paddy fields, has traditionally been owned collectively by a lineage—a group of relatives usually comprising three generations: a grandmother and her husband; their children; and their grandchildren. When a woman dies, land is bequeathed to her sisters, nieces, and daughters in accordance with the decision of the lineage head, who is selected from among male members of the second generation. The basic principle of land allocation is to maintain equity among lineage members. Individual land rights, other than usufruct rights, are highly restricted in this system, partly to maintain paddy land within the lineage. The original lineage ownership system, however, had become rare in our study areas at the time of our survey in 1996. At that time, a woman's daughters usually inherited paddy fields jointly; we call this form of land tenure joint family ownership. Furthermore, single-family ownership, in which daughters individually inherit shares of the land, had become widespread for paddy fields in many areas. For upland commercial tree fields, single-family ownership (in which both daughters and sons or only sons inherit the land individually) is more common than lineage and joint family ownership. In addition, "private" ownership has been widely created through land purchases and by clearing natural forests, particularly for upland

---

9. This is surprisingly similar to the transfer of land as gift among the matrilineal Akan in western Ghana (see Quisumbing et al. 2001a and Chapter 8 in this volume). Similar to the ceremonies surrounding gift transfers, *hibah* requires the agreement of all parties concerned, including one's matrilineal relatives, as well as expensive feasts.

10. The Minang themselves do not consider their culture to be static, and take pride in the flexibility of *adat* (customary law). Continuous discussions and reinterpretation of *adat* help the community make judgments that allow both continuity and development in their *adat* (Errington 1984: 99–100). Whereas some laws are unchangeable (the *cupak usali,* or original measure), *cupak buatan* (the constructed measure) is subject to change through consensus, provided that it does not contradict or threaten the core *cupak cusali.*

TABLE 5.2 Land tenure categories and their major characteristics in Sumatra

Ownership categories	Inherited by	Joint ownership
Lineage	Sisters, nieces, and daughters	Yes
Joint family	Daughters	Yes
Single family I	Daughters	No
Single family II	Daughters and sons	No
Single family III	Sons	No
Private	Any family member	No

fields. According to the customary land tenure system, as explained earlier, the labor effort involved in forest clearance establishes private ownership. Individualized rights on cleared forestland, however, are subject to erosion over time, unless it is planted to trees in Sumatra (Angelsen 1995; Otsuka et al. 2001).

According to a community-level survey by Otsuka et al. (2001), individual land rights are very weak under the lineage ownership system: cultivators are usually not allowed to rent out, pawn, or sell land or to plant trees without permission from the lineage members. In the case of joint family ownership of upland fields, cultivators are at best allowed to rent out land under share tenancy and to plant trees without permission. Land rights are stronger under single-family ownership, in which cultivators have the right to rent out and sometimes to pawn without obtaining permission from the family members. If permission is obtained, land can be sold under the single-family ownership system. In contrast, almost perfectly individualized rights (including rights to sell without permission) are granted to privately purchased land and cleared forestland, even though land rights tend to decline in the latter case if land is left fallow for a long time. Tree planting has promoted the conversion from lineage ownership to joint family ownership and further to single-family ownership, because efforts to plant trees are rewarded by strong individual rights under the customary land tenure rules (Otsuka et al. 2001). In fact, after trees are planted, owners of single-family land are often granted the rights to sell the land. In other words, tree planting helps establish strong individual land rights, when such rights are originally weak. An important issue is the implication of such evolutionary changes in land tenure institutions for gender equity.

We use the data from the inheritance subsample to show the land tenure distribution of plots by land use type.[11] In the Kerinci subsample, 42 percent of

11. The data on land tenure in lowland rice fields in Bungo Tebo from the intensive inheritance survey of the subsample are more reliable than those from the survey of all sample households, because the inheritance survey focused on land tenure on individual plots, whereas the household survey was longer and more comprehensive, and covered a wide range of issues. It is therefore likely that the survey of all households was more prone to respondent fatigue and related biases.

owned lowland rice fields are owned under the joint family system; ownership by daughters and sons is the predominant category (Table 5.3). Around 27 percent of owned plots are under single-family ownership; again, ownership by daughters and sons is the major category. Thus, it seems that even in the category of "ancestral land," under which paddy land has traditionally been classified, the inheritance system seems to have evolved to include both daughters and sons as legitimate heirs. Both young and mature cinnamon fields are more likely to be owned by a single family (by both daughters and sons) or can be acquired privately, whether through purchase or forest clearance.

In Bungo Tebo, lineage land is found only in upland rice fields, accounting for 70 percent of upland rice plots (Table 5.4). Joint family land is found only in lowland rice fields, accounting for 55 percent of lowland rice plots. Almost 50 percent of lowland rice plots are owned jointly by daughters, with the remainder owned jointly by daughters and sons. Only 7 percent of lowland rice fields are under single-family ownership. In contrast, ownership of rubber plots is more individualized. Single-family ownership and private purchase are the dominant tenure categories for young and mature rubber plots. Rubber plots have also been acquired by forest clearance, accounting for 13 percent of young rubber plots and 9 percent of mature rubber plots. Finally, bush-fallow areas are mostly under single-family ownership (41 percent of plots), followed by private ownership acquired by forest clearance (31 percent) and private purchase (23 percent). For both rubber and bush-fallow areas, single-family ownership is dominated by ownership by sons.

TABLE 5.3 Land tenure distribution of owned/cultivated plots, by land use type, in Kerinci: Subsample of households (percent)

Land tenure category	Lowland rice	Young cinnamon	Productive cinnamon
Joint family	42	0	0
Daughters	4	0	0
Daughters and sons	38	0	0
Sons	0	0	0
Single family	27	33	38
Daughters	1	1	1
Daughters and sons	23	27	35
Sons	3	5	2
Borrowing	5	11	12
Private—purchase	7	25	18
Private—forest clearance	1	19	22
Share/fixed rent tenancy	18	12	10
Total	100	100	100

TABLE 5.4 Land tenure distribution of owned/cultivated plots, by land use type, in Bungo Tebo: Subsample of households (percent)

Land-tenure category	Lowland rice	Upland rice	Young rubber	Mature rubber	Bush-fallow
Communal/lineage	0	70	0	0	0
Joint family	55	0	0	0	3
Daughters	49	0	0	0	0
Daughters and sons	6	0	0	0	3
Sons	0	0	0	0	0
Single family	7	0	34	29	41
Daughters	1	0	7	0	8
Daughters and sons	1	0	3	2	7
Sons	5	0	24	27	26
Private—purchase	10	0	33	49	23
Private—forest clearance	0	0	13	9	31
Renting	15	0	0	9	0
Borrowing	12	20	13	4	0
Other	1	10	7	0	2
Total	100	100	100	100	100

The distribution of plots by land tenure status seems to indicate that, in Kerinci, the inheritance systems have been gradually shifting to a more egalitarian system in which both sons and daughters can inherit land. In Bungo Tebo, on the other hand, the evolution of inheritance systems seems to have gone further, with women specializing in lowland paddy land and sons in agroforestry and bush-fallow areas. Note that in both locations the evolution has taken place based on the traditional ruling that earned property (such as fields obtained by purchase and forest clearance) can be disposed of at will to children of either sex.

Socioeconomic Characteristics

According to Table 5.5, the average farm size, including lowland and upland areas, is larger in Bungo Tebo than in Kerinci. The average size of currently operated lowland rice land is 0.40 hectares in Kerinci and 0.93 hectares in Bungo Tebo. Note that some rice land in the area is not currently being cultivated by the sample households. Some plots are cultivated by family members by rotation under joint family ownership and some plots are temporarily pawned, lent out, and rented out. If we include land that is not being currently cultivated, the average size of lowland rice plots is 0.98 hectares in Kerinci and 1.10 hectares in Bungo Tebo. Note that farm size data were collected by interviews and not by direct measurement, so the data may be subject to measurement errors. Unlike in the Ghana study sites, where farmers do not possess a clear numerical concept of farm size, farmers in Sumatra have, at the very least,

TABLE 5.5 Demographic characteristics of sample households in Kerinci and Bungo Tebo

Characteristics	Kerinci	Bungo Tebo
Number of sample households	100	162
Farm size of subsample households (hectares)		
Lowland	0.40	0.93
Upland[a]	1.85	5.60
Household size	3.94	4.46
Number of working members[b]	3.34	3.64
Composition of working members (percent)		
Respondents		
Husband	33	34
Wife	38	38
Children of respondents		
Sons	17	14
Daughters	12	14
Average schooling attainment of working members (years)		
Respondents		
Husband	7.50	6.55
Wife	7.56	4.72
Children of respondents		
Sons	9.53	7.78
Daughters	11.00	7.75

[a] Includes bush-fallow area.

[b] Members aged 15–65 years who are not in school.

rough ideas of farm sizes in terms of hectares. Thus, we do not expect serious data problems with respect to farm size in the Sumatra sites.

The average household size is relatively small in both sites, though it is somewhat larger in Bungo Tebo. The small household size is explained partly by the fact that, unlike for the Philippines, we included only coresident household members in the computation of household size. However, we collected data on the age, education, occupation, and marital status of all children, regardless of place of residence. Many unmarried children reside and work in the cities and other areas outside the village. This is especially the case in Kerinci. Working members include all the resident household members aged 15–65 years working both on-farm and in nonfarm jobs.

In general, the respondents (husbands and wives) have less schooling than do their children. In Kerinci, husbands and wives have almost the same level of schooling, whereas their daughters have slightly more schooling than do sons. This situation is similar to that in the Philippines. The smaller proportion of female children in the household compared with male children suggests that married daughters live outside their natal household. In Bungo Tebo, husbands in the respondents' generation have higher levels of schooling than their wives, whereas sons and daughters have equal levels of schooling. In this less developed region, the discrimination against women in schooling seems to have disappeared. The determinants of gender differences in schooling and their consequences for individual incomes and household expenditures are the central issues to be investigated in this study.

Changes in Land Use

Table 5.6 shows the pattern of land use before land acquisition and land use at present in Kerinci. In general, land acquired initially as forestland and bush-fallow land is currently planted with either young cinnamon trees aged 1–3 years or productive cinnamon trees that are more than 3 years old. The shift in land use patterns in favor of cinnamon production indicates the profitability of cinnamon production relative to alternative land uses, particularly bush-fallow (Suyanto, Tomich, and Otsuka 2001a).

Table 5.7 demonstrates land use changes in Bungo Tebo. Before the current operators acquired the sample plots, about one-fifth of our selected rubber and bush-fallow plots were primary forests and rubber fields and bush-fallow fields each accounted for two-fifths. Virtually all unexploited forestland in Indonesia is officially classified as state land. However, from a local village perspective these primary forests are communally owned and under the control of a village chief. Thus, community members who wish to clear uncultivated forestland are expected to obtain permission from the village chief. In practice, however, these forests are open access to community members, so that very few easily accessible primary forests remained in the study area at the time of our survey.[12] About one-half of both cleared forest plots and acquired bush-fallow plots were planted to rubber trees. The productive life span of a rubber tree can be 60 years or more.[13] Moreover, once established, rubber trees generate seedlings and, with proper thinning and other management practices, a rubber forest can be sustained for a long time. Hence, with very few exceptions, acquired rubber fields remained planted to rubber either through replanting or through regeneration to fill gaps with young rubber trees. As shown in Table 5.7, 99 percent of the present rubber fields in our sample were already planted to rubber before the current cohort of trees was planted, which indicates that many rubber fields were cleared and replanted after the trees became unproductive.

---

12. See the model of Anderson and Hill (1990), which describes how unused open-access land would be exploited when property rights are conferred on those who have opened the land.

13. The average life of rubber trees in our sites seems significantly longer than the case reported by Barlow and Muharminto (1982) of 15–25 years for regular tapping after reaching a tappable age of about 10 years. They also point out that the productive life of rubber trees is negatively related to the intensity of tapping.

TABLE 5.6 Land use before acquisition and at present in Kerinci: Subsample of households

Land use before acquisition	Number of plots	Proportion of land use at present (percent)		
		Young cinnamon[a]	Productive cinnamon[b]	Bush-fallow
Forest	81	29	54	17
Cinnamon fields	212	34	66	0
Bush-fallow	163	37	50	13

[a] Cinnamon trees aged 1–3 years.

[b] Cinnamon trees over 3 years old.

TABLE 5.7 Land use before acquisition and at present in Bungo Tebo: Subsample of households

Land use before acquisition	Number of plots	Proportion of land use at present (percent)	
		Rubber	Bush-fallow
Forest	103	46	54
Rubber fields	202	99	1
Bush-fallow	218	59	41

Labor Use

In order to explore why different paths have been chosen in the evolution of land tenure institutions and inheritance systems in Kerinci and Bungo Tebo villages, we examine the relative contributions of men and women to labor inputs in lowland and upland rice cultivation and to the two major tree crops, cinnamon and rubber, in these two regions (Table 5.8).[14] In Kerinci, wet rice, young cinnamon, and mature cinnamon fields were sampled; in Bungo Tebo, upland rice, young rubber, and mature rubber fields were included. Since the focus of the original study in Bungo Tebo was on the relative profitability of upland rice and agroforestry (rubber), data on labor input and net revenue in lowland rice fields were not collected (Suyanto, Tomich, and Otsuka 2001a, 2001b). In Kerinci, wet rice and cinnamon use male and female labor relatively equally. In wet rice cultivation, male family labor accounts for 58 percent of family labor input and female labor comprises 42 percent. Whereas young cinnamon uses

---

14. The labor input data come from the whole sampled fields used for the computation of net revenue from food crops and agroforestry discussed in Suyanto, Tomich, and Otsuka (2001a, 2001b).

TABLE 5.8 Proportion of labor input in rice production and agroforestry, by gender, in Kerinci and Bungo Tebo

Type of labor	Kerinci			Bungo Tebo		
	Wet rice	Young cinnamon	Mature cinnamon	Upland rice	Young rubber	Mature rubber
Family labor (percent)						
Men	58	55	75	32	83	91
Women	42	45	25	68	17	9
Total	100	100	100	100	100	100
Total person-days per hectare	64	47	7	150	39	53
Total labor (percent)[a]						
Men	54	47	60	30	68	92
Women	46	53	40	70	32	8
Total	100	100	100	100	100	100
Total person-days per hectare	222	68	25	176	52	95

NOTE: Data are from sampled fields.

[a] Family and hired labor.

slightly more male family labor—55 percent versus 45 percent—women are significantly less involved in mature cinnamon cultivation, accounting for only 25 percent of family labor input. Yet the labor requirements for the management of mature cinnamon are much smaller than those for young cinnamon. When both hired and family labor are considered, wet rice and young cinnamon use relatively equal amounts of male and female labor.

In Bungo Tebo, upland rice is very intensive in female family labor: women contribute 68 percent, compared with men's contribution of only 32 percent. Although relevant data were not collected on lowland rice cultivation, it is known that female labor dominates. Both young and mature rubber plots utilize substantial inputs from male family members: men contribute 83 percent of family labor in young rubber and 91 percent in mature rubber. The relative proportions of male and female labor input do not change substantially when we consider family and hired labor combined. The relatively large amount of male labor is required because it is physically difficult and risky for women to work in the jungle rubber fields covered by densely grown trees. In contrast, cinnamon trees are grown in rows and, hence, cinnamon fields are easily accessible by women. Such differences reflect the comparative advantages of men and women in the cultivation of wet rice and tree crops.

From the observations made above, it seems reasonable to hypothesize that the land inheritance system has changed from a matrilineal system to an egalitarian or bilateral system in order to provide proper work incentives to men and women. Thus, in Kerinci, where men and women work equally in both lowland and upland fields, sons and daughters inherit both lowland and upland more or less equally. In Bungo Tebo, in contrast, where women work primarily in rice fields and men work primarily in rubber fields, daughters tend to inherit rice fields whereas sons tend to inherit rubber fields.

Household Income Sources

Farm income consists of incomes from tree crop, rice, and livestock production, as well as agricultural wage earnings and land rentals, whereas nonfarm income comprises incomes from formal wage employment and from informal employment in retail, rural transport, and domestic services earned by the resident working members, as well as remittances from family members working outside the village. Table 5.9 exhibits the breakdown of total household income into different components in both Kerinci and Bungo Tebo villages. Unfortunately, we were unable to ascertain the nonfarm incomes of each household member. It is, however, certain that men earn more nonfarm income than women do, particularly in Kerinci.

Although both sites depend heavily on farm income, the average household farm income in Kerinci is about twice that in Bungo Tebo. Income from cinnamon production is particularly high. However, yearly income from cinnamon fluctuates widely, because cinnamon is harvested every eight years or so. Thus, actual income from cinnamon can be quite different from permanent income. Farmers sell standing cinnamon trees to local traders, who offer prices to farmers based on their own assessment of the value of cinnamon in the field. Taking advantage of this practice, we employed traders in our survey and requested them to assess the value of standing cinnamon trees in all productive cinnamon fields in our samples. As shown in Table 5.9, the value of cinnamon stock is about nine times as large as the actual flow income from cinnamon harvesting. Cinnamon is also produced in Bungo Tebo, but cinnamon income is very small. Rubber income in Bungo Tebo is much smaller than cinnamon income in Kerinci. Thus, locational rents arising from the production of profitable cinnamon seem to explain a large part of the income gap between the two research sites. Kerinci is also better endowed with productive lowland paddy fields, so that rice income is also much larger than in Bungo Tebo. In order to compensate for the smaller incomes from tree crop and rice production, albeit only partially, livestock and poultry production is a more important income source in Bungo Tebo.

Both sites are located in rural areas and it takes more than an hour by vehicle to drive to the nearest local town. Thus, nonfarm income sources are limited and, hence, the nonfarm income shares are relatively small. Remittances to and from nonresident family members are also small. Note that, unlike in the Philippines, there are very few landless households in our sample in Sumatra,

TABLE 5.9 Sources of household income in Kerinci and Bungo Tebo:
Intensive survey, 1997

	Kerinci		Bungo Tebo	
Income sources	Rupiahs/year (thousand)	Percent	Rupiahs/year (thousand)	Percent
Farm income	7,417	83	3,148	71
Cinnamon income	4,472	50	253	6
(Value of cinnamon stock)	(39,883)	(0)		
Rubber, tree, and other crops[a]	1,576	18	1,662	37
Upland rice	0	0	65	1
Lowland rice	634	7	248	6
Livestock and poultry	280	3	689	16
Agricultural wage and rental income[b]	455	5	231	5
Nonfarm income	1,552	17	1,273	29
Nonagricultural enterprise	454	5	155	4
Nonagricultural wage	781	9	964	22
Remittances	317	3	154	3
Total	8,969	100	4,421	100

NOTE: The exchange rate was approximately US$1 = 2,500 rupiahs.

[a] Includes income from banana, coconut, firewood, pepper, durian, rattan, papaya, coffee, tobacco, vegetables, peanuts, potato, rattan, and other fruit crops.

[b] Includes income from land rental.

essentially because Sumatra has abundant land resources compared with the Philippines.

The Sample Individuals

Distribution of Sample Individuals by Gender

In the intensive inheritance and expenditure survey, the respondents were asked about pre-marriage wealth (schooling and landownership) of their parents and in-laws, the schooling and inheritance of their spouses, and the schooling of and proposed bequests to their children. Each respondent was also asked about the characteristics of all of his or her siblings, such as date of birth, educational attainment, and areas of paddy land, agroforestry land, and bush-fallow land that they had received or expected to receive from their parents. In many cases, respondents received land at marriage but stood to inherit more land after their parents' death.

Since 60 households each were chosen for this survey, we obtained relevant information on 120 fathers and mothers of the respondents (Table 5.10).

TABLE 5.10 Demographic characteristics of sample individuals in Kerinci and Bungo Tebo: Intensive survey, 1997

Individuals	Kerinci			Bungo Tebo		
	Number	Year of birth	Schooling (years)[a]	Number	Year of birth	Schooling (years)[a]
Parents of respondents						
Father	60	n.a.	3.7 (2.9)	60	n.a.	2.9 (1.7)
Mother	60	n.a.	2.8 (2.6)	60	n.a.	1.7 (1.6)
Respondents' generation						
Sons	147	1956	8.9 (4.2)	141	1957	7.1 (3.3)
Daughters	145	1958	8.0 (4.0)	106	1956	4.6 (2.8)
Children of respondents[b]						
Sons	42	1984	5.8 (3.6)	50	1984	4.9 (3.0)
Daughters	28	1981	7.4 (3.2)	58	1984	4.8 (2.9)

NOTE: n.a. means not available.

[a] Numbers in parentheses are standard errors.

[b] Children aged 7–21 years.

The sample size of the respondents' generation is larger because we gathered information about the siblings of the respondents. We will therefore use a total of 539 sample individuals in the analysis of the determinants of land inheritance and schooling investment.

We also obtained data on the characteristics of the children of respondents, such as age, sex, and years of schooling. In our analysis of school enrollment, we included all 178 children aged 7–21 years regardless of residence at the time of the survey. For these children, parental investments in schooling are in progress. We excluded older children aged 22 years and over because there are only 8 such children in Kerinci and 8 in Bungo Tebo.

Schooling Attainment

Table 5.10 presents years of schooling of three generations of subsample household members (parents of the respondents, respondents and their siblings, and children of the respondents) in the Kerinci and Bungo Tebo villages. In both regions, fathers obtained one more year of schooling than mothers, though schooling levels in Bungo Tebo were lower than in Kerinci. Years of completed schooling increased in the respondents' generation: in contrast to their fathers, who on the average had 3.3 years of schooling, male respondents have 8.0 years of schooling. Female respondents have lower educational attainments than male respondents, at 6.3 years on the average. Educational attainments are lower and the gender gap is more pronounced for both generations in Bungo Tebo than in Kerinci. In fact, there is no significant difference in schooling between males and females in the respondents' generation in Kerinci.

In Kerinci, among children aged 7–21 years, we found that daughters are older by three years than sons, and thus their completed schooling is longer than sons' by 1.6 years on the average. Possibly because the average age of daughters is higher, and because of earlier age at marriage, the proportion of daughters in the household is smaller than that of sons. However, these results should be viewed with caution owing to the small sample sizes; that is, they cannot be used to draw inferences about the demographic structure of the population. In Bungo Tebo, the average age and schooling attainment of daughters and sons aged 7–21 years are the same. We also speculate that, by the time investments in the schooling of children are completed, children will have obtained significantly more schooling than their parents did. The major reasons are the expansion in public schools in rural areas, the declining cost of schooling, and households' increased incomes. Overall, we found that schooling investments in the daughters and sons of the respondents appear to have become egalitarian.

Land Inheritance

In contrast to the gender differences in schooling, mothers' inherited landholdings were generally larger than their husbands' in the parents' generation (Table 5.11). In Bungo Tebo, mothers inherited significantly larger areas of paddy land than did fathers, whereas they inherited approximately the same size of upland fields. Thus, possible income loss arising from mothers' fewer years of schooling might have been compensated for by larger inheritance of paddy land.

Patterns of land inheritance have significantly changed in the respondents' generation. In Kerinci, daughters and sons have inherited approximately equal areas of paddy land, but daughters have slightly larger inherited agroforestry areas and smaller bush-fallow areas. This is incentive compatible, since it is primarily men who clear bush-fallow land and establish cinnamon fields. In Bungo Tebo, daughters maintain the matrilineal custom of inheriting paddy land, having significantly larger areas than their brothers, but they receive substantially smaller areas of agroforestry land and bush-fallow land. Such an inheritance pattern is consistent with the comparative advantages of men and women in paddy and tree crop production in this area.

It is clear that both land inheritance and schooling investment in Kerinci are egalitarian between men and women. It is, however, unclear whether women's income is significantly lower than men's in Bungo Tebo, because women inherit larger areas of paddy land and smaller sizes of upland plots than men. The quantitative assessment of the possible difference in total income between men and women in Bungo Tebo is a major task to be carried out in Chapter 6.

TABLE 5.11 Landholdings of parents' and respondents' generations in Kerinci and Bungo Tebo

Generation	Kerinci		Bungo Tebo	
	Mean landholdings (hectares)	Standard deviation	Mean landholdings (hectares)	Standard deviation
Parents of respondents				
Father				
Inherited paddy	0.61	1.10	0.11	0.26
Inherited agroforesty land	0.44	1.02	0.57	1.60
Inherited bush-fallow area	0.03	0.23	0.42	1.14
Mother				
Inherited paddy	0.67	1.07	0.47	0.57
Inherited agroforesty land	0.40	0.96	0.41	1.45
Inherited bush-fallow area	0.06	0.34	0.51	1.85
Respondents				
Number of potential heirs	4.87	2.56	4.17	2.30
Sons				
Inherited paddy	0.23	0.30	0.07	0.20
Inherited agroforesty land	0.23	0.64	0.33	0.86
Inherited bush-fallow area	0.12	0.75	0.39	0.96
Daughters				
Inherited paddy	0.21	0.31	0.20	0.29
Inherited agroforesty land	0.28	0.74	0.18	0.82
Inherited bush-fallow area	0.02	0.11	0.11	0.39

The Scope of the Sumatra Study

As in the Philippine study, our basic hypothesis is that parents are concerned with both the efficiency and the equity consequences of wealth transfers to their heirs. As land resources become scarce with increases in population, intensive farming systems, such as agroforestry and irrigated rice farming, become more profitable than extensive farming systems, such as bush-fallow and rainfed rice farming. As Otsuka and Place (2001) emphasize, the shift to intensive farming systems requires investments in land improvement, such as tree planting and irrigation. Furthermore, new farming systems require more work effort for management and care. In order to promote investments in land improvement and subsequent management, appropriate incentive systems must be developed, such that those who invest in land recoup the benefits in future.[15]

---

15. Note that only a minimum amount of investment is required to construct and maintain simple gravity irrigation systems in our sites.

We hypothesize that in Kerinci the matrilineal inheritance system has been replaced by the egalitarian system, because men and women now work equally in both lowland rice and upland cinnamon fields. We also hypothesize that in Bungo Tebo the matrilineal system has been maintained for rice fields but replaced by the patrilineal system for rubber fields, because women work in rice fields and men work in rubber fields. To the extent that parents are egalitarian with respect to wealth transfers, we expect that schooling investments in daughters and sons tend to be adjusted so as to equalize the total incomes of sons and daughters not only in Kerinci but also in Bungo Tebo. Chapter 6 aims to substantiate these arguments statistically using regression analyses of the determinants of land inheritance and schooling and the determinants of agricultural incomes and household expenditures.

In Chapter 7, we will first examine how changes in inheritance systems toward gender equality and in land tenure systems toward individualized ownership systems affect the equity of land distribution across households. We will then analyze patterns of household expenditures in order to test the hypothesis that male and female members are treated equally within a household.

6 Gender Equity in the Inheritance of Paddy Land and Agroforest and in Schooling

This chapter explores statistically the implications of the shift from communal to individualized tenure for the distribution of land and schooling between sons and daughters in western Sumatra. In this area the inheritance system is evolving from a strictly matrilineal system to a more egalitarian system in which sons and daughters inherit the type of land that is more intensive in their own work effort. Whereas gender bias is either nonexistent or small in land inheritance, daughters tend to be disadvantaged in schooling. The gender gap in schooling, however, appears to be closing for the generation of younger children.

This chapter has four main sections. The first section describes the regression specification and identifies the determinants of land inheritance and schooling investments in the respondents' generation. The second section identifies the determinants of schooling investments in the children's generation. The third section explores the determinants of household agricultural incomes and expenditures in order to assess the effects of gender differences on land inheritance and schooling. The last section provides the summary and conclusions.

Determinants of Wealth Transfers in the Respondents' Generation

Readers who are not interested in the technical details of statistical estimation may proceed directly to the "Summary of Findings" at the end of this section on page 145.[1]

Specification of Estimated Functions

Suppose that parents can transfer either assets (land) or human capital (or education, represented by schooling) to their children. To investigate the determinants of the distribution of education and land among sons and daughters, we estimate a transfer equation of the following form:

$$T^*_{ij} = \beta_0 + \beta_1 X_{cij} + \beta_2 X_{fj} + \beta_3 X_{mj} + \gamma_1 D X_{fj} + \gamma_2 D X_{mj} + \varepsilon_{ij}, \quad (6.1)$$

---

1. This section draws heavily on Quisumbing and Otsuka (2001).

where $\mathbf{T}^*_{ij}$ is a vector of transfers, $\mathbf{T}^*_{ij} = [E^*_{ij}, p^*_{ij}, a^*_{ij}, b^*_{ij}]$, and $E^*_{ij}, p^*_{ij}, a^*_{ij}, b^*_{ij}$ are levels of education, paddy land, agroforestry land, and bushfallow land, respectively, inherited by child i in family j. Regression parameters β_k and γ_m are vectors of coefficients for each type of transfer; $\mathbf{X}_c$ is a vector of child characteristics such as sex, birth year, and dummies for the eldest and youngest children; $\mathbf{X}_f$ and $\mathbf{X}_m$ are vectors of exogenous human and physical wealth of father and mother at the time of marriage, respectively; D is the daughter dummy; and ε_{ij} is the error term in each equation.[2]

To account for the possibility that husband and wife do not have identical preferences regarding bestowals on children, an empirical specification consistent with a collective model of the household is used.[3] Thus, father's and mother's wealth at the time of marriage, which are exogenous to decisions made within marriage, enter separately into the regressions. Parental wealth consists of human capital, as proxied by years of schooling, and each parent's inherited holdings of paddy land, agroforestry land, and bush-fallow areas. In our sites in Indonesia, assets at marriage devolve to their respective owners in case of divorce; these have been used as proxies for threat points or bargaining power (Thomas, Contreras, and Frankenberg 2002).[4] Divorce is relatively common in most of Indonesia, owing to the system of bilateral descent, which gives women the right to their children, and by inheritance rights and work patterns, which give women the economic independence to support themselves (Malhotra 1997).[5] However, the incidence of divorce is low in our Sumatra sites. Parents' inherited landholdings are divided by the number of potential heirs to account for the effect of population pressure (larger family sizes) on transfers to the next generation. If the coefficients on the same wealth variables for father and mother are significantly different from each other, the unitary model of household decisionmaking is rejected.

We also include the number of brothers and sisters in the regression, to test whether sibling rivalry affects the allocation of land and education to children

---

2. If parents trade off different types of transfers among children, error terms across transfer equations may be correlated. Since the regressors are identical in all the transfer equations, a systems estimator such as SUR (Seemingly Unrelated Regressions) could have improved efficiency. However, because the dependent variables are censored and we are not aware of a tractable systems Tobit estimator, we estimated the transfer equations using single-equation Tobit.

3. For a review of collective models of the household, see Haddad, Hoddinott, and Alderman (1997). This formulation draws on McElroy and Horney's (1981) and McElroy's (1990) specification of the Nash bargaining model and is similar to Thomas (1990, 1994).

4. This may not be true in all societies, however. Fafchamps and Quisumbing (2002) show that, in rural Ethiopia, the overlap between assets at marriage and the distribution of assets upon divorce is not complete.

5. According to the 1991 Demographic and Health Survey (1992), rural divorce rates have declined through time. In 1976, the rural divorce rate (42 percent) was considerably higher than the urban rate of 33 percent; in 1991 it had declined to 23 percent, closer to the urban rate of 19 percent (Malhotra 1997).

(Butcher and Case 1994).[6] Parental land assets and schooling are interacted with the daughter dummy to test whether fathers or mothers with more physical and human capital treat children of different sexes differentially, that is, to test for gender preference with respect to the influence of parental resources.[7] This specification yields several tests of the unitary model. The first tests whether paternal and maternal resources affect sons equally, or $\beta_2 = \beta_3$. The second tests whether paternal and maternal resources have different effects on daughters relative to sons, or $\gamma_1 = \gamma_2$. That is, if the coefficients on the interaction terms with parental characteristics are significantly different from each other, the unitary model is also rejected. The last test involves comparing the sum of the coefficient on the parental wealth variable and the coefficient on its relevant interaction term with the daughter dummy with the corresponding sum for the opposite-sex parent. This sum, which captures the total effect of the parental characteristic, is the effect on daughters. If the sums are significantly different from each other, the household behavior is inconsistent with the unitary model.

Equation (6.1) is estimated both in levels and with family fixed effects. Since land transfers are subject to censoring (many children do not receive any land), a Tobit procedure is used for the land regressions in levels. However, it is possible that omitted family-level variables are correlated with regressors, and thus their estimated effects on transfers may be biased. For families with at least two children, the within-family allocation can be used as the source of variation in the sample from which to estimate intrahousehold differences in transfers.[8] A fixed-effects estimation procedure could control for these unobservables using family-specific dummy variables.[9] In this specific application, however, only the child's sex and birth year, the eldest and youngest dummies, and the interaction between child sex and parent characteristics remain as explanatory variables. That is, the effects of variables that do not vary across

---

6. The gender composition of the sib set is arguably endogenous, even if gender is randomly determined for the individual, because it depends on the choice of family size. The number of brothers and sisters could be correlated with unobserved parental characteristics that also affect the quantity-quality tradeoffs in fertility decisions. For an extensive discussion, see Rosenzweig and Wolpin (2000).

7. For example, Thomas (1990, 1994) finds that maternal education and nonlabor income have a bigger impact on the height of a daughter, relative to a son, and that paternal education has a bigger impact on a son, relative to a daughter.

8. Families with at least two children are included, so that birth order and sex dummies are relevant in the family fixed-effects specification. The fixed-effects procedure eliminates selectivity bias because family size, which affects selection into the sample, is a family-specific variable (Heckman and MaCurdy 1980; Pitt and Rosenzweig 1990).

9. That is, the observed transfer, T_{ij}, to child i in family j would be given by $T_{ij} = t_j + \beta X_{ij} + u_{ij}$, where the family-specific effect is represented by a dummy variable, t_j, which is taken to be constant for a family. However, this specification, although controlling for additive unobservables, does not consider interactions between observables and unobservables (Hsiao 1986).

children cannot be identified.[10] For simplicity, we report only the level results in this chapter, because there are no crucial differences in the estimation results between the two methods.[11]

Determinants of Land Inheritance and Schooling Investments

Table 6.1 presents regression results on the levels of education and inherited land of the respondents and their siblings in the Kerinci sample, and Table 6.2 shows similar results for Bungo Tebo. Schooling equations were estimated using ordinary least squares, with standard errors corrected for household clustering.[12]

From Table 6.1 the following observations can be made. First, the gender effect is insignificant. None of the coefficients on the daughter dummy is significant according to the two-tailed t-test, which suggests the absence of "social" discrimination leading to gender bias against daughters. If we apply a one-tailed test, however, the coefficient is significantly negative at the 5 percent level in the schooling regression, in both the levels and fixed-effect estimates. Thus, we cannot deny the tendency for daughters to be disfavored socially in schooling investments. It is also important to note that an increase in the number of sisters reduces the inherited paddy and agroforestry areas, whereas an increase in the number of brothers has no such effect. These findings suggest that, when land becomes scarce, sons, who are typically better educated, tend to seek nonfarm jobs, whereas daughters, who are less educated, tend to stay in the village and compete for the family's land resources. In fact, such behavior is consistent with the tradition of matrilineal communities in Sumatra. As will be shown shortly, the effects of the number of sons and daughters are different in Bungo Tebo.

Second, mother's paddy landownership has a positive effect on the schooling of sons. Mothers seem to exhibit greater concern for their children's schooling than do fathers, and those who are endowed with larger paddy areas tend to send their children for further study. F-statistics reported in the bottom panel

---

10. On the other hand, if transfers were affected by family-level heterogeneity, a random-effects procedure would be appropriate. The relevant model would be $T_{ij} = t + \beta X_{ij} + u_j + v_{ij}$, where the family-specific constant terms, u_j, are randomly distributed. The family-specific terms (u_j) are not estimated directly, but estimates of the variance components are used to compute the generalized least squares (GLS) estimator for the random-effects model. A Lagrange multiplier statistic tests for the appropriateness of the random-effects model compared with ordinary least squares (OLS) without group effects, and a Hausman test compares the random-effects model with a fixed-effects specification.

11. Since the dependent variable is censored in the land transfers equations, we used a fixed-effects Tobit estimator, because Honoré (1992) has shown that the ordinary Tobit estimator is inconsistent in the presence of fixed effects. This trimmed least-absolute-deviations estimator is preferred because it is both consistent and asymptotically normal under suitable regularity conditions and assumes neither a particular parametric form nor homoskedasticity.

12. Censoring of the dependent variable is not an issue for the respondents' generation, since all have attended school and schooling decisions have been completed. It is a more important issue for the children's generation and will be discussed subsequently.

TABLE 6.1 Determinants of schooling and land inheritance, by respondents and siblings, in Kerinci: Levels estimates

Variables	Years of schooling[a]	Paddy land[b] (hectares)	Agroforestry[b] (hectares)	Bush-fallow[b] (hectares)
Constant	-1444.18	-858.52	-2006.04	-6925.12
Daughter	-1.53	0.02	0.08	3.70
Birth year	1.40	0.88**	2.05*	7.13
Birth year squared[c]	-335.83	-225.56**	-524.05**	-1835.61
Eldest	-0.60	-0.05	-0.23	-0.70
Youngest	-0.73	-0.02	-0.15	-1.09
Number of brothers	-0.01	0.01	0.00	-0.74
Number of sisters	0.38	-0.03*	-0.09*	-1.32
Father's schooling	-0.15	0.01	0.02	0.60*
Mother's schooling	0.28	0.01	0.06	-0.90
Father's paddy land	1.59	0.38**	-0.17	-0.37
Mother's paddy land	3.73*	0.62**	-0.71	0.33
Father's agroforestry land	-2.44	-0.15	1.27**	1.43
Mother's agroforestry land	-0.20	0.44**	0.69	0.37
Father's bush-fallow land	-10.35**	0.18	1.25	8.20
Mother's bush-fallow land	-4.45	1.64**	1.11	21.62
Daughter × father's schooling	-0.03	-0.00	-0.02	-1.09
Daughter × mother's schooling	0.28	-0.01	-0.02	-2.38
Daughter × father's paddy land	-2.71**	-0.13	-0.47	-40.24
Daughter × mother's paddy land	-1.96	0.25	-0.40	4.82
Daughter × father's agroforestry land	4.23**	0.01	0.76*	-40.97
Daughter × mother's agroforestry land	0.21	0.40	0.40	-12.08
Daughter × father's bush-fallow land	6.06**	-0.36	-0.75	-6.14
Daughter × mother's bush-fallow land	3.38	-1.84**	-0.48	37.88

σ		2.31	0.71	0.24
Number of observations	292	292	292	292
Uncensored		19	160	254
Log-likelihood		−58.35	−229.03	−28.79
F-statistic (p-value)	29.34 (.00)**			
χ² (p-value)		71.01 (.00)**	172.79 (.00)**	180.94 (.00)**
R²	.28			
Pseudo R²		.38	.27	.76
Hypothesis tests: F-test (p-value)				
F-tests "son effects"				
Father's schooling = mother's schooling	0.95 (.33)	5.79 (.02)*	0.44 (.51)	0.10 (.76)
Father's paddy = mother's paddy	0.93 (.34)	0.13 (.72)	1.21 (.27)	4.86 (.03)*
Father's agroforestry land = mother's agroforestry land	0.42 (.52)	0.06 (.81)	0.83 (.36)	1.84 (.18)
Father's bush-fallow land = mother's bush-fallow land	0.35 (.56)	1.02 (.31)	0.00 (.95)	3.79 (.05)*
F-tests "daughters relative to sons"				
Gender interaction terms with schooling equal	0.60 (.44)	0.15 (.70)	0.00 (.98)	0.01 (.94)
Gender interaction terms with paddy equal	0.10 (.75)	0.22 (.64)	0.01 (.93)	4.90 (.03)*
Gender interaction terms with agroforestry equal	1.51 (.22)	2.11 (.15)	0.27 (.61)	2.72 (.10)
Gender interaction terms with bush-fallow equal	0.10 (.75)	0.43 (.51)	0.01 (.92)	2.92 (.09)
F-tests "daughter effects"				
Schooling plus interaction terms equal	6.01 (.02)*	0.71 (.40)	0.32 (.57)	0.04 (.85)
Paddy plus interaction terms equal	3.23 (.08)	0.23 (.63)	0.45 (.50)	21.63 (.00)**
Agroforestry plus interaction terms equal	1.81 (.18)	1.99 (.16)	10.30 (.00)**	1.04 (.31)
Bush-fallow plus interaction terms equal	0.46 (.50)	0.68 (.41)	0.01 (.93)	0.00 (.95)

NOTES: Estimated coefficients are shown; * indicates significance at the 5 percent level; ** at the 1 percent level, two-tailed t-test.

a Ordinary least squares with robust standard errors, clustered on households.

b Tobit estimates.

c (Birth year/1,000) squared.

TABLE 6.2 Determinants of schooling and land inheritance, by respondents and siblings, in Bungo Tebo: Levels estimates

Variables	Years of schooling[a]	Paddy land[b] (hectares)	Agroforestry[b] (hectares)	Bush-fallow[b] (hectares)
Constant	-4118.16	-312.19	348.23	-3140.05
Daughter	-2.28**	0.47**	1.70	-4.12*
Birth year	4.16	0.32	-0.37	3.20
Birth year squared[c]	-1051.11	-80.04	99.96	-817.56
Eldest	-0.45	0.03	-0.12	-0.22
Youngest	0.00	0.07	0.94	-0.73*
Number of brothers	0.30	0.01	-0.58**	-0.70**
Number of sisters	0.17	-0.06**	0.07	-0.04
Father's schooling	0.28	0.05*	0.18	0.32**
Mother's schooling	0.02	0.01	0.37*	-0.01
Father's paddy land	-0.56	0.87*	3.28	-1.07
Mother's paddy land	4.05*	0.86**	-3.90	-1.03
Father's agroforestry land	1.31	-0.10	3.52**	-0.59
Mother's agroforestry land	0.32	-0.14	1.85**	1.19**
Father's bush-fallow land	-1.25*	-0.20	-1.02	1.32**
Mother's bush-fallow land	-1.00*	0.09	-0.02	1.62**
Daughter × father's schooling	-0.14	-0.02	-2.22*	0.53*
Daughter × mother's schooling	-0.00	-0.04	-16.45	0.50
Daughter × father's paddy land	-0.98	0.73	31.42	0.47
Daughter × mother's paddy land	-1.96	0.64	3.30	-4.58
Daughter × father's agroforestry land	0.93	0.01	9.07	2.06
Daughter × mother's agroforestry land	0.75	0.21	4.78*	2.47*
Daughter × father's bush-fallow land	0.62	-0.05	...[d]	1.95
Daughter × mother's bush-fallow land	2.35**	-1.08	...[d]	-1.10

σ		0.31	1.44	1.23
Number of observations	247	247	247	247
Uncensored	247	93	44	51
Log-likelihood		−82.29	−107.89	−121.16
F-statistic (p-value)	18.75 (.00)**			
χ^2 (p-value)		148.28 (.00)**	140.17 (.00)**	139.37 (.00)**
R^2	.38			
Pseudo R^2		.47	.39	.37
Hypothesis tests: F-test (p-value)				
F-tests "son effects"				
Father's schooling = mother's schooling	0.92 (.34)	1.19 (.28)	0.91 (.34)	4.93 (.03)*
Father's paddy = mother's paddy	1.29 (.26)	0.00 (.98)	3.49 (.06)	0.00 (.99)
Father's agroforestry land = mother's agroforestry land	0.75 (.39)	0.04 (.84)	5.05 (.03)*	4.22 (.04)*
Father's bush-fallow land = mother's bush-fallow land	0.11 (.74)	1.48 (.22)	0.53 (.47)	0.25 (.62)
F-tests "daughters relative to sons"				
Gender interaction terms with schooling equal	0.13 (.72)	0.06 (.80)	1.52 (.22)	0.01 (.91)
Gender interaction terms with paddy equal	0.05 (.82)	0.01 (.91)	0.99 (.32)	0.30 (.58)
Gender interaction terms with agroforestry equal	0.01 (.92)	0.52 (.47)	0.44 (.51)	0.05 (.83)
Gender interaction terms with bush-fallow equal	1.87 (.18)	2.10 (.15)	. . .[d]	4.13 (.04)*
F-tests "daughter effects"				
Schooling plus interaction terms equal	0.08 (.78)	2.71 (.10)	1.48 (.22)	3.04 (.08)
Paddy plus interaction terms equal	1.90 (.17)	0.03 (.87)	1.58 (.21)	0.31 (.58)
Agroforestry plus interaction terms equal	0.50 (.48)	0.66 (.42)	0.86 (.36)	1.71 (.19)
Bush-fallow plus interaction terms equal	6.24 (.02)*	1.20 (.27)	. . .[d]	4.27 (.04)

NOTES: Estimated coefficients are shown; * indicates significance at the 5 percent level; ** at the 1 percent level, two-tailed t-test.

[a] Ordinary least squares with robust standard errors, clustered on households.

[b] Tobit estimates.

[c] (Birth year/1,000) squared.

[d] Variables not included owing to nonconvergence.

of Table 6.1 show that the coefficient on mother's paddy land is significantly different from that on father's, indicating that parents do not necessarily treat sons equally.

Third, father's bush-fallow land has a negative effect on the schooling of sons. The larger bush-fallow area of fathers is associated with a lower schooling attainment of sons, which would reflect the relatively low returns to schooling when ample areas of uncultivated land exist. This finding is consistent with the hypothesis that uncultivated land and schooling are substitutable means of transferring wealth from one generation to another. The coefficient on father's bush-fallow land is significantly different from the mother's coefficient.

Fourth, it may seem that mothers express less gender preference than fathers with respect to their asset holdings. Four interaction terms between the daughter dummy and mother's human and physical assets are all insignificant except for one case, indicating that mothers do not generally discriminate between daughters and sons based on their ownership of assets. In contrast, three interaction terms between the daughter dummy and father's landownership are significant in the schooling regression. The results imply that fathers who own larger paddy areas do not want to send daughters to school, whereas if they own large upland fields they are more likely to send daughters, rather than sons, to school. Thus, fathers do not necessarily discriminate against their daughters. Despite the differential effects of the ownership of paddy land and bush-fallow land by fathers and mothers, it is only in the case of gender interactions with parental paddy land that father's and mother's effects are significantly different from each other. This indicates that parental resources do have differential effects on daughters relative to sons.

To sum up, the findings that some father- or mother-specific asset ownership variables are significantly different from each other in the wealth transfer decisions imply that the unitary model of household behavior is rejected. These differences are associated with specific types of assets, the strongest effect being observed with paddy land. However, the insignificance or, at best, the weak significance of the daughter dummy, as well as its generally insignificant interactions with parental wealth variables, indicates that wealth transfers in this community are largely egalitarian, free from both social and parental discrimination with respect to gender. These qualitative conclusions remain unchanged with the fixed-effects estimation.

Lastly, land inheritance persists over generations. Larger parental holdings per capita of specific types of land typically lead to larger areas bequeathed to children.

Despite distinct differences in climatic conditions, population pressure, and type of tree crops grown between the two regions, the estimation results for Bungo Tebo shown in Table 6.2 are not markedly different, with major exceptions being the significant and negative coefficients on the daughter dummy in the schooling and bush-fallow regressions, the positive and significant coefficient in the paddy land regression, and the insignificance of the interaction terms between the daughter dummy and father's landownership. In other words, daughters are significantly disadvantaged with respect to schooling and inheritance of bush-fallow land, but are favored with respect to inheritance of paddy land. The observed practice that daughters receive larger areas of paddy land, whereas sons are compensated by more years of schooling, is consistent with the tradition of the matrilineal inheritance system. That sons inherit more bush-fallow land is a new custom, consistent with the requirement of men's labor for future development of such land. The phenomenon that having more sisters decreases one's inheritance of paddy land, whereas more brothers decrease receipts of agroforestry and bush-fallow areas, is also consistent with the differences in comparative advantage in lowland and upland farming between daughters and sons. These differences are likely to reflect both efficiency and egalitarian motives of parents. It is also important to emphasize that the negative and significant effects of the number of brothers on inherited agroforestry and bush-fallow areas in Bungo Tebo are not observed in Kerinci (see Table 6.1). These contrasting results can be explained by the fact that sons are far more educated in Kerinci than in Bungo Tebo (see Table 5.5), so that sons in the former region can easily find nonfarm jobs outside the villages when land becomes scarce.

Because of transaction costs, missing markets, and information failures, we expect that parental assets directly related to the outcome would have the most important effect (for example, parental schooling on child schooling, paddy land on paddy). However, larger parental holdings per capita of specific types of land lead to larger areas bequeathed to children only in Bungo Tebo. This may be because the villages in Kerinci are better integrated into the market economy than are those in Bungo Tebo.

We reject the unitary model only for differences in the effects of parental schooling and differences in the interaction terms with bush-fallow land in the case of Bungo Tebo. Judging from the insignificant differences in the effects of asset ownership by fathers and mothers and the insignificant effects of their interaction terms with the daughter dummy, the rejection of the unitary model is weaker in Bungo Tebo than in Kerinci. This is not surprising because households in Kerinci still cling more strongly to traditional matrilineal systems, which give greater bargaining power to wives rather than husbands. Our field interviews indicate that this is in part owing to proximity to Solok, or the High Region, which is the traditional seat of Minangkabau culture. In general, not only are parents egalitarian but they also have a propensity to pool their resources in making wealth transfer decisions in Bungo Tebo.

Summary of Findings

1. A gender bias in schooling investments and land inheritance is not significant in the Kerinci sample villages, indicating a fairly egalitarian distri-

bution of intergenerational transfers between sons and daughters. The equitable inheritance of paddy land and upland areas is consistent with the
approximate equality of male and female labor inputs in paddy and cinnamon production. There is, however, a weak indication that sons, who
are slightly favored in schooling investments, tend to seek nonfarm employment outside the village, whereas daughters who are endowed with
land tend to stay.

2. In contrast, daughters in Bungo Tebo are disfavored with respect to
   schooling and bush-fallow land, but are favored with respect to inheritance
   of paddy land. This is consistent with the relative importance of male
   labor in the future development of bush-fallow land and daughters' comparative advantage in lowland rice production.

3. The effects of father- or mother-specific asset ownership are significantly
   different in some wealth transfer decisions in both Kerinci and Bungo
   Tebo, suggesting that the unitary model of household behavior does not
   hold in a strict sense.

Determinants of Schooling in the Children's Generation

Readers who are not interested in the technical details of statistical estimation
may proceed directly to the "Summary of Findings" at the end of this section
on page 152.

The persistence of gender bias against daughters in schooling, particularly
in Bungo Tebo, is worrisome, because low schooling levels limit women's ability to obtain nonagricultural employment. Does this bias persist in the generation of the respondents' children? For this purpose, we examine whether the
child's gender continues to affect schooling attainment in favor of sons in the
children's generation. Altogether we have 178 observations on children of
school age, that is, those aged 7–21 years.[13]

Unlike the respondents and their siblings, schooling decisions for the respondents' children are not yet complete. To take into account incomplete
schooling decisions, we use two individual-level outcomes: (1) the deviation of
each child's completed years of schooling from the cohort mean; and (2) actual
years of completed schooling, controlling for child age.[14] In the first specification, we are measuring how well each child is doing relative to other children

---

13. We did not include children who are 22 years and older because there are only eight children in that age bracket in Kerinci and Bungo Tebo, respectively.

14. We follow the methodology in Quisumbing and Maluccio (2003). We do not explicitly
deal with the right-handed censoring that occurs because a child was still enrolled in school at the
time of the survey. If we assume that an enrolled child will complete at least the grade currently attained, observed years of schooling will be right censored (King and Lillard 1987). Because we are
more interested in gender differentials than in schooling progression, deviations from cohort means
should be able to capture differential outcomes by gender relative to children of the same age.

of the same age. In the second, we control for the correlation between age and schooling completion by including linear and quadratic terms in child age. Although it could be argued that both measures are capturing the same phenomenon, an advantage of the deviation from the cohort mean is that it is not prone to censoring, unlike schooling attainment, which could be censored at zero in cases where many children have never attended school. In order to test whether family-specific unobservables or family random effects are important, we estimated both fixed- and random-effects estimates. In both regions, the Lagrange multiplier test indicates that family-level heterogeneity is important. Moreover, the Hausman test does not lead us to reject the hypothesis that the fixed- and random-effects coefficients are significantly different from each other (with the exception of schooling attainment in Bungo Tebo). This suggests that there are no differences between estimates that assume that patterns of gender discrimination can be explained by factors that vary randomly across families and estimates that take into account unobserved family characteristics.

According to the estimation results of the schooling functions shown separately for Kerinci and Bungo Tebo in Tables 6.3 and 6.4, respectively, the gender gap against daughters in schooling has practically disappeared in the children's generation. In Kerinci, using the random-effects estimates, we find that girls tend to do even better in terms of years of schooling. The only significant interactions with the daughter dummy are found in the random-effects regressions: daughters do better relative to boys of the same age when their mothers have more bush-fallow area. In general, there are few significant variables in the regressions, the major exceptions being birth year and its squared term in the regressions on years of schooling. Such results are consistent with the egalitarian bequest motives of parents, but may also result from the imprecision of the estimates owing to the small sample size.[15]

It is also remarkable that the daughter dummy is insignificant in Bungo Tebo (Table 6.4), and that none of the interactions with the daughter dummy is significant. It seems that parents no longer exhibit preferential treatment for either daughters or sons with respect to child schooling in this region as well.

In Kerinci, we find that the coefficients on the parental wealth variables continue to be significantly different from each other in the case of paddy land and bush-fallow land (random-effects estimates). In all the regressions, the interactions of the daughter dummy with parents' bush-fallow land are significantly different from each other. In Bungo Tebo, in both levels and random-effects estimates, the coefficients on parental paddy land are significantly different from each other. Thus, it seems that egalitarian bequest motives coexist with a collective model of household behavior in Sumatra.

---

15. For example, in Kerinci, coefficients on mother's paddy land and mother's bush-fallow land, and the interactions of these variables with the daughter dummy, are large but imprecisely estimated. Magnitudes of the corresponding coefficients are smaller in Bungo Tebo.

TABLE 6.3 Determinants of the schooling attainment of the respondents' children in Kerinci

Variables	Deviation from cohort mean[a] (levels)	Years of schooling[a] (levels)	Deviation from cohort mean[a] (random effects)	Years of schooling (random effects)
Constant	-2.81	-13.64	-3.98	-15.20
Daughter	2.49	3.91	2.14	3.32**
Birth year	-0.06	1.59**	0.11	1.80**
Birth year squared	0.01	-0.03**	0.00	-0.03**
Number of brothers	-0.28	-0.22	-0.23	-0.25
Number of sisters	-0.09	0.02	-0.29	-0.12
Father's schooling	0.13	0.15	0.17	0.21
Mother's schooling	0.21	0.36	0.14	0.27*
Father's paddy land	-0.87	-0.44	-1.78	-1.52
Mother's paddy land	3.63	3.00	3.93	3.32
Father's agroforestry land	-0.77	-0.65	-0.21	-0.14
Mother's agroforestry land	-1.27*	-1.09	-1.49**	-1.30**
Father's bush-fallow land	0.94	1.36	0.68	0.92
Mother's bush-fallow land	-6.21	-5.88	-6.07*	-5.96*
Daughter × father's schooling	-0.12	-0.15	-0.15	-0.18
Daughter × mother's schooling	-0.15	-0.31	-0.06	-0.19
Daughter × father's paddy land	0.60	-0.57	2.40	1.59
Daughter × mother's paddy land	-3.49	-3.10	-4.06	-3.72
Daughter × father's agroforestry land	0.69	0.64	0.06	0.02
Daughter × mother's agroforestry land	1.03	1.49	1.80	2.24

	(1)	(2)	(3)	(4)
Daughter × father's bush-fallow land	−0.87	−1.28	−0.71	−0.92
Daughter × mother's bush-fallow land	6.68	5.96	6.18*	5.69*
Number of observations	70	70	69	69
F-statistic (p-value)	4.39 (.00)**	10.02 (.00)**	29.97 (.09)	621.12 (.00)**
χ^2 (p-value)				
R^2	.40	.89		
Breusch–Pagan Lagrange multiplier test (p-value)			5.59 (.02)*	6.91 (.01)**
Hausman test (fixed effects vs. random effects) (p-value)			5.61 (.90)	12.79 (.31)
Hypothesis tests: F-test (p-value)				
F-tests "son effects"				
Father's schooling = mother's schooling	0.03 (.87)	0.24 (.62)	0.03 (.87)	0.11 (.74)
Father's paddy = mother's paddy	1.06 (.31)	0.74 (.39)	4.72 (.03)*	3.86 (.05)*
Father's agroforestry land = mother's agroforestry land	0.36 (.55)	0.41 (.53)	2.20 (.14)	2.07 (.15)
Father's bush-fallow land = mother's bush-fallow land	4.40 (.04)*	5.19 (.03)*	4.61 (.03)*	5.49 (.02)*
F-tests "daughters relative to sons"				
Schooling interaction terms equal	0.00 (.95)	0.13 (.72)	0.03 (.87)	0.00 (.99)
Paddy interaction terms equal	0.83 (.37)	0.38 (.54)	4.72 (.03)*	3.39 (.07)
Agroforestry interaction terms equal	0.09 (.77)	0.80 (.38)	2.20 (.14)	2.30 (.13)
Bush-fallow interaction terms equal	4.70 (.04)*	5.10 (.03)*	4.61 (.03)*	4.92 (.03)*
F-tests "daughter effects"				
Schooling plus interaction terms equal	0.24 (.63)	0.28 (.60)	0.16 (.68)	0.13 (.72)
Paddy plus interaction terms equal	0.38 (.54)	2.10 (.15)	0.13 (.71)	0.07 (.79)
Agroforestry plus interaction terms equal	0.06 (.81)	0.42 (.52)	0.03 (.87)	0.84 (.36)
Bush-fallow plus interaction terms equal	0.46 (.50)	0.00 (.99)	0.09 (.76)	0.12 (.73)

NOTES: Estimated coefficients are shown; * indicates significance at the 5 percent level; ** at the 1 percent level, two-tailed t-test.

[a] Ordinary least squares with standard errors corrected for clustering.

TABLE 6.4 Determinants of the schooling attainment of the respondents' children in Bungo Tebo

Variables	Deviation from cohort mean[a] (levels)	Years of schooling[a] (levels)	Deviation from cohort mean[a] (random effects)	Years of schooling (random effects)
Constant	-1.62	-9.99	-1.62	-8.55
Daughter	-0.49	-1.33	-0.47	-0.80
Birth year	0.24	1.66**	0.25	1.50**
Birth year squared	-0.01	-0.04**	-0.01	-0.03*
Number of brothers	-0.19	-0.12	-0.19	...
Number of sisters	-0.10	-0.05	-0.11	...
Father's schooling	0.05	0.04	0.05	...
Mother's schooling	-0.04	-0.07	-0.05	...
Father's paddy land	-2.82	-3.51**	-2.83*	...
Mother's paddy land	1.50**	0.78*	1.48**	...
Father's agroforestry land	0.30*	0.39**	0.29	...
Mother's agroforestry land	1.54**	2.20**	1.56	...
Father's bush-fallow land	0.22	0.17	0.23	...
Mother's bush-fallow land	0.62	0.79	0.64	...
Daughter × father's schooling	0.04	0.05	0.04	-0.01
Daughter × mother's schooling	0.12	0.24	0.12	0.20
Daughter × father's paddy land	1.27	1.43	1.41	1.88
Daughter × mother's paddy land	-0.47	0.94	-0.56	-0.82
Daughter × father's agroforestry land	-0.48	-0.54	-0.44	0.14
Daughter × mother's agroforestry land	-0.11	-0.80	-0.15	-0.70
Daughter × father's bush-fallow land	-0.16	-0.19	-0.4	-0.07
Daughter × mother's bush-fallow land	0.02	0.22	0.00	0.62

	108	108	107	107
Number of observations				
F-statistic (p-value)	12.29 (.00)**	7.82 (.00)**		15.02 (.00)**
χ^2 (p-value)			27.31 (.16)	
R^2	.25	.75		
Breusch–Pagan Lagrange multiplier test (p-value)			12.09 (.00)**	14.68 (.00)**
Hausman test (fixed effects vs. random effects) (p-value)			3.39 (1.00)	357.43 (.00)**
Hypothesis tests: F-test (p-value)				
F-tests "son effects"				
Father's schooling = mother's schooling	0.32 (.57)	0.72 (.40)	0.30 (.59)	n.a.
Father's paddy = mother's paddy	7.80 (.01)**	11.62 (.00)**	8.97 (.00)**	n.a.
Father's agroforestry land = mother's agroforestry land	10.29 (.00)**	22.01 (.00)**	0.64 (.42)	n.a.
Father's bush-fallow land = mother's bush-fallow land	0.51 (.48)	1.83 (.18)	0.47 (.49)	n.a.
F-tests "daughters relative to sons"				
Schooling interaction terms equal	0.16 (.69)	0.58 (.45)	0.09 (.76)	0.38 (.54)
Paddy interaction terms equal	0.84 (.37)	0.04 (.84)	0.90 (.34)	0.62 (.43)
Agroforestry interaction terms equal	0.28 (.60)	0.09 (.77)	0.02 (.89)	0.15 (.70)
Bush-fallow interaction terms equal	0.10 (.76)	0.30 (.59)	0.02 (.90)	0.22 (.64)
F-tests "daughter effects"				
Schooling plus interaction terms equal	0.00 (.97)	0.10 (.76)	0.01 (.93)	n.a.
Paddy plus interaction terms equal	1.62 (.21)	1.78 (.19)	2.12 (.15)	n.a.
Agroforestry plus interaction terms equal	7.01 (.01)**	4.14 (.05)**	0.98 (.32)	n.a.
Bush-fallow plus interaction terms equal	0.61 (.48)	0.97 (.33)	0.32 (.57)	n.a.

NOTES: Estimated coefficients are shown. n.a. means not applicable. * indicates significance at the 5 percent level; ** at the 1 percent level, two-tailed t-test.

a Ordinary least squares with standard errors corrected for clustering.

It may well be that the closing of the gender gap in schooling reflects the general trend of increasing returns to female education in the Indonesian economy. Using a nationally representative dataset, Deolalikar (1993) found that women in Indonesia are acquiring secondary and tertiary education in relatively larger numbers than are men, in response to the greater relative returns to female higher education. Again, using nationally representative data, Behrman and Deolalikar (1995) found that private rates of return to schooling investments in females in Indonesia are higher than those for males. Specifically, the marginal increases in wage rates and earnings with postprimary schooling are greater in percentage terms for females than for males.

Summary of Findings

1. In contrast to the respondents' generation, the gender gap in schooling has disappeared among children aged 7–21 years. This means that parents tend to invest more or less equally in the schooling of their children.
2. We found that the effects of father' and mothers' wealth on the schooling attainment of children are statistically different. Thus, the unitary model of the household cannot be accepted in the case of Sumatra.

Determinants of Household Income Expenditures

Readers who are not interested in the technical details of statistical estimation may proceed directly to the "Summary of Findings" at the end of this section on page 162.

Specification of the Regression Functions

We estimate agricultural income functions separately for the two research sites. In Kerinci, we estimate an income determination function for lowland rice production but not for upland cinnamon production. Because cinnamon trees are harvested every eight years or so, a number of households in our sample had obtained no income from cinnamon production during the survey year. Instead, we explore the determinants of the value of the stock of standing cinnamon trees. The regression runs are based on plot-level data obtained from households included in the extensive household survey. In Bungo Tebo, we were unable to collect data on income from lowland rice production in the household survey. Thus, we estimate a lowland rice income determination function based on data from a subsample in the intensive survey and an income function for rubber based on plot-level data from the household survey. Because of the smaller sample size, we have to apply a simpler specification to the estimation of the lowland rice income function in Bungo Tebo.

Our regression specification for the function explaining the value of cinnamon stock in Kerinci is as follows:

Value of cinnamon stock $= a_0 + a_1$ (age of tree) $+ a_2$ (age of tree-squared)
$$+ a_3 \text{ (plot size)} + a_4 \text{ (altitude)}$$
$$+ \Sigma a_i \text{ (two dummies for land use before}$$
current tree planting)
$$+ \Sigma a_j \text{ (three tenure dummies)}$$
$$+ a_{10} \text{ (cinnamon + paddy area)}$$
$$+ a_{11} \text{ (ratio of cinnamon area)}$$
$$+ a_{12} \text{ (number of working members)}$$
$$+ a_{13} \text{ (ratio of female workers)}$$
$$+ a_{14} \text{ (ratio of high school workers)}$$
$$+ a_{15} \text{ (ratio of college workers)}$$
$$+ \Sigma a_k \text{ (ratio of working members in four}$$
different age categories) $+ \varepsilon$, (6.2)

where the two dummies for previous land use are forest and bush-fallow land and the default is cinnamon field; the tenure dummies are privately purchased, privately acquired by opening forest for cultivation, and share tenancy, with the default being single-family ownership; the age categories for the working members are 15–25 years (the control), 26–35, 36–45, 46–55, and 56–65; and ε is an error term. Logarithms are taken for all continuous variables except for ratios.

Tree age and its squared term are included because age affects the productivity of trees and, thus, the value of harvests. We included plot and household characteristics as explanatory variables, assuming that they are either exogenous or predetermined. Plots located in areas characterized by high altitudes are unfavorable for cinnamon production, so that the profitability of its production will be low. This is also true for rubber production in Bungo Tebo. In order to control for the effects of soil fertility, we include the dummies for land use before the trees currently grown were planted. We expect that the fertility would be higher for cinnamon plots that were previously uncultivated forests. Tenure dummies are represented by the manner of land acquisition. To the extent that private ownership provides stronger management incentives than single-family ownership, the dummy variables for private acquisition of land would have positive coefficients. On the other hand, the share tenancy dummy would have a negative coefficient, if the Marshallian inefficiency of share tenancy exists in cinnamon production.[16]

Total lowland paddy and cinnamon areas owned by the household are used as proxies for the wealth of these farm households, whereas the ratio of cinnamon to total area is used to capture the difference in the land value between lowland and upland plots. These variables may also affect income through their

---

16. See Hayami and Otsuka (1993) for a survey of the share tenancy literature.

effects on the demand for family labor. The supply of family labor is represented by the number of working family members. We did not include hired labor, because it is endogenous. We also included characteristics of the working members such as gender, age, and schooling composition, which are represented by ratios, in order to examine whether these characteristics are critically important in the management of cinnamon fields. Of particular interest for this study is the effect of the gender composition of family workers.

Essentially the same specification is applied for the estimation of the rubber income function in Bungo Tebo, with a few exceptions. First, because of the strong multicollinearity between the dummy for forest prior to the establishment of currently growing trees and the dummy for private acquisition by opening forest, we drop the former variable. Thus, the coefficient on the latter variable will capture both tenure and fertility effects. Second, whereas in Kerinci single-family ownership refers mostly to land inherited by daughters and sons (Table 6.3), in Bungo Tebo it refers mostly to agroforestry land inherited by sons (Table 6.4).

For the estimation of the lowland rice income function, we replace the tree age variables by the rainfed plot dummy (as distinguished from an irrigated plot), and altitude by walking distance from the residence. Tenure dummies pertain to single-family ownership, privately purchased, borrowed, share tenancy, and leasehold tenancy, with the joint family ownership category as the control.

The simplified form of the lowland rice income function in Bungo Tebo is specified as follows:

$$\text{Lowland rice income} = \beta_0 + \beta_1 \text{ (paddy area)} + \Sigma\beta_i \text{ (four tenure dummies)}$$
$$+ \beta_6 \text{ (number of working members)}$$
$$+ \beta_7 \text{ (ratio of female workers)}$$
$$+ \beta_8 \text{ (ratio of workers with high school education)}$$
$$+ \beta_9 \text{ (ratio of college-educated workers)}$$
$$+ \Sigma\beta_j \text{ (ratio of working members in four}$$
$$\text{different age categories)} + \eta, \quad\quad (6.3)$$

where η is an error term and the tenure dummies are the same as those in the Kerinci lowland rice income function, except for the omission of the nonexistent leasehold tenancy dummy variable. The sample size is 53, since seven households have incomplete data. Ten households did not cultivate any paddy land, and so we applied a linear specification and employed the Tobit estimation method. Also note that paddy area is almost identical to plot size because most sample households cultivate only one plot.

Estimation Results of the Agricultural Income Functions

The estimation results of the four agricultural income functions are shown in Table 6.5. Age of trees has a positive and significant impact on the value of cin-

TABLE 6.5 Determinants of agricultural incomes in Kerinci and Bungo Tebo

Variables	Kerinci — Value of cinnamon stock (double log)	Kerinci — Lowland rice income (double log)	Bungo Tebo — Rubber income (double log)	Bungo Tebo — Lowland rice income (linear tobit)
Constant	7.44*	6.82**	5.55**	2743.79
	(1.74)	(14.65)	(2.62)	(1.38)
Dummy for rainfed plot		−0.14		
		(−0.89)		
Walking time		0.01		
		(0.05)		
Age of tree	3.06*		−0.00	
	(1.80)		(−0.00)	
Age of tree squared	−0.19		0.00	
	(−0.45)		(0.03)	
Plot size	0.78**	0.70**	0.71**	
	(11.94)	(8.83)	(6.67)	
Lowland rice area				2642.25**
				(3.03)
Altitude	−0.76		0.25	
	(−1.39)		(1.35)	
Previous land use dummies				
Forest before[a]	0.35			
		(0.96)		
Bush-fallow before[a]	−0.04		0.15	
		(−0.35)		(0.74)
Privately purchased	−0.16		−0.01	
		(−1.18)	(−0.13)	
Opened for cultivation	0.01		0.38	
		(0.05)		(1.34)
Leasehold tenancy	0.28		0.28	
		(1.62)		(1.35)
Borrowed			−0.14	
			(−0.50)	
Tenure dummies				
Single		0.17		3930.98**
			(1.27)	(3.19)
Privately purchased		0.21		1843.42
		(1.02)		(1.32)
Borrowed		0.02		3469.51**
		(0.08)		(3.62)

TABLE 6.5 *Continued*

| | Kerinci | | Bungo Tebo | |
Variables	Value of cinnamon stock (double log)	Lowland rice income (double log)	Rubber income (double log)	Lowland rice income (linear tobit)
Share tenancy		0.17		1371.47
		(0.98)		(1.33)
Leasehold tenancy		0.09		
		(0.51)		
Cinnamon + paddy area	0.24**	0.04		
	(2.52)	(0.52)		
Ratio of cinnamon area	−0.14	−0.41		
	(−0.32)	(−1.60)		
Rubber plus paddy area			−0.30**	
			(−3.20)	
Ratio of rubber area			−0.59*	
			(−2.18)	
Working members	0.19	−0.05	0.28*	−615.49
	(0.90)	(−0.27)	(1.94)	(−1.50)
Ratio of female workers	−0.13	−0.09	0.19	−1656.33
	(−0.00)	(−0.31)	(0.65)	(−0.64)
Ratio of working members with				
High school education	−0.48*	−0.18	−0.03	−1139.02
	(−2.02)	(−0.89)	(−0.14)	(−0.96)
College education	−0.57*	−0.02	−0.07	9393.03
	(−2.19)	(−0.07)	(−0.09)	(0.89)
Ratio of working members				
Aged 26–35	0.58*	0.25	−0.20	−1631.62
	(1.77)	(0.78)	(−0.59)	(−1.25)
Aged 36–45	−0.21	0.40	−0.91*	753.69
	(−0.47)	(0.92)	(−2.18)	(0.43)
Aged 46–55	0.84*	0.41	0.18	−949.49
	(1.82)	(0.97)	(0.48)	(−0.42)
Aged 56–65	0.52	−0.38	−1.21**	309.20
	(1.20)	(−1.07)	(−3.05)	(0.13)
R^2	.79	.55	.48	.50
Number of observations	171	113	119	53

NOTES: Numbers in parentheses are *t*-values; * indicates significance at the 5 percent level; ** at the 1 percent level, two-tailed *t*-test.

[a] Land use before acquisition.

namon stock but does not have a significant impact on rubber income. The effect of the average age of trees is unclear because a number of regenerated trees are grown in many old rubber fields. As expected, plot size increases the value of cinnamon stock and incomes from lowland rice and rubber production. All of these estimated coefficients are significantly smaller than unity, suggesting that agricultural production is subject to decreasing returns to scale.[17] Somewhat unexpectedly, variables representing land quality, that is, altitude and prior land use patterns, are insignificant in the estimation results of the cinnamon and rubber income functions.

There is no evidence that land tenure institutions affect the investment and management incentives for agroforestry fields, despite the significant differences in land rights. Using the same datasets, Suyanto, Tomich, and Otsuka (2001a, 2001b) also find that land tenure institutions do not affect the net value of cinnamon fields (that is, value of cinnamon stock minus the cost of management) or the residual profit from rubber production. They argue that tree planting increases the strength of expected land rights when such rights are originally weak, providing sufficiently strong investment and management incentives. For instance, although land rights are weaker under single-family ownership than under private ownership, tree planting enhances the expected land rights, so that those who invested in tree planting under single-family ownership would be able to bequeath land to any designated person or even to sell to nonfamily members in future.

Whereas the land tenure dummies are insignificant in the Kerinci lowland rice income function, the single-family ownership dummy and the dummy for borrowing are significant in the Bungo Tebo lowland rice income function. The positive effect of the single-family ownership dummy indicates that incentives to manage paddy land are stronger under single-family ownership than under joint family ownership. On the other hand, it is difficult to explain theoretically why borrowing of paddy land, mostly from other family members for short periods, increases income, except possibly through the mining of land quality for short-run benefits (Hayami and Otsuka 1993). It may also be possible that the (unobserved) quality of borrowed land and of labor on borrowed land is higher.

The total operational area occupied by cinnamon and paddy production increases the value of cinnamon stock, but the total area occupied by rubber and paddy, as well as the ratio of the rubber area, decreases income from rubber plots significantly. Since gestation periods of 8–10 years are required for cinnamon production, it is likely that only wealthy landed farmers can afford to produce high-valued trees. On the other hand, the management of large jungle rubber fields requires large amounts of family labor (see Table 5.8), so that large landowners may fail to manage their fields effectively. Consistent with this

---

17. In the case of lowland rice production in Bungo Tebo, the elasticity of rice income with respect to plot size is 0.51, assessed at the mean values of income and plot size. This elasticity is also significantly smaller than unity.

interpretation, the number of family workers has a positive and significant coefficient.

An important finding is that the ratio of female family workers has no significant effects on agricultural incomes. This is expected for cinnamon and paddy production in Kerinci, since men and women work more or less equally in paddy and upland fields. In Bungo Tebo, it may well be that the gender composition of family workers does not affect rubber and paddy income significantly because of the division of labor for rubber and paddy fields between male and female workers. The use of hired labor may also neutralize the effect of family gender composition. In any case, there does not seem to be any significant difference between male and female workers' contribution to agricultural incomes.

We found that, in general, the schooling attainment of family members does not affect incomes from rubber and lowland rice production (similarly to the Filipino case). There is, however, evidence that working members who have finished high school and college education are much less involved in cinnamon production. In Kerinci, because they have better access to nonfarm occupations, educated household members seem to have larger opportunity costs than do those in Bungo Tebo. Among working members, those in the age brackets 26–35 and 46–55 are more heavily involved in cinnamon production, whereas those in the age brackets 36–45 and 56–65 are less involved in rubber production.

Estimation Results of the per Capita Expenditure Function

Our main interest is to identify the determinants of total household income, but we note that intermittent earnings from cinnamon production lead to high variability in current household agricultural incomes. Thus, we use household expenditure as our dependent variable because it is a good proxy for household permanent income. To adjust for the possible effects of household size, we use expenditure per capita. We do not use expenditure per adult equivalent, because we believe that it is preferable to estimate the effects of age and gender composition on expenditures through regression rather than imposing consumption weights on specific age/gender groups a priori.

According to the estimation results shown in Table 6.6, the coefficients on total operational landholdings are positive and significant in both Kerinci and Bungo Tebo.[18] As expected, the ratio of paddy land has positive coefficients in each of the expenditure functions, but none of them is significant. The ratio of female family workers has no significant effect on total expenditure per capita, which indicates that female workers earn as much as male workers in both farm

---

18. In our regression runs, we tried both the currently operated farm area as well as total farm area (the land under current cultivation together with land to which households have cultivation rights but that they themselves do not cultivate, such as land on rotation and lent, rented-out, or pawned land). The results of the regression runs are fairly similar.

TABLE 6.6 Determinants of log per capita expenditures in Kerinci and Bungo Tebo

Variables	Kerinci	Bungo Tebo	
Constant	13.56**	13.93**	13.90**
	(23.54)	(39.55)	(37.09)
Log farm size	0.25**	0.11*	0.11*
	(2.82)	(1.78)	(1.74)
Ratio of paddy area	0.27	0.14	0.14
	(0.52)	(1.18)	(1.16)
Log household size	−0.24	−0.51**	−0.49**
	(−0.79)	(−3.22)	(−2.91)
Ratio of female workers	0.57	−0.08	0.11
	(0.82)	(−0.20)	(0.26)
Ratio of working members with			
High school education	0.05	0.63**	
	(0.16)	(2.44)	
Junior high school education			0.58*
			(1.80)
Senior high school education			0.70*
			(1.98)
College education	1.08*	1.61	1.52
	(2.22)	(1.00)	(0.92)
Ratio of working members			
Aged 26–35	−0.19	0.09	0.09
	(−0.35)	(0.22)	(0.27)
Aged 36–45	0.24	−0.39	−0.38
	(0.34)	(−0.89)	(−0.86)
Aged 46–55	0.79	−0.52	−0.47
	(1.28)	(−1.16)	(−0.97)
Aged 56–65	−0.11	0.27	0.27
	(−0.18)	(0.88)	(0.85)
Number of observations	100	162	162
R^2	.39	.54	.53

NOTES: Numbers in parentheses are *t*-values; * indicates significance at the 5 percent level; ** at the 1 percent level, two-tailed *t*-test.

and nonfarm jobs. As in the Philippines, it seems that women have access to the nonfarm labor market in Sumatra. "Social" discrimination in the labor market does not appear to be an issue in Sumatra, unlike in Ghana (which is discussed in Part III).

Per capita expenditure increases significantly with the increased proportion of working members with college schooling in Kerinci, and it increases significantly with the ratio of working members with high school education in

Bungo Tebo. In Kerinci, 37 percent of working children have finished junior high school (7–9 years of schooling), 39 percent have finished senior high school (10–12 years of schooling), and 14 percent have finished college. In Bungo Tebo, the corresponding figures are 51 percent for junior high school, 24 percent for senior high school, and 0 percent for college. In our estimations, we combine the junior and senior high school categories because their effects are indistinguishable (see the last column of Table 6.6 in the case of Bungo Tebo).

A Comparison of Income between Men and Women

We found no statistical evidence that women are disfavored in either agricultural production or nonfarm jobs in the Kerinci and Bungo Tebo villages. As far as Kerinci is concerned, there are no significant differences in schooling and land inheritance between sons and daughters, which ought to lead to equality of income between men and women in this site.

In Bungo Tebo, a typical daughter inherits 0.13 more hectares of lowland area, whereas a typical son receives 0.15 additional hectares of upland rubber fields (Table 5.11). In addition, sons receive 2.5 more years of schooling than daughters on the average (Table 5.10). Using the coefficient on plot size in the lowland rice income function in Bungo Tebo estimated by the Tobit regression (Table 6.5), we found that 0.13 additional hectares of paddy land results in an increment of about 46,800 rupiahs (US$18.7). Similarly, using the mean plot size of upland fields and mean rubber income, we estimated that 0.15 additional hectare of rubber fields yields 30,900 rupiahs (US$12.4). Thus, daughters receive slightly larger agricultural incomes than sons.

Next, we want to explore the effect on household expenditures of additional years of schooling for sons. It is difficult to estimate this effect because we use discrete schooling-level ratios in the expenditure function. Thus, in order to assess the probable range of the effect of an additional 2.5 years of schooling from the average female level of 4.6 years to the average male level of 7.1 years, we assume that a typical household consists of five persons and that one person has completed three more years of schooling at junior high school after completing six years at primary school. Since we used logarithms for per capita expenditure and simply the ratio for schooling in the regression analysis, the exponent defined by the {coefficient of ratio for junior high school × (5/1)} corresponds to the ratio of total household expenditures with and without completing junior high school. Using the average total household expenditure in the sample, we estimated that sons' income gain associated with an additional three years of schooling is 133,128 rupiahs (US$53.3) per year. The actual difference in schooling between sons and daughters is not 3.0 years but 2.5 years, so the difference in income is somewhat less than the above estimate—US$44.4.

Thus, altogether, sons receive slightly more income than daughters in Bungo Tebo. The difference of US$38.1 (12.4 − 18.7 + 44.4) is not, however, very large. In fact, it amounts to only 10.1 percent of average annual household income per working member and 2.5 percent of average household expenditure.

As in the Philippines case, we also use simulation methods to examine the implications for per capita expenditures of different distributional patterns of land and education among sons and daughters (Table 6.7). We estimate log per capita expenditures for various counterfactual scenarios of the distribution of schooling, paddy land, cinnamon land, and rubber land, and compare the difference from the baseline. Since we use estimated coefficients to arrive at expenditures estimates, we also use bootstrapped standard errors in our comparisons (Efron 1979; StataCorp 2001).

In the first scenario, we simulate the impact of giving sons and daughters the same level of schooling. In the second, we examine the potential effect of increasing the family's paddy land by 1 hectare, and in the third and fourth scenarios we simulate the effect of increasing the family's landholdings of cinnamon land in Kerinci and rubber land in Bungo Tebo, respectively. The second to fourth scenarios can be interpreted as changing the distribution of land inheritance categories between land traditionally inherited by women (paddy land) and agroforestry land (cinnamon and rubber), which is increasingly being inherited by men.

TABLE 6.7 Estimates of changes in log per capita expenditures under different scenarios of landownership and educational attainment

Simulation	Kerinci	Bungo Tebo	Difference from baseline		Difference in rupiahs	
			Kerinci	Bungo Tebo	Kerinci	Bungo Tebo
Baseline	13.70	13.44				
	(0.12)	(0.05)				
Give sons and daughters same education	13.70	13.44	0.004	0.003	1.004	1.003
	(0.12)	(0.06)	(0.005)	(0.032)		
Increase paddy land by 1 hectare	13.76	13.54	0.06	0.10	1.062	1.105
	(0.12)	(0.08)	(0.036)	(0.060)		
Increase cinnamon land by 1 hectare	13.73	13.48	0.03*	0.04	1.030	1.041
	(0.12)	(0.07)	(0.014)	(0.047)		
Increase rubber land by 1 hectare	n.a.	13.48	n.a.	0.04	n.a.	1.041
		(0.07)		(0.047)		

NOTES: Numbers in parentheses are bootstrapped standard errors, 1,000 replications. n.a. means not applicable. * indicates significance at the 5 percent level; ** at the 1 percent level.

Our results show that there is no significant effect on permanent incomes (as proxied by per capita expenditure) from changing the distribution of schooling between sons and daughters or from changing the family's endowment of paddy and rubber land. The effect of increasing cinnamon land is statistically significant, but it is small in magnitude. These results suggest that altering the distribution of schooling and types of land between sons and daughters does not have perceptible effects on households' permanent income.

Our results are consistent with the findings of Deolalikar (1993) and Behrman and Deolalikar (1995) cited earlier. Indeed, there might be increasing returns to female schooling in our study villages because we do not see any significant impact on households' permanent income from giving equal amounts of schooling to sons and daughters.[19]

Summary of Findings

1. The size of area cultivated increases agricultural incomes significantly, indicating that the size of landholdings remains an important determinant of household income in rural areas of Indonesia. We must also point out that the impact of farm size is somewhat offset by decreasing returns to scale.
2. In general, land tenure institutions do not affect agricultural incomes significantly, implying that the shift from matrilineal toward bilateral inheritance systems has no substantive impact on household incomes.
3. The gender composition of household working members does not have significant impacts on agricultural incomes, and schooling composition has either no effect or a negative effect. These results suggest that neither human capital attributes nor gender are critically important in the management of cinnamon, rubber, and lowland rice production.
4. With respect to household expenditure, gender composition has no significant effect but schooling has a significantly positive effect, which means that women are not disfavored in either farm or nonfarm jobs and that human capital is important in nonfarm jobs.
5. In Bungo Tebo, where women are favored in land inheritance and disfavored in schooling, there is a small income gap in favor of sons. This indicates that human capital is becoming more important than land as a source of income in rural households.
6. Changing the distribution of schooling between sons and daughters does not seem to affect per capita expenditures. Neither does changing the distribution of the family's inherited land, except in the case of cinnamon, and even then the effect is small in magnitude. Thus, even if inheritance

---

19. Although we do not have data on the extent of women's participation in the nonfarm labor market, it seems that women are increasingly involved in nonfarm employment and much less involved in upland rice farming in Bungo Tebo, whereas in Kerinci women are presumed to be equally involved in both farm and nonfarm employment.

patterns may be evolving toward inheritance of agroforestry areas by men, the impact on household permanent incomes is negligible.

Summary and Conclusions

The income determination functions for cinnamon, rubber, and lowland paddy indicate that, whereas the size of landholdings remains an important determinant of household income, the gender and human capital of household working members do not have significant impacts on agricultural incomes. Thus, as in the Philippines, human capital is not critically important in agricultural production. Human capital is, however, an important determinant of permanent income, as proxied by household expenditure, which strongly indicates that human capital is important in nonfarm jobs. It seems that those household members who are endowed with human capital tend to participate in nonfarm employment.

We found that parents have been changing their decisions about land transfer and schooling investments between sons and daughters over time. In all likelihood, such changes represent responses to changes in the relative profitability of rice farming, agroforestry, and bush-fallow farming systems and the relative returns to schooling in the nonfarm sector. In Kerinci, although women were disadvantaged in schooling in the parents' generation, there is a fairly egalitarian distribution of land and schooling between sons and daughters in the respondents' generation. In Bungo Tebo, in contrast, daughters are disfavored in schooling investments but are favored in paddy land inheritance. An income gap exists in favor of sons owing to the larger income effect of the difference in schooling. However, changing the distribution of land and schooling does not have significant effects on permanent income, as proxied by per capita expenditure.

Among the children of respondents, however, the gender gap in schooling has disappeared. These findings indicate that parents are basically egalitarian and are adjusting their schooling investments to secular increases in returns to schooling. We also speculate that the absence of a wage gap against women in Indonesia leads to an equalization, over time, of schooling between men and women.

Our results show that parental transfer decisions, although egalitarian, do not support the unitary model of household behavior. We found that fathers and mothers have different preferences in wealth transfers depending on the amount of resources they brought to the marriage. This indicates that the collective model of household behavior applies in the case of rural Sumatra.

7 Inter- and Intrahousehold Equity in Sumatra

We found that land is a major source of income for agricultural households in our Sumatra sites. We also found that land tenure institutions have been evolving toward individualized ownership systems, which would have contributed to improved efficiency of the management of land and tree resources. The issue that immediately arises is the effect of such evolutionary changes in land tenure institutions on the equity of income distribution among rural households. The first objective of this chapter is to explore interhousehold inequality in the distribution of land and consumption expenditures, the latter being a proxy for the permanent income of households.

We postulated that parents have egalitarian motives for the transfer of wealth to their sons and daughters. This hypothesis was generally supported by the analysis of land inheritance and schooling investments in Chapter 6. We now test the same basic hypothesis using the analysis of current expenditure patterns. Thus, the second purpose of this chapter is to assess statistically whether there is a significant bias in the intrahousehold distribution of consumption expenditures among family members. We will also examine the validity of the unitary model of household decisionmaking with respect to expenditure allocations in Sumatra.

This chapter has three main sections. We first explore the structure of interhousehold landownership and consumption expenditure inequalities among sample households by applying the Gini decomposition analysis formulated in the Philippine study. We then identify the determinants of consumption expenditure shares statistically. The last section provides the summary and conclusions.

Landownership Inequality among Households

Because access to land resources is a major determinant of household incomes in rural communities, the distribution of land will be an important determinant of household income distribution. In this section, we examine the distribution of operational landholdings and consumption expenditures, rather than income,

164

primarily because income from cinnamon production in Kerinci is subject to large yearly fluctuations and thus would not be representative of permanent income. In order to identify the implications of different land tenure institutions for equity, we apply the Gini decomposition analysis to the distribution of operational land-holdings. For simplicity, we treat lowland and upland areas separately, because lowland areas are much more valuable than upland areas.[1]

Tables 7.1 and 7.2 show the distribution of operational landholdings by land type (that is, lowland paddy land and upland areas devoted to commercial trees) and by land tenure type in Kerinci and Bungo Tebo, respectively. It is clear that Kerinci has a higher degree of landholding inequality than Bungo Tebo for upland landholdings: the Gini coefficient for cinnamon land in Kerinci is 0.51, whereas the coefficient for rubber in Bungo Tebo is 0.40. Kerinci is more developed and upland areas are more scarce, so this observation suggests that land scarcity contributes to the increasing inequality of the inter-household distribution of land. In contrast, fertile lowland is scarcer in Bungo Tebo than in Kerinci: consistent with our inference, the Gini coefficient of low-land rice is 0.44 in Kerinci, which is smaller than the coefficient of 0.57 in Bungo Tebo. In order to examine the validity of our inference, it is useful to compare the pseudo-Gini coefficients of land distribution under traditional family ownership with those under more recently emerging private ownership.

In Kerinci, cinnamon land comprises 73 percent of the total landholdings of our sample households. Particularly unequally distributed is private land acquired by the opening of forestland and by private purchase. Since private purchase requires cash, only the wealthy landed class can afford to purchase land (Suyanto, Tomich, and Otsuka 2001a). In Kerinci, uncultivated forests are located quite far from village centers, and hired labor is employed to clean forests and to manage cleared land. Thus, wealthier farmers tend to own larger areas of opened land. In contrast, land under single-family ownership is much more equally distributed. These observations support the hypothesis that privatization of land tenure institutions leads to an inequitable distribution of land. The activation of share tenancy contracts, however, tends to counteract such trends, because tenancy contracts usually facilitate land transfer from land-rich to land-poor households (Hayami and Otsuka 1993).

In Kerinci, the pseudo-Gini coefficient of lowland rice fields is much smaller than that of upland cinnamon fields. As may be expected, land distribution under single-family ownership is highly equal. The inequitable distribution of joint family land is somewhat anomalous, but can be explained by the fact that we used joint family land currently cultivated by our sample house-

---

1. We are unable to aggregate paddy and forestry land owing to the absence of price data for purchase or sale transactions. Whereas forestry land can be acquired through purchase, paddy land is almost always acquired through inheritance.

TABLE 7.1 Overall Gini ratio of operational landholdings and contribution, by land component, in Kerinci

Tenurial group	Land share (percent)	Pseudo-Gini	Contribution (percent)
Cinnamon			
Privately purchased	30	0.66	39
Opened for cultivation	13	0.67	18
Share tenancy	9	0.34	6
Borrowed	10	0.44	8
Single-family ownership	38	0.39	29
All cinnamon	100	0.51[a]	100
Lowland rice			
Joint family ownership	25	0.46	25
Single-family ownership	29	0.31	20
Privately purchased	13	0.77	23
Borrowed	5	0.33	2
Share tenancy	16	0.45	16
Leasehold tenancy	12	0.46	14
All lowland rice	100	0.44[a]	100

[a] Identical to the overall Gini ratio.

TABLE 7.2 Overall Gini ratio of operational landholdings and contribution, by land component, in Bungo Tebo

Tenurial group	Land share (percent)	Pseudo-Gini	Contribution (percent)
Rubber			
Single-family ownership	20	0.56	26
Opened for cultivation	5	0.09	3
Privately purchased	59	0.46	68
Leasehold tenancy	13	0.03	3
Borrowed	3	−0.04	0
All rubber	100	0.40[a]	100
Lowland rice			
Joint family ownership	23	0.58	23
Single-family ownership	9	0.12	2
Privately purchased	19	0.68	22
Share tenancy	4	0.36	2
Leasehold tenancy	26	0.69	32
Borrowed	19	0.60	19
All lowland rice	100	0.57[a]	100

[a] Identical to the overall Gini ratio.

holds during the survey year. If we considered the entire area of jointly owned fields under rotational use, the distribution would be much more equal.

In Bungo Tebo, the distribution of rubber land is highly unequal for privately purchased land but not for forestland opened for cultivation. In this area, ample uncultivated forestland used to exist, at least until recently, and all the households had more or less equal access to forestland, which used to be basically open access. This explains the relatively equal distribution of this type of land. Private purchase is quite common in this region, as is clear from its high share in total landholdings. Very often, land under single-family ownership is obtained after receiving permission from members of the extended family. The fact that the pseudo-Gini coefficient of single-family ownership is very high suggests that households endowed with less family land tend to have sold their land to households endowed with larger areas of land. It seems that the development of private ownership contributes to the widening gap in landownership among households in Bungo Tebo as well.

In the case of paddy land, the distribution of privately purchased land is skewed but the incidence of land purchase is much less than for rubber fields. Particularly equally distributed are single-family land and, to the lesser extent, share tenancy land, but their land shares are small. Somewhat unexpectedly, the distributions of joint family owned, leasehold, and borrowed lands are unequal. As a result, the overall distribution of paddy land is relatively equal.

Overall, we have found that land acquired through one's initiatives such as privately purchased land and land opened for cultivation is a major source of inequality in landholdings, particularly if uncultivated land is scarce. Thus, we can fairly conclude that privatization of land tenure institutions is associated with a more unequal land distribution.

It is important to point out that the Gini coefficient of landholding distribution is higher than the expenditure Gini, which is shown in Table 7.3: in Kerinci, the expenditure Gini is 0.37; in Bungo Tebo it is 0.18. These observations suggest that, whereas land income contributes substantially to household income inequality, nonfarm income, which is another source of finance for household expenditures, may tend to equalize the distribution of permanent income, for which expenditures are a proxy. Note also that the difference in the expenditure Gini between Kerinci and Bungo Tebo is relatively high. As was demonstrated by the analysis of the determinants of per capita consumption expenditure in Table 6.6, college education is a significant factor affecting household expenditure in Kerinci. Thus, wealthy households with highly educated children may enjoy significantly larger permanent incomes in Kerinci.

Summary of Findings

1. Land scarcity contributes to increasing inequality in the interhousehold distribution of land. Indeed, the pseudo-Gini coefficient of land under traditional family ownership is less than under private ownership, which has more recently emerged. This is because private land is acquired either by

TABLE 7.3 Expenditure shares in Kerinci and Bungo Tebo

	Kerinci	Bungo Tebo	All villages
Expenditure items (percent)			
Food	54	58	56
Health	3	2	3
Education	1	1	1
Clothing	2	4	4
Tobacco	6	5	5
Other[a]	34	30	31
Total	100	100	100
Total consumption expenditure			
(thousand rupiahs/year)	5,598	3,802	4,747
Gini coefficient of inequality	0.37	0.18	0.34

NOTE: Exchange rate was approximately US$1 = 2,500 rupiahs.

[a] Includes jewelry, remittances, durables, transportation, pilgrimage, recreation.

purchase or by forest clearance, which requires cash or the resources to hire labor for clearing.

2. Although the privatization of land tenure institutions may increase land distribution inequality, share tenancy contracts, as well as single-family ownership, tend to counteract this trend.

3. Whereas land income may contribute to interhousehold expenditure inequality, nonfarm income tends to equalize the distribution of permanent income.

Determinants of Consumption Expenditure Shares

Specification of Estimated Functions

Readers who are not interested in the technical details of statistical estimation can proceed directly to the "Summary of Findings" at the end of this section on page 174.

Having examined the distribution of expenditures across households, we now turn to the distribution of expenditures within the household. As with the Philippines study, we estimate a system of household expenditure functions to examine the manner in which parents allocate their resources to male and female children. We focus on identifying whether some expenditure items are geared toward certain demographic categories. The expenditure shares regressions also provide an additional test of the unitary and the collective household models.

Because of censoring of the dependent variable and endogeneity of per capita expenditure (PCE), we estimate each expenditure share function as a simultaneous Tobit system, although we do not estimate all the expenditure functions as a system. Each expenditure share regression is estimated as a Tobit, with the predicted values of the natural logarithm of PCE ($\ln PCE^*$) as one of the regressors. To the extent that households smooth consumption over their lifetime, PCE can effectively represent household permanent income, which is a measure of long-run household resource availability. Because PCE is considered to be a choice variable, we calculate its predicted value using instrumental variables that affect PCE but not the expenditure shares. The instruments are the log of farm size, the ratio of paddy area to the total, the ratio of female working members, the average years of schooling of male and female working members, and the ratios of working members in four age categories (26–35 years, 36–45 years, 46–55 years, and 56–65 years). The first-stage regression on ln *PCE,* estimated using ordinary least squares (OLS), was presented in Table 6.6 and discussed in Chapter 6; parameter estimates using the simultaneous Tobit method are slightly different but are not presented here because the coefficients of interest are those on the Tobit regression.

In the second-stage regression we estimate a series of expenditure share functions, specified as

$$\mathbf{W} = \gamma_0 + \gamma_1 \ln PCE^* + \gamma_2 \ln \text{household size}$$
$$+ \gamma_3 \ln \text{father's schooling} + \gamma_4 \ln \text{mother's schooling}$$
$$+ \gamma_5 (\text{father's paddy land})^{\frac{1}{2}} + \gamma_6 (\text{mother's paddy land})^{\frac{1}{2}}$$
$$+ \gamma_7 (\text{father's agroforestry land})^{\frac{1}{2}}$$
$$+ \gamma_8 (\text{mother's agroforestry land})^{\frac{1}{2}}$$
$$+ \sum_{i=9}^{17} \gamma_i (\text{proportion in each gender/age group category})$$
$$+ \Sigma\gamma_{20} (\text{Kerinci village dummy}) + \theta, \tag{7.1}$$

where $\mathbf{W}$ is a vector of expenditure shares, γ are parameters, and θ is an error term.

Household size is expected to capture the effect of the strength of size economies or diseconomies in household consumption expenditures. We use the data on land areas received at marriage and on the schooling of fathers and mothers as indicators of spouses' exogenously determined bargaining power, because both human and physical asset ownership critically determine the spouses' potential income earnings. Because land rights differ significantly by gender across paddy land and agroforestry land in Sumatra, and because we have no way of aggregating land areas in these categories, we include two categories of land in our regressions: paddy land (traditionally inherited by women) and upland (the sum of agroforestry and bush-fallow land). Recall that women receive more paddy land than their husbands (particularly in Bungo Tebo), who, in turn, tend to have larger holdings of upland areas at marriage.[2]

---

2. We also estimated the expenditure share regressions with the sum of total landholdings for each spouse as explanatory variables. Aggregating land categories does not enable us to reject the null hypothesis that the coefficients on husband's and wife's land are equal.

As in the Philippines chapter, we do not use the logarithm of fathers' and mothers' inherited landholdings because some respondents and their spouses do not inherit any land. Instead, owing to the possible declining marginal effects of inherited land, we use the square root of the levels of fathers' and mothers' inherited land. We test the unitary versus the collective model of the household by testing whether the coefficients on the husband's and the wife's human and physical capital are significantly different from each other, after controlling for the effects of per capita household expenditures.

After controlling for levels of household income (as proxied by per capita expenditure), the assets of husband and wife should have no effect on allocations if the unitary model holds in a static framework, so that $\gamma_3 = \gamma_4 = 0$, $\gamma_5 = \gamma_6 = 0$, and $\gamma_7 = \gamma_8 = 0$ hold. In a more general (for example, dynamic) framework, however, the equality of husband's and wife's effects to zero may not hold. We therefore use a more general version of the test of the unitary model, namely that the difference between the husband's and the wife's asset effects is zero. Our demographic groupings are males and females separately in age brackets 0–5, 6–9, 10–19, and 20–65, using males in age bracket 20–65 as the control category. We pool data from the two sites to increase the degrees of freedom, and include a dummy variable for Kerinci.

Data on Expenditure Shares

We divide household expenditure items into food, health, education, clothing, tobacco, and other (Table 7.3). Food comprises 54 percent of total household expenditures in Kerinci and 58 percent in Bungo Tebo. The education budget share is only 1 percent of the total because our data on educational expenditures include only direct costs, which are low owing to public provision of primary education. Other expenditures, which include jewelry, remittances to children and other family members, consumer durables, transportation, pilgrimage, and recreation, comprise about one-third of the total.

Total expenditure in Kerinci is 1.4 times that of Bungo Tebo. Household income in Kerinci is higher owing to the higher profitability of cinnamon production compared with rubber production and better access to nonfarm jobs. Kerinci is closer to town centers, which allows villagers to engage actively in nonfarm activities and purchase higher-valued urban consumer goods. An important issue here is how expenditure in each category is affected by the age and gender composition of the household. We examine this issue in the next subsection.

Estimation Results

The regression results of the expenditure shares functions are shown in Table 7.4. We include food, health, schooling, child clothing, and tobacco (which is grouped separately because it is commonly considered to be an "adult good" in expenditure analyses). According to the estimation results, the share of food in total expenditure tends to decline with an increase in PCE, consistent with Engel's law. Expenditures on child clothing also decline with an increase in PCE, but coefficients for the other expenditure categories, although negative, are insignificant. As in the Philippines, larger households have a significantly lower food share, suggesting that increases in household size may result in economies of size in food consumption. Coefficients of household size for the other expenditure categories, however, are insignificant.

The effects of father's and mother's schooling, paddy land, and agroforestry land on expenditure shares are not significant except in a few cases.[3] Father's schooling has a positive and significant effect on the expenditure share of child clothing, whereas father's paddy land decreases the food expenditure share. Mother's schooling has a negative impact on the share of household resources devoted to tobacco—a good consumed mostly by men—and mother's paddy land increases the share spent on education. The general insignificance of the coefficients on parental characteristics suggests that, once per capita expenditures are controlled for, parental characteristics do not have much additional explanatory power.

We examine the validity of the unitary model of household behavior in Sumatra by testing whether the coefficients on father's and mother's schooling and those on father's and mother's landholdings are the same. After controlling for per capita expenditures, if the coefficients on father's and mother's characteristics are not significantly different, we cannot reject the unitary model in favor of the collective model. Equality of coefficients suggests that the human and physical assets brought into marriage by mothers and fathers have equal effects on consumption expenditures. The computed χ^2 statistics shown in the bottom panel of Table 7.4 are all below critical values at the 5 percent level of significance, which indicates that father's and mother's schooling and father's and mother's paddy and agroforestry land have the same effects on the expenditure shares. Thus, the unitary model cannot be rejected with respect to decisions on budget shares. Yet we have evidence that father's and mother's schooling and landholdings have different effects on the schooling attainment of younger children. In the case of individual educational outcomes, the collective model of the household—a model in which household members have different preferences—applies. It is possible that, although parents may agree on the overall allocation of household resources to education, as revealed by education budget shares, they have different opinions about who in the household benefits from resources devoted to education. Thus, tests of the unitary model using household-level data may be weaker because they do not reveal parental preferences as closely as do individual-level data.

---

3. Father's and mother's schooling and landholdings are proxies for the relative income contributions of spouses. We do not use each spouse's income shares because they may be endogenous to expenditure share functions.

TABLE 7.4 Determinants of expenditure shares in Kerinci and Bungo Tebo, 1997

Variables	Food	Health	Education	Child clothing	Tobacco
Constant	3.65**	0.42	0.03	0.62*	0.31
	(4.52)	(0.84)	(0.20)	(2.0)	(0.54)
Ln PCE*[a]	-0.20**	-0.03	-0.01	-0.05*	-0.02
	(-3.33)	(-0.78)	(-0.58)	(-2.31)	(-0.58)
Ln household size	-0.22**	-0.03	0.01	0.002	0.02
	(-4.78)	(-1.03)	(1.43)	(0.15)	(0.52)
Ln father's schooling	0.01	-0.001	0.01	0.02*	0.02
	(0.53)	(-0.07)	(1.02)	(2.10)	(0.84)
Ln mothers' schooling	-0.03	0.01	0.0004	0.01	-0.04*
	(-1.10)	(0.85)	(0.01)	(1.21)	(-2.16)
SQRT father's paddy land[b]	-0.06*	0.003	0.006	0.01	0.02
	(-1.96)	(0.12)	(0.87)	(1.60)	(0.71)
SQRT mother's paddy land[b]	0.004	0.02	0.01*	0.01	-0.008
	(0.12)	(1.01)	(2.41)	(0.99)	(-0.28)
SQRT father's agroforestry land[b]	-0.002	0.006	-0.004	0.002	-0.0006
	(-0.19)	(0.59)	(-0.87)	(0.53)	(-0.01)
SQRT mother's agroforestry land[b]	0.01	0.008	-0.007	-0.01	-0.02
	(0.45)	(0.48)	(-1.33)	(-1.11)	(-0.88)
Proportion of household members					
Males aged 0–5	0.21	-0.02	0.02	0.04	0.08
	(1.35)	(-0.15)	(0.53)	(0.91)	(0.62)
Males aged 6–9	0.16	-0.03	0.07	0.08	0.17
	(0.83)	(-0.19)	(1.39)	(1.48)	(1.12)
Males aged 10–19	0.14	0.06	0.07	0.09*	0.05
	(1.04)	(0.62)	(1.74)	(2.54)	(0.40)

Males aged 65+	0.24	0.18	-0.007	0.02	0.10
	(0.91)	(1.46)	(-0.12)	(0.22)	(0.57)
Females aged 0–5	0.15	-0.04	0.009	0.07	0.09
	(0.86)	(-0.24)	(0.20)	(1.62)	(0.70)
Females aged 6–9	0.13	0.02	0.05	0.12**	0.12
	(0.77)	(0.23)	(1.19)	(2.91)	(1.01)
Females aged 10–19	0.17	-0.005	0.09**	0.10**	0.10
	(1.23)	(-0.05)	(2.58)	(2.65)	(0.91)
Females aged 20–64	-0.14	0.09	0.06	0.08	0.15
	(-0.76)	(0.67)	(1.31)	(1.72)	(1.07)
Females aged 65+	-0.39	-0.04	0.04	0.01	-0.05
	(-1.92)	(-0.18)	(0.89)	(0.08)	(-0.24)
Kerinci village dummy	0.07*	-0.008	0.006	0.01	0.04
	(2.12)*	(-0.35)	(0.77)	(0.84)	(1.53)
Log-likelihood function	319.29	401.85	351.52	406.69	273.87
Nonlinear Wald test (χ^2 statistic)					
Husband's schooling = wife's schooling	1.27	0.26	0.37	0.30	2.92
Husband's paddy = wife's paddy	2.03	0.19	0.81	0.13	0.51
Husband's agroforestry = wife's agroforestry	0.23	0.02	0.32	1.56	0.65
Number of observations	99	99	99	99	99

NOTES: Estimator is simultaneous equations Tobit, with log per capita expenditure predicted. Numbers in parentheses are z-statistics; * indicates significance at the 5 percent level; ** at 1 the percent level.

[a] PCE* refers to the predicted values of per capita expenditure.

[b] SQRT refers to the square root of the areas of mothers' and fathers' inherited landholdings of paddy and agroforestry land, respectively.

In general, the shares of household members in different age/sex categories do not significantly affect the budget shares devoted to food, housing, and clothing. However, having females aged 10–19 years increases the budget share on education—a result that corroborates our earlier finding of increased parental investment in girls' education. Having males aged 10–19 years and females aged 6–9 years and 10–19 years increases budgetary allocations to child clothing. Except for the result on education, which indicates a slight preference for girls, there is no evidence that males and females in the same age brackets affect expenditure patterns differentially. In other words, parental discrimination against females cannot be discerned from the coefficients on demographic categories. This is consistent with the egalitarian cultural values of Indonesian society, which were amply attested to by the analysis of the determinants of land inheritance and schooling investments in Chapter 6.

Summary of Findings

1. In general, the shares of household members in different age/sex categories do not significantly affect the shares of expenditure on food, housing, child clothing, schooling, and tobacco. This indicates that rural household expenditure allocation tends to be egalitarian in Sumatra.
2. The unitary model of the household—a model in which individuals within the household share the same preference or a single decisionmaker decides for all—cannot be rejected in the case of expenditure allocations.

Summary and Conclusions

The first objective of this chapter was to assess whether there exists a large and widening interhousehold inequality in the distribution of land and expenditures. We found that landholding inequality tends to be higher for the type of land that is scarce, and that the inequality is higher for privately owned land than for family-owned land. Furthermore, expenditure is more unequally distributed in Kerinci than in Bungo Tebo. One factor responsible for the inequality of land distribution is the privatization of landownership associated with the increased scarcity of land. Another important factor is proximity to urban centers, which in Kerinci enables households with educated members to diversify their income sources.

The second objective was to assess whether there is significant bias in the intrahousehold allocation of expenditures among male and female family members. We found that none of the ratios of male and female members falling into the same age categories have, in general, significantly different impacts on the expenditure shares. Overall, as in the Philippines, the intrahousehold allocation of expenditures in Sumatra may well be described as egalitarian. This conclusion is consistent with the largely egalitarian transfer of parental wealth to sons and daughters found in Chapter 6.

The last objective was to test whether the unitary household model applies to Indonesian households. We did not find significant differences between the coefficients on parental schooling or on landholdings. Thus, our results do not lead us to reject the unitary model so far as household expenditures are concerned. This conclusion is different from the "weak" rejection of the unitary model in the analysis of land inheritance and schooling investments between sons and daughters.

PART III

The Ghana Case

8 The Study Villages and Sample Households in Cocoa-Growing Areas

This chapter provides the context for the statistical analyses to be conducted in Chapters 9 and 10. The Ghana case is particularly interesting because customary land tenure institutions have been evolving not only toward individualized ownership but also toward gender equity in landownership.

We first describe the major characteristics of the study villages and the survey design in our Ghana sites. We find that joint ownership of land by the extended family has been replaced by more individualized ownership through inter vivos gifts from husband to wife and children. This new form of intergenerational transfer is de facto inheritance. We also find that the strength of land rights is closely linked with the mode of land acquisition; in particular, strong land rights are associated with land received as gifts. In the second section, we describe the prevailing land tenure institutions and socioeconomic characteristics of the sample households. We also present information on changing land use, as well as on labor use in mature cocoa and food crop cultivation, in order to explain the evolution of land tenure institutions, particularly the increased tendency for husbands to give gifts of land to their wives and children. In the third section, we explore intergenerational changes and cross-sectional differences in schooling and land inheritance by gender using individual survey data. Lastly, we set out the hypotheses to be tested statistically in Chapters 9 and 10.

Study Villages and Survey Structure

Study Villages

In 1996–97, we conducted a survey of households in 10 selected villages that had been surveyed by the World Bank in 1987–88 in the Wassa area of western Ghana (Migot-Adholla et al. 1993). Wassa is the last frontier of westward movement of the cocoa area in this country as migrants moved in search of cultivable forestland (Hill 1963), and, with the exception of reserved areas, virgin forests have already disappeared in our study sites (see Figure 8.1). Our

FIGURE 8.1 Map of survey area in Ghana

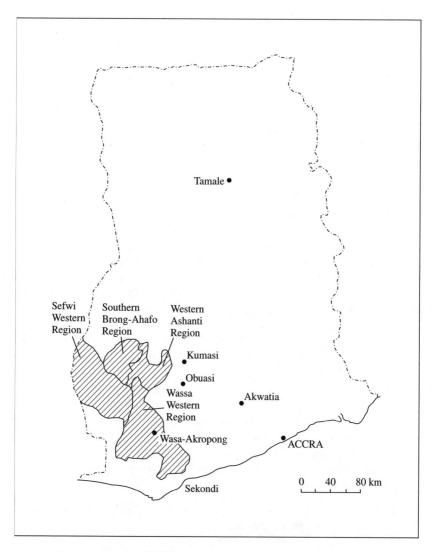

SOURCE: Quisumbing et al. (2001b).

study sites are mostly hilly and the deterioration of forest environments has resulted in soil erosion and other negative environmental externalities. The establishment of cocoa agroforestry on sloping land, however, will reduce soil erosion and contribute to the partial restoration of tree biomass and biodiversity (Gockowski, Nkamleu, and Wendt 2001).

A recent study of land tenure institutions in western Ghana (Quisumbing et al. 2001a) shows that they have evolved toward increasing individualization in our sites. Concerns have often been raised about the impact of such changes on the distribution of land rights by gender. For example, a recent literature review by Gray and Kevane (1999) states that increasing commercialization, population growth, and concurrent increases in land value seem to have adversely affected women's land rights in Africa. This is consistent with the argument that a shift in land tenure toward individualized rights tends to weaken women's land rights (Lastarria-Cornhiel 1997). This view is often supported by the gradual disappearance of matrilineal inheritance and the rise of patrilineal inheritance systems, for example in some parts of Sub-Saharan Africa (Place and Otsuka 2001a, 2001b). In our study areas, however, Quisumbing et al. (2001a) find that individualization of land rights has resulted in women's acquiring stronger land rights, induced by the increase in the demand for women's labor in cocoa production.

Traditionally, Akan households in this region have practiced uterine matrilineal inheritance, in which land is transferred from a deceased man to his brother or nephew (sister's son) in accordance with the decision of the extended family or matriclan.[1] This implies that children do not inherit land from their parents, particularly their fathers, but sons can inherit land from their matrilineal relatives. In contrast, among patrilineal groups who are migrants to the area, inheritance occurs strictly along paternal lines. In the past few decades among Akans, however, land has often been transferred from a husband to his wife and children as an inter vivos gift if the wife and children help the husband establish cocoa fields (Quisumbing et al. 2001a). This is a marked departure from the uterine matrilineal inheritance system practiced in this area.

The increase in the demand for women's labor as a result of the expansion of labor-intensive cocoa cultivation in place of land-intensive shifting cultivation seems to have created incentives for husbands to give their wives and children land as gifts. Although the marketing of cocoa is controlled by the government, domestic prices have moved closer to international prices, creating additional incentives to expand cocoa cultivation. The individualization of land tenure institutions was further strengthened by the Intestate Succession Law (ISL) in 1985, which provides for the following division of the farm: three-sixteenths to the surviving spouse, nine-sixteenths to the surviving children, one-eighth to the surviving parent, and one-eighth in accordance with customary inheritance law. However, the common interpretation of the ISL by cocoa farmers in our study sites is one-third each for the spouse, children, and maternal family. Although this modified ISL appears well enforced, we must not

---

1. The preferred order of inheritance if a man dies intestate is, first, his uterine brother; second, if there is no uterine brother, the son of a uterine sister; third, one of the sons of the deceased mother's sister. See Awusabo-Asare (1990).

overlook the fact that a one-third division of land was practiced well before the enactment of the ISL.

We find that that the incidence of gifts increases in areas where matrilineal inheritance is practiced, in order to strengthen individual land rights (Quisumbing et al. 2001a). We also find that these evolutionary changes in customary land tenure institutions have taken place to achieve greater efficiency in the use and allocation of land for food crop production under shifting cultivation and cocoa agroforestry. We would then expect that investments in the education of sons and daughters will have adjusted to changes in land inheritance practices, insofar as land transfer and education are major alternative forms of intergenerational wealth transfers.

Survey Structure

We originally intended to create a panel dataset by revisiting those households surveyed in the earlier World Bank study. However, land tenure status in the previous survey was not clearly defined, and parcels owned by women in male-headed households were not included.[2] Furthermore, because of the changing distribution of land across tenure types (particularly as a result of increases in the incidence of gifts), the World Bank samples no longer corresponded to the actual distribution of land by tenure status in 1996. Also, considering the complexity of the prevailing land tenure institutions, we found the sample size of 150 randomly selected households in the earlier survey too small for our purpose. Thus, after conducting a census survey of 1,878 households in the 10 survey villages, we chose 281 households based on stratified random sampling across the exhaustive tenure categories of pure owners, pure tenants, pure caretakers (who manage mature cocoa fields, usually for absentee owners), owners cum tenants cultivating both owned and rented land, owners cum caretakers, and tenants cum caretakers.[3] Sample sizes were allocated to the 10 villages in proportion to the village population and, to the extent possible, the earlier sample households that agreed to be reinterviewed were included. In this way, a representative sample of tenure distribution was obtained.

For each sample household, we collected information on the land tenure status and land use of all parcels, which are defined as contiguous areas of land

---

2. The only parcels managed by women in the World Bank study were in female-headed households. Also problematic are the lack of distinction between patrilineal and matrilineal inheritance rules and between female household heads and female plot managers in male-headed households, and the lack of information on the intensity of tree planting. Neither was the productivity of cocoa and food crop cultivation considered separately.

3. A total of 281 households were interviewed, but 23 were dropped for various reasons (including noncompletion of questionnaires for all three rounds). This brings the total to 258 households. The household tenure status can be created for only 257 households, because the tenure variable for some fields is missing in one household. Our subsequent discussion refers to the 257 remaining households, although sample sizes may be smaller for some of the analyses given missing information for some households.

acquired at the same time through a single mode of acquisition. Typically, a sample household holds more than one parcel. There are close to 800 parcels divided into over 2,000 fields, of which 80 percent are managed by the same person and 20 percent by other household members or persons outside the household who may or may not be of the same sex as the parcel "manager." We also collected land use histories for all these parcels, including previous land use and dates when land was converted to different uses. In order to obtain detailed production data from all the fields currently held by the household, we randomly sampled mature and young cocoa fields and food-producing fields. If different fields were managed separately by men and women or by tenants, owners, and caretakers, we chose more than one field from the same household.[4] We applied a stratified random sampling method, because 2,000 fields are cultivated by our sample households.

To investigate changes in intergenerational transfers over time, we designed a retrospective household survey of land inheritance, gifts, temporary allocation of family land, and schooling over three generations. We paid particular attention to different types of land transfers, since the strength of individual land rights is linked closely to the mode of land transfers, with gift transfers having the strongest individual rights and allocated family land the weakest. The retrospective survey on inheritance was patterned after similar surveys in the Philippines (Quisumbing 1994; Chapter 2 in this volume) and Sumatra (Chapter 5 in this volume) and included questions on the parents, siblings, and children of the respondents, yielding information on three generations (the parents', respondents', and children's generations).[5] The respondents were asked about the pre-marriage wealth (schooling and landownership) of their parents and in-laws (and other familial sources of inheritance), the schooling and inheritance of their spouses, and the schooling of and proposed bequests to their children. Respondents were also asked to list all of their siblings, their dates of birth, their educational attainment, and the areas of different types of land that they received or expected to receive from their parents or other relatives. In many cases, respondents received land at marriage but stood to inherit more land after their parents' death.

Since one can inherit land from the matriclan as well as from one's own parents, inheritance was distinguished according to its source. Unlike in our other survey sites, the survey in Ghana was administered only to the head of household (usually male), because low levels of literacy among wives made it difficult for them to answer questions involving retrospective or recall information (for example, dates or years of birth). In most cases, we requested the wife to join the interview for retrospective questions pertaining to her family.

---

4. A field is defined as a portion of a parcel characterized by the same cropping pattern.
5. The grandchild generation is called the child generation for brevity.

An interesting feature of the Ghana survey is the complexity of inheritance sources and potential heirs resulting from the uterine matrilineal system and the practice of polygyny. Under this system, a person can inherit from a number of matrilineal relatives, depending on the order of succession. The practice of serial marriage means that an individual may have several sets of maternal and paternal half-siblings. In our study sample, about 9 percent of household heads have two wives.

Based on the above considerations, and after extensive pretests in the field, the inheritance retrospective was designed to capture the possibility of acquiring land from four sets of matrilineal relatives: mother, maternal uncle, maternal grandmother, and other matrilineal relatives. Only one source of paternal inheritance was identified: the father. Respondents (heads of households) were also asked to list all their paternal and maternal full- and half-siblings. Interestingly, individuals were often uncertain how many half-siblings they had, particularly if one of their parents had moved to another village upon remarriage. Since not only siblings but also cousins, nieces, and nephews can inherit land from the matriclan, the number of heirs is potentially very large. To simplify matters, the analysis is restricted to the siblings and half-siblings that the respondent can name; thus parental landholdings are not divided by the number of potential heirs to capture the effects of population pressure.

Land Tenure Institutions in the Survey Villages

Prevailing Land Tenure Institutions

Table 8.1 shows the distributions of all fields of the sample households and of fields selected by land use type for the detailed input and output survey. Cocoa trees begin to produce output from the fourth to fifth year. We classify cocoa fields into mature cocoa fields from which cocoa can be harvested and young cocoa fields intercropped with food crops. Although the number of mature cocoa fields is smaller than the number of young cocoa fields, mature cocoa fields are much larger. This is because cocoa trees are planted gradually from one portion of the parcel to the next, with new fields being merged with other tree-planted fields. Fallow land occupies a large area, whereas land devoted entirely to food crops is less common. This is because food crops and cocoa are traditionally intercropped: food crops are planted while the cocoa trees are still young; once the cocoa trees are too tall to allow adequate sunlight for food crops, food is no longer grown as an intercrop. Growing food and cocoa intercrops also takes advantage of weeding labor, because the ground around young cocoa trees has to be kept free from weeds. Since cultivators often do not know the length of the fallow period on all their parcels, our data on the duration of the fallow period for all selected fields are incomplete. However, available information indicates that the fallow period commonly ranges from 5 to 10 years.

TABLE 8.1 Distribution and size of operational landholdings for all sample fields and selected sample fields, by land use type, in Ghana

	All fields		Selected fields		
Land use type	Number	Size (hectares)	Number	Size (hectares)	Number of households
Mature cocoa	504	1.85	276	2.02	213
Young cocoa	701	0.60	218	0.67	187
Food only	197	0.52	112	0.53	106
Fallow only	548	2.37	0	n.a.	n.a.
Food and fallow	12	0.54	6	0.43	6
Other[a]	39	1.65	0	n.a.	n.a.
Total	2,001	1.42	612	1.25	249

NOTE: n.a. means not applicable.

[a] Fields entirely planted to kola or palm oil trees.

We over-sampled food crop fields for the collection of detailed production data. Usually various food crops are grown together in an intermingled manner in the same field and we identified 12 crop types, including maize, plantain, cassava, and yams. We collected one-year production data, but a few crops, such as plantain, need more than a year to bear fruit and are continuously cultivated for two to three years in our survey area. Thus, in order to control for the effects of crop mix when we estimate the income function of food crops, we used estimates of the proportions of various crops as explanatory variables, assuming that various crops grown together in multiple-crop fields account for equal proportions of land area. We admit that the assumption of equal proportions was adopted primarily because of data requirements; other more plausible assumptions would have required collecting additional data. As may be expected, there are only a small number of mixed fallow crop fields.

Table 8.2 shows the distribution of all the sample fields by land use and land tenure regime. Both the mode of land transfer and land rights systems have evolved in western Ghana (Quisumbing et al. 2001a). When virgin forests were abundant, forest areas were appropriated by individual members primarily for food crop production. Relatively strong individual land rights were granted in return for the substantial labor input required to clear forests. Traditionally, in the Akan uterine matrilineal system this type of land was either bequeathed to nephews or temporarily allocated to other male members of the extended family, leaving wives and children without any rights to a man's property if he were to die intestate. Of our sample villages, seven are indigenous villages inhabited primarily by Akan people subject to matrilineal inheritance, and three are migrant villages inhabited mostly by migrants generally subject to patrilineal inheritance. There are, however, short-distance migrants who are Akans. Our

TABLE 8.2 Distribution of all sample fields under different land tenure regimes, by land use type, in Ghana (number of fields)

Land tenure type	Mature cocoa	Young cocoa	Food only	Fallow only	Food/ fallow	Other	Total
Allocated family land	42	62	42	83	3	6	238
Inherited family land	29	27	5	43	2	3	109
Appropriated village land	52	74	18	64	0	8	216
Purchased village land	26	19	7	24	0	2	78
Received as a gift	188	293	72	202	5	16	776
Privately purchased	12	25	5	19	0	0	61
Acquired through renting	16	8	0	7	0	0	31
Currently renting	78	185	23	88	0	3	377
Caretaking	61	5	8	10	1	1	86
Borrowing from nonrelatives	. . .	3	17	8	1	. . .	29
Total	504	701	197	548	12	39	2,001

sample comprises 85.0 percent matrilineal households, 9.4 percent patrilineal households, and 5.6 percent mixed households.

According to Table 8.2, temporarily allocated family land is more important than inherited land. However, inherited family land is now being given more frequently to men's children and wife compared with allocated land, which requires the consent of the family members. More recently, appropriated community land is also increasingly being transferred directly to wives and children. Such inter vivos transfers are termed "gifts" in our study. Individual rights on such land are firmly established. According to retrospective data collected by Quisumbing et al. (2001b) on land acquired, by mode of acquisition, the incidence of gifts has increased since the late 1960s.

When forests were abundant, migrants acquired land by purchasing forest-land from village chiefs. More recently, however, renting has become a more common mode for migrants to obtain access to cultivable land. Tenants are contracted to plant and establish cocoa trees and, more often than not, after the parcel has been completely planted with trees the parcel itself is divided equally or in a 2:1 ratio between the owner and tenant (Robertson 1982; Boadu 1992). Migrants, as well as young Akan men, also work as caretakers in mature cocoa fields, for which they usually receive one-third of the harvested crop output. A nonnegligible number of fields is borrowed from nonrelatives.

In order to measure the strength of land rights under different land tenure institutions, we used group interviews to ask whether the following six rights exist: (1) to plant and replant trees; (2) to rent out land; (3) to pawn; (4) to bequeath; (5) to give; and (6) to sell. In general, each group discussion included more than 50 villagers, including the chief, sub-chiefs, elders, and others. By and large, it took 5–15 minutes for the group to arrive at a consensus answer to each question about each land right, because participants rarely discussed definitions of land rights. These rights are ordered from the weakest (that is, the right to plant) to the strongest (that is, the right to sell). For example, if the cultivator holds the right to bequeath, this person certainly holds the rights to plant trees, rent out parcels, and pawn. Table 8.3 shows the average number of rights or cases in which farmers have these rights without approval from family members or the village chief. The number of rights should be interpreted as ordinal numbers, because the importance of each right could be different. The weakest land rights are observed in temporarily allocated family land, on which even tree planting is not allowed. Thus, if land rights at the time of tree planting determine investment incentives, we expect to observe that cocoa trees are seldom planted on allocated family land. Land rights are also weak in inherited land among matrilineal Akan households.

Yet about one-half of allocated and inherited fields are planted to cocoa according to Table 8.2. These observations suggest that not only current land rights but also expected changes in land rights affect tree-planting decisions. Although we did not formally collect data on land rights on borrowed land, our field interviews indicate that borrowed land has even weaker rights than allocated and inherited land. In fact, usufruct rights are well established in the case of family land so long as fields are used for crop cultivation, but not in the case of borrowed land.

Patrilineal households are endowed with fairly strong rights on inherited land. It seems that land rights are more easily individualized in patrilineal society, because the interests in the same piece of land are shared primarily by a small circle of individuals, consisting of a father and his sons. Strong land rights

TABLE 8.3 Index of land rights under different land tenure regimes in Ghana

Land tenure type	Indigenous village	Migrant village
Temporarily allocated family land[a]		
Food crop land from father	0.0	0.2
Food crop land from family	0.8	0.6
Inherited family land		
Akan (matrilineal)	1.0	1.0
Non-Akan (patrilineal)	0.0	6.0
Village forestland		
Appropriated by indigenes	5.0	5.2
Purchased by migrants	6.0	6.0
Tree-planted land transferred		
as gift from father	6.0	6.0

NOTES: Based on group interviews. Six rights are considered: (1) to plant or replant trees, (2) to rent out, (3) to pawn, (4) to bequeath, (5) to give, and (6) to sell. This table shows the average number of cases in which farmers have rights without approval from family members or a village chief.

[a] Food crop land includes fallow land.

are also observed in formerly village forestland, whether appropriated by indigenes or purchased by migrants. Strong land rights accrue on cleared forestland because efforts to clear forest are rewarded by strong individual land rights. Equally strong land rights are observed in tree-planted land received as a gift. Gifts are usually made by a man to his children and sometimes to his wife, after seeking agreement from members of the extended family.[6] The strong rights are conferred as rewards for efforts to plant and grow trees. In fact, the proportion of fields planted to cocoa trees is relatively high in fields received as gifts (Table 8.2). This observation indicates that incentives to plant trees on allocated family land and inherited land may be strong if, by planting trees, individual land rights are strengthened to permit the transfer of family land as a gift (Otsuka et al. 2001).

Socioeconomic Characteristics

Table 8.4 presents the socioeconomic characteristics of our sample households. Ethnicity is based on the self-declared ethnicity of the household head. Although we did not examine this issue carefully, there are a small number of intermarriages between Akans and non-Akans. Akans predominate in our sample, accounting for 211 households compared with only 44 non-Akan households. Thus, the small sample size of the non-Akan households should be considered when interpreting the significance of the results of our econometric analyses. Households' total landholdings—comprising all land owned or operated—are not significantly different between Akans and non-Akans. On a per capita basis, however, Akans operate larger farm areas, primarily owing to the larger household size of non-Akans. This is to be expected since Akans are indigenous to the community whereas non-Akans would typically have to purchase land, acquire it through rental agreements, or ask the village chief's permission to clear forests. Akan households' easier access to land means that they cultivate more land per capita than do non-Akan households.

Although about 11 percent of households are headed by women in both Akan and non-Akan groups, one-fifth of all parcels are managed by women—meaning that the parcel was acquired by a woman. Non-Akan households have a slightly higher proportion of household members aged 15–65 years, although there are also household members over 65 years of age who report themselves as still working.

Male working members in both the respondent and child generations report higher completed years of schooling than female working members do.

---

6. Such inter vivos gifts are formalized by the recipient's presenting ritual drinks to family elders and other witnesses in the *aseda* (thanksgiving) ceremony. The drink is the physical expression of appreciation for the gift, and is crucial so that the transfer of land rights by gift will not be contested in the future. When a husband gives land to his wife and children, it is their responsibility to provide the drinks, although a husband may secretly do so if the recipients cannot afford it.

TABLE 8.4 Demographic characteristics of sample households, by ethnic group, in Ghana

Characteristics	Akan	Non-Akan
Number of sample households	211	44
Total land owned and operated		
by the household (hectares)	12.72	12.70
Total land operated by the household (hectares)	10.99	9.40
Area planted to mature cocoa	3.56	3.41
Area planted to young cocoa[a]	1.61	1.63
Area planted to food only	0.39	0.38
Bush-fallow area[b]	5.17	3.95
Other[c]	0.25	0.02
Household size	5.6	6.9
Person–land ratio (land in hectares/capita)	2.43	1.74
Percent female-headed households	11.37	11.36
Percent female-managed parcels	19.91	22.41
Number of household members aged 15–65 years[d]	2.8	3.6
Number of working members aged 15–65 years who		
are not students[e]	2.3	2.7
Years of schooling of working members		
Respondents		
Male	7.3	5.2
Female	3.8	2.9
Children of respondents		
Sons	8.0	7.3
Daughters	5.0	6.9

[a] Young cocoa is usually intercropped with food crops.

[b] Includes a few cases where a portion of fallow land is planted to food. The respondent, however, describes the land as bush-fallow.

[c] Includes land planted to other trees, for example kola and palm oil.

[d] This definition excludes household members who are over 65 years and still working. A student is someone who reported being a "student" as his/her main or secondary occupation in the first round of data collection.

[e] This percentage distribution could be calculated only for those households that had at least one working member aged 15–65 years who was not a student.

However, years of schooling are higher in the child generation, and the gender gap has begun to close. We examine intergenerational changes in schooling in greater detail in Chapter 9.

Changes in Land Use

Table 8.5 shows the proportion of cocoa fields in the total land area in 1997 compared with land use patterns before acquisition. Cocoa trees have been planted in 45 percent of allocated parcels and 53 percent of inherited parcels,

TABLE 8.5 Distribution of land use before acquisition and in 1997, by land tenure type, in Ghana (percent)

	Before acquisition (percent of total land area)			In 1997	
				Cocoa (percent of total	Fallow (percent of shifting cultivation
Land tenure type	Forest	Cocoa[a]	Other[b]	land area)[a]	area)
Allocated family land	10.8	3.2	86.1	44.8	64.8
Inherited land	11.4	25.2	63.3	52.8	86.0
Appropriated village land	92.8	0.9	6.3	60.6	78.0
Purchased village land	87.2	1.9	10.9	59.2	77.4
Land received as a gift	17.9	5.6	76.5	63.3	72.4
Privately purchased	14.5	9.1	76.4	60.7	79.2
Acquired through renting	42.3	15.4	42.3	77.4	100.0
Currently renting	19.0	6.3	74.7	70.3	79.3
Caretaking	0.0	90.7	9.3	77.6	52.6
Borrowing from nonrelatives	0.0	0.0	100.0	10.3	30.8

[a] Both mature and young cocoa fields.

[b] Includes food production and fallow fields.

which suggests that the current land tenure status of parcels alone does not determine the incidence of tree planting. The proportion of cocoa fields in 1997, however, is somewhat higher in parcels on appropriated and purchased village land, land received as gift, and privately purchased land. The proportions are particularly high in the case of renting and caretaking, because tenants are assigned to plant trees and workers are employed to take care of mature trees. On land received as a gift, the proportion of cocoa fields prior to acquisition was very small; most of the parcels that were transferred as gifts were inherited and allocated family land used for shifting cultivation and were given by the father of the recipient, especially in Akan households (45 percent). This confirms that gifts are being used as a way to transfer land to designated heirs rather than let it revert to the matriclan after death. Land received as a gift is not completely planted to cocoa, because at present this is not required to receive permission from the extended family to transfer the land parcel as a gift.

Current Labor Use

In order to explore why land tenure institutions have evolved to strengthen women's and children's land rights, we need to understand the cocoa growing cycle and the relative contribution of women and children to labor in mature cocoa and young cocoa and in food crop cultivation. Data on gross revenue, paid-out costs, and the cash income (or net revenue) per hectare of mature co-coa fields, together with data on labor hours and the relative contribution of women and children within the household, are shown in Table 8.6. Paid-out costs, consisting mainly of payments to hired labor, account for roughly 15 per-cent of gross revenue. Chemical fertilizers were not applied and only a small number of farmers utilize pesticides, albeit in small amounts. Thus, credit for purchasing current inputs is not critically important in our sample villages. Cur-rent income, defined as total revenue less paid out costs, represents the return to land and family labor, which depends on management activities in the past as well as at present. There is no strong association between average age of trees and revenue, even though there appears to be some declining trend.

For mature cocoa, the major task is harvesting, which may start as early as October and is completed in March. Cocoa farming is highly labor intensive: assuming a 7-hour workday, the average labor input amounts to 70 days per hectare, which is high by any standard. There is no strong trend in labor re-quirements associated with aging of trees. The family labor of women and chil-dren, particularly the wife, accounts for about one-third of labor total inputs. The labor market for harvesting is relatively active and hired labor contributes roughly 40 percent of total labor inputs.[7]

Turning to food crop and young cocoa fields (Table 8.7), both gross rev-enue and income are much higher from pure food crop fields than from mixed crop fields, except in the first two years of cocoa cultivation. The relatively high revenue from young cocoa fields clearly demonstrates the advantage of cocoa and food intercropping. Paid-out costs and labor hours, however, are much higher in the initial year of cocoa cultivation, owing to the high labor require-ment of establishing cocoa fields. Although total labor input and income per hectare are higher in pure food cultivation than in cocoa cultivation, the inten-sity of cultivation is much higher in cocoa cultivation. Typically food crops are produced in two consecutive seasons under shifting cultivation and land is left fallow for nearly eight years on the average. Therefore, roughly speaking, the average net revenue per year in shifting cultivation is 90,000 cedis and the av-erage labor input is 220 hours, both of which are far smaller than the annual revenue and labor hours in cocoa cultivation.[8] Family labor contributed by women and children is especially important for food crops and for young co-

---

7. Wages, however, are substantially different among the 10 villages, even for the same tasks, which indicates segregation of local labor markets resulting from labor market imperfections or high transaction costs. Because of the noncomparability of wages, we did not impute the cost of family labor using prevailing wages to estimate profits.

8. Using the income data, Otsuka et al. (2001) estimate the internal rate of return to cocoa tree planting by assuming that (1) the opportunity cost of using land for cocoa cultivation is the in-come from food cultivation, which is carried out in the first two years and then followed by eight years of fallow, and (2) the termination year of cocoa cultivation is the twenty-fifth year. The esti-mated return is as high as 30 percent.

TABLE 8.6 Gross revenue, paid-out costs, income, and labor inputs per hectare at the field level for mature cocoa production, by average age of cocoa trees, in Ghana

Average age of cocoa trees	Number of observations	Gross revenue (thousand cedis/hectare)	Paid-out costs (thousand cedis/hectare)	Income[a] (thousand cedis/hectare)	Total labor hours per hectare	Percent women and children
4	15	402	62	340	460	27
5	21	636	56	580	669	34
6	19	534	59	475	695	36
7	14	515	36	479	314	32
8	19	658	49	609	602	35
9	18	488	43	445	627	30
10	9	674	37	637	468	33
11	12	531	69	462	571	34
12	12	674	126	548	451	32
13	10	341	43	298	458	34
14	6	497	26	471	398	23
15	7	338	47	291	503	34
16	7	564	60	504	582	35
17	6	319	39	280	446	43
18	7	412	51	361	362	29
19	5	408	88	320	432	25
20–24	23	343	58	285	378	27
25–29	13	396	37	359	328	22
30+	18	381	54	327	467	33

NOTE: The exchange rate was US$1 = 2050 cedis.

[a] Income is defined as gross revenue minus paid-out costs.

TABLE 8.7 Gross revenue, paid-out costs, income, and labor inputs per hectare for food crop production on young cocoa and pure food crop fields in Ghana

Type of crop and years of cultivation	Number of observations	Gross revenue (thousand cedis/hectare)	Paid-out costs (thousand cedis/hectare)	Income[a] (thousand cedis/hectare)	Total labor hours per hectare	Percent women and children	Average fallow period[b] (years)
Young cocoa							
Less than 1 year	52	253	79	174	1,401	41	15.60 (5)
1st year	40	489	32	457	894	51	9.96 (72)
2nd year	49	443	36	407	616	35	11.91 (54)
3rd year	28	271	66	205	687	32	7.87 (24)
4th year	14	207	46	161	274	15	7.86 (7)
Food crops	98	494	38	456	1,106	48	7.73 (56)

NOTE: The exchange rate was US$1 = 2050 cedis.

a Income is defined as gross revenue minus paid-out costs.

b We obtained information about fallow periods prior to the current cultivation from only a limited number of cases, shown in parentheses.

coa in its first two years, accounting for close to half. Labor contributed by women and children declines as cocoa matures, but still accounts for about one-third, as the data for mature cocoa indicate (Table 8.6).[9]

From the above observations, it seems reasonable to hypothesize that the land tenure system has evolved to grant women strong land rights in order to provide proper work incentives in cocoa cultivation. Are such changes also reflected in intergenerational land transfer patterns? We turn to this question in the next section.

The Sample Individuals

Distribution of Sample Individuals by Gender

In the inheritance and expenditure survey, the respondents were asked about the pre-marriage wealth (schooling and landownership) of their parents and in-laws, the schooling and land inheritance of their spouses, and the schooling of and proposed bequests to their children. Respondents were also asked about the characteristics of all of their siblings, such as their dates of birth, educational attainment, and areas of bequeathed (inherited) land, gift land, and allocated land received from their patrilineal and matrilineal relatives.

Table 8.8 presents summary statistics on the schooling of the parents', respondents', and children's generations. Only households for which parental information is complete are included in the analysis, and, for the respondents' generation, only children who survived to 21 years of age are included in the regression analysis. The age cutoff is imposed so that schooling decisions will have been completed in the respondents' generation, although, in practice, children leave school much earlier. The general level of schooling in the parents' generation is low—84 percent of fathers and 94 percent of mothers have never been to school—and fathers have more years of schooling than mothers. Among Akan households, fathers had 1.6 years of schooling, compared with 0.3 years for mothers; among non-Akans, fathers had 1.1 years and mothers 0.4 years. Schooling attainment has increased in the respondents' generation, but it is still low. The mean completed years of schooling for husbands in Akan areas is 7.2, and that of wives is 3.8; completed schooling is lower among non-Akans—4.6 years for husbands and 2.5 years for wives. The gender gap, however, seems to have narrowed in the respondents' generation, reflecting the tendency for women's schooling levels to increase through time. The gap be-

---

9. Unlike in our case studies in the Philippines and Sumatra, we did not collect household income data by source in Ghana. But in Chapter 9 we will estimate the cocoa and food incomes of a "typical" household—disaggregated by male and female plot managers—and compare them with average household expenditure, in order to assess the importance of returns to land and family labor as sources of income among farming households in Ghana.

TABLE 8.8 Demographic characteristics of sample individuals, by ethnic group of individual, in Ghana

| | Akan | | | | | Non-Akan | | | | |
| | | Year of birth | | Years of schooling | | | Year of birth | | Years of schooling | |
	N	Mean	Standard deviation	Mean	Standard deviation	N	Mean	Standard deviation	Mean	Standard deviation
Parents of head and resident spouses										
Father	301	n.a.	n.a.	1.6	3.5	86	n.a.	n.a.	1.1	3.1
Mother	315	n.a.	n.a.	0.3	1.5	74	n.a.	n.a.	0.4	1.8
Respondents and spouses										
Male	147	1951	14.3	7.2	4.3	38	1948	14.0	4.6	5.2
Female	153	1958	12.0	3.8	5.0	38	1957	11.3	2.5	3.7
Older children[a]										
Male	41	1967	6.7	8.6	4.9	14	1967	4.5	7.6	5.9
Female	35	1965	8.1	6.9	5.0	19	1965	6.1	7.1	4.6
Younger children[b]										
Male	58	1979	2.6	7.6	2.9	14	1978	3.6	6.9	3.7
Female	58	1980	2.4	6.4	3.2	19	1979	2.2	6.5	3.5
School-age children[c]										
Male	121	1982	6.9	5.3	3.6	21	1981	5.1	5.1	4.1
Female	141	1983	4.0	4.3	3.1	27	1981	4.2	5.5	3.4

NOTES: The table is based on the subsample of 197 intact households with information for all three generations. n.a. means not applicable.

[a] Children aged over 21 years.

[b] Children aged 13–21 years.

[c] Children aged 7–21 years.

tween males and females is narrower still in the children's generation, though it is larger for older children of the household head, and smaller for the younger children. Among Akans, for example, differences in schooling between male and female children are 1.7 years for those over 21 years of age, 1.2 years for those aged 13–21 years, and only 1.0 year for those aged 7–21 years.

Table 8.9 presents information on land owned by each generation. At the time of marriage or independent farming, Akan fathers had 8.3 hectares of land, in contrast to mothers, who had only 1.6 hectares. Non-Akan fathers had 5.1 hectares, and mothers had 0.6. This is consistent with our previous analysis of household patterns of land acquisition (Quisumbing et al. 2001a): men typically start farming independently by clearing forests, whereas women heads of household are less likely to acquire forestland. Non-Akans, who are migrants to the study area, held smaller areas because they did not have access to family land. In the respondents' generation, land sizes at the time of marriage had declined markedly for both males and females, and proposed sizes of land to be bestowed on children had likewise declined, although not by as much as the decline between the parents' and the respondents' generation. However, it is interesting to note that disparities in landholding sizes between males and females are growing smaller, especially for Akan households. Whereas fathers had five to nine times as much land as mothers in the parents' generation, husbands had

TABLE 8.9 Land owned, by gender and ethnic group, in Ghana (hectares)

Generation and gender	Akan			Non-Akan		
	N	Mean	Standard deviation	N	Mean	Standard deviation
Parents' generation[a]						
Males	209	8.3	10.7	60	5.1	6.7
Females	282	1.6	3.4	66	0.6	1.8
Respondents' generation[b]						
Males	725	2.3	5.2	197	1.0	2.3
Females	579	0.9	1.7	135	0.6	0.8
Children's generation[c]						
Males	169	1.3	1.9	36	1.5	2.1
Females	176	0.9	1.8	47	0.7	0.7

NOTE: The table is based on the subsample of 197 intact households with information for all three generations.

[a] Size of landholdings at the time of marriage or independence from family.

[b] Land received from family in the form of inheritance, allocation, or gift. The sample consists of respondents and their siblings who were either living at the time of the survey or deceased but aged 21 years or over at the time of death.

[c] Includes land jointly given by father and mother. Living children aged 7 years or over only; children of intact couples only.

only a little bit more than twice as much land as their wives. In the children's generation, Akan sons stand to inherit about 40 percent more than their sisters, though non-Akan sons will continue to inherit more than twice the land of their sisters. Thus, it seems clear that gender gaps in both land and schooling are narrowing through time, particularly among Akans, largely because of the increased importance of gifts in the face of growing population pressure on limited land resources.

Although the land transfer questionnaire distinguished four sources of matrilineal inheritance, in practice there were very few observations in each of the separate categories, so the analysis aggregated all the matrilineal categories.[10] The distribution of land received from both maternal and paternal kin is presented in Table 8.10 by mode of transfer—inheritance, allocation, and gift. The importance of each type of land transfer differs between Akans and non-Akans. For Akan males and females, inheritance and gifts are the most important means of land transfer. Although inherited areas may appear slightly larger than those received as gifts, the difference is not significant.[11] Inheritance is the predominant form of land transfer for non-Akans. Although gift transfers exist, they are not as important for transferring wealth directly to one's children as they are among Akans, for whom gifts are a means of subverting the matrilineal inheritance system. Taking all land categories together, males receive more land than females.

Finally, we examine the transfer or bestowal intentions of respondents in Table 8.11. Regardless of ethnicity, most land to be bestowed on children comes from the father, because mothers bring less land to the marriage. Whereas mothers' land tends to be more equally divided between sons and daughters, fathers bestow their land preferentially on sons.

The Scope of the Ghana Study

As in the Sumatra study, our basic hypothesis is that parents are concerned with both the efficiency and the equity of wealth transfers to their heirs. We have already seen that the land tenure system has evolved toward more individualized land rights systems. We hypothesize that the uterine matrilineal inheritance system has evolved to grant greater land rights to women because of the increased demand for women's labor in cocoa cultivation. We also expect that gender differences in land transfers will vary according to the mode of land transfer, whether inheritance, allocation, or gift. If parents do not practice discrimina-

---

10. Distinguishing among the different sources of matrilineal inheritance greatly improved survey response, however, because it was easier for respondents to identify a piece of land as coming from a specific relative, say a maternal uncle, than from a larger category called the matriclan.

11. It is, however, possible that respondents may not be able to distinguish between inherited land and land received as a gift. The key defining variable appears to be whether or not an *aseda* ceremony was performed; this thanksgiving ceremony almost always accompanies gift transfers.

TABLE 8.10 Average area of land received from family by respondents and siblings in Ghana (hectares/person)

	Akan head				Non-Akan head			
	Inherited	Allocated	Gift	Total	Inherited	Allocated	Gift	Total
Males in respondents' generation								
From mother and matrikin								
Mean	0.71	0.11	0.38	1.20	0.18	0.02	0.06	0.25
Standard deviation	3.64	0.65	1.45	4.00	1.01	0.30	0.41	1.12
N	725	725	725	725	197	197	197	197
From father								
Mean	0.57	0.07	0.47	1.11	0.59	0.02	0.13	0.73
Standard deviation	1.91	0.82	1.97	2.99	1.68	0.13	0.86	1.86
N	725	725	725	725	197	197	197	197
Total								
Mean	1.28	0.18	0.85	2.31	0.76	0.04	0.18	0.98
Standard deviation	4.27	1.04	2.51	5.17	2.06	0.33	1.00	2.26
N	725	725	725	725	197	197	197	197
Females in respondents' generation								
From mother and matrikin								
Mean	0.11	0.05	0.13	0.30	0.12	0.00	0.00	0.12
Standard deviation	0.55	0.57	0.73	1.27	0.36	0.00	0.00	0.36
N	579	579	579	579	131	131	131	131
From father								
Mean	0.36	0.02	0.20	0.59	0.43	0.00	0.00	0.43
Standard deviation	0.91	0.16	0.62	1.05	0.57	0.00	0.00	0.57
N	579	579	579	579	131	131	131	131
Total								
Mean	0.48	0.07	0.33	0.88	0.55	0.00	0.00	0.55
Standard deviation	1.11	0.59	0.98	1.66	0.80	0.00	0.00	0.80
N	579	579	579	579	131	131	131	131

NOTE: The sample consists of respondents and their siblings who were either living at the time of the survey or deceased but aged 21 years or over at time of death.

TABLE 8.11 Mean area of land to be bestowed on children aged 7 years or over, by ethnic group of parent (hectares)

	Akan father	Akan mother	Non-Akan father	Non-Akan mother
Son				
Mean	1.12	0.10	1.45	0.21
Standard deviation	1.80	0.30	1.80	0.35
N	159	169	47	36
Daughter				
Mean	0.77	0.10	0.80	0.20
Standard deviation	0.74	0.22	0.90	0.30
N	157	176	66	47

NOTE: The data pertain only to children from intact households. Land bestowal includes land already bequested. The proportion of children on whom some land has already been bestowed is 4 percent.

tion against daughters, we expect parental resources not to have a significant effect on land transfers to children of either gender. But if society or particular ethnic groups discriminate against women, we may observe allocations of family land biased against females in that ethnic group. Thus, although we cannot predict whether schooling investments in daughters and sons will adjust to equalize the total returns of sons and daughters from cocoa and food crop cultivation, we can examine the patterns of investment in both land and schooling. Chapter 9 aims to substantiate these arguments statistically, using regression analyses of the determinants of land inheritance and schooling and the determinants of agricultural incomes and household expenditures.

In Chapter 10, we will examine how the parallel changes in the inheritance system toward gender equality and in the land tenure system toward individualized ownership systems affect the equity of land distribution across households. We will also analyze patterns of household expenditures in order to test whether particular demographic groups are favored with respect to the allocation of household expenditures.

9 Gender Equity in Intergenerational Transfers of Cocoa Land and in Schooling

This chapter explores statistically the implications of the shift from communal to individualized tenure systems for the distribution of land and schooling between sons and daughters in western Ghana. Although traditional matrilineal inheritance rules deny landownership rights to women, women have increasingly acquired land through gifts and other means, thereby reducing the gender gap in landownership (Quisumbing et al. 2001b). The gender gap in schooling has also declined significantly over time, even though it persists. We attribute such changes to the declining trend of "social" discrimination as well as weak parental discrimination.

This chapter has five main sections. The first section describes the regression specification and identifies the determinants of land inheritance and schooling investments in the respondents' generation. The second section identifies the determinants of schooling investments and proposed land transfers in the children's generation. The third section examines the extent to which the gender gap is the result of social and parental "discrimination." The fourth section explores the determinants of household agricultural incomes and expenditures in order to assess the effects of gender differences in land inheritance and schooling. The last section summarizes major findings and draws conclusions.

Determinants of Wealth Transfers in the Respondents' Generation

Readers who are not interested in the technical details of statistical estimation may proceed directly to the "Summary of Findings" at the end of this section on page 208.[1]

Specification of Estimated Functions

Formally the specification of the transfer equations is the same as equation (6.1):

$$T^*_{ij} = \beta_0 + \beta_1 D + \beta_2 X_{cij} + \beta_3 X_{fj} + \beta_4 X_{mj}$$
$$+ \gamma_1 D X_{fj} + \gamma_2 D X_{mj} + \varepsilon_{ij}, \tag{9.1}$$

---

1. This section draws heavily on Quisumbing, Payongayong, and Otsuka (2001).

where $\mathbf{T}_{ij}^{*}$ is a vector of transfers $\mathbf{T}_{ij}^{*} = [E_{ij}^{*}, I_{ij}^{*}, G_{ij}^{*}, A_{ij}^{*}]$ and $E_{ij}^{*}, I_{ij}^{*}, G_{ij}^{*}, A_{ij}^{*}$ are levels of schooling and areas of inherited, gift, and allocated land, respectively, received by child i in family j. Regression parameters $\boldsymbol{\beta}_{k}$ and $\boldsymbol{\gamma}_{m}$ are vectors of coefficients for each type of transfer; $\mathbf{X}_{c}$ is a vector of child-specific characteristics such as birth year, number of brothers, number of sisters, a dummy for being a half-sibling (child of either parent from a previous union), and dummies for the eldest child; $\mathbf{X}_{f}$ and $\mathbf{X}_{m}$ are vectors of exogenous human and physical wealth of father and mother at the time of marriage, respectively; D is the daughter dummy; and ε_{ij} is the error term in each equation.[2]

We distinguish between inherited land, gift land, and temporarily allocated family land, partly because individual land rights in the three types of land are substantially different and partly because the influence of parents on each type of land transfer is likely to be different. Allocated land is usually fallow land controlled by the extended family, whereas inherited land was previously cultivated by a deceased family member. Allocated land is allocated by the extended family to the individual for his or her temporary use and thus rights are weaker than those on inherited land. How much such land is transferred is determined primarily by the decision of the extended family in accordance with traditional rules of land inheritance and allocation. Such traditional rules have been circumvented by gifts from living donors, which reward the efforts of wife and children to establish cocoa fields by granting strong landownership rights to them. Gift transfers are also made among the members of the extended family, and extended family members, who have shared interests in the same piece of land, need to approve gift transfers to designated recipients. Once the wife or children receive the gift land, however, they can bequeath it to heirs of their choice in the future. Thus, if there is any "social" discrimination against female children by the extended family, we expect to observe that daughters receive less family land that is not directly correlated with land owned by their father and mother. This implies that the daughter dummy would have negative coefficients in the land transfer regressions. By planting trees, parents can transfer their cultivated land directly to their children. Therefore, if there is any parental discrimination against female children, we expect to observe that

---

2. If parents trade off different types of transfers among children, error terms across transfer equations may be correlated. Since the regressors are identical in all the transfer equations, a systems estimator such as SUR (Seemingly Unrelated Regressions) could have improved efficiency. However, the dependent variables are censored and we are not aware of a tractable systems Tobit estimator, so we estimated the transfer equations using single-equation Tobit. In Chapter 3, we estimated a recursive simultaneous equation model in which education is estimated first, and its predicted values are then used in the land inheritance regression, which is then estimated as a Tobit. Estimating both functions simultaneously exploits the correlation between error terms in the two equations and provides additional evidence on whether or not schooling and land are viewed as substitutes by parents. Thus, although we can examine substitutability or complementarity between different types of transfers, unlike Filmer (1999) we do not have information with which to examine whether intergenerational transfers reinforce or compensate for innate ability.

interaction terms between parental landownership and the daughter dummy would have negative coefficients. We are also interested in the significance of the total effect on girls, which is the sum of the social and parental discrimination effects against female children.

In the case of schooling investments, it is not the extended family but parents who are decisionmakers. Thus, the concept of social discrimination applied to land transfers is not relevant. Yet, if returns to schooling are lower for women than for men owing to societal discrimination in farm and nonfarm jobs, its effect will be captured by the daughter dummy. There is also a possibility that parents discriminate against daughters autonomously, that is, independently from resource ownership. Parental discrimination associated with resource ownership will be captured by the interaction terms between the daughter dummy and landownership or schooling, to the extent that land and schooling accurately reflect the physical and human wealth of parents.

To account for the possibility that husband and wife do not have identical preferences regarding bestowals on children, an empirical specification consistent with a collective model of the household is used.[3] Thus, father's and mother's wealth at the time of marriage, which are exogenous to decisions made within marriage, enter separately into the regressions. Parental wealth consists of human capital, as proxied by years of schooling, and each parent's holdings of land at the time of marriage. Most land held at the time of the parents' marriage is either recently cleared forestland or food crop land that has been allocated by the extended family. Inheritance would have taken place later in the parents' life and gifts would not have been common when the parents of the respondents got married. We do not distinguish between each type of parental land in our analysis. We also include the number of brothers and sisters in the regression, to test whether sibling rivalry affects the allocation of land and schooling to children (Butcher and Case 1994; Garg and Morduch 1998a, 1998b; Morduch 2000).[4]

Similar to the discussion in Chapter 6, three tests of the unitary versus the collective model can be proposed. The first, $\beta_3 = \beta_4$, tests whether the effects of the same physical or human capital variables for father and mother on sons are significantly different from each other. If the null hypothesis is rejected, this leads to a rejection of the unitary model of household decisionmaking.[5] The

---

3. For a review of collective models of the household, see Haddad, Hoddinott, and Alderman (1997). This formulation draws on McElroy's (1990) specification of the Nash bargaining model and is similar to Thomas (1990, 1994).

4. The gender composition of the sib set is arguably endogenous, even if gender is randomly determined for the individual, because it depends on the choice of family size. The number of brothers and sisters could be correlated with unobserved parental characteristics that also affect the quantity-quality tradeoffs in fertility decisions. For an extensive discussion, see Rosenzweig and Wolpin (2000).

second, $\gamma_1 = \gamma_2$, tests whether parental resources have different impacts on girls relative to boys. A final test of the unitary model involves comparing the sum of the coefficient on the parental wealth variable and the coefficient on its relevant interaction term with child gender with the corresponding sum for the opposite-sex parent. This sum captures the total effect of the parental characteristic, and is the effect on daughters, in contrast to the effect on sons, which simply compares the coefficients on the wealth variables. If the sums are significantly different from each other, this is inconsistent with the unitary model.

Equation (9.1) is estimated both in levels and with family fixed effects. Since land transfers are subject to censoring (many children do not receive any land), a Tobit procedure is used for the land regressions in levels. However, it is possible that omitted family-level variables, such as the total land area controlled by the extended family, are correlated with regressors, and thus their estimated effects on transfers may be biased. For families with at least two children, the within-family allocation can be used as the source of variation in the sample from which to estimate intrahousehold differences in transfers.[6] A fixed-effects estimation procedure could control for these unobservables using family-specific dummy variables.[7] In this specific application, however, only the child's sex and birth year, the half-sibling and eldest dummies, the interaction between child sex and ethnic group, and the interaction between child sex and parent characteristics remain as explanatory variables. That is, the effects of variables that do not vary across children cannot be identified. Because Tobit is inconsistent in the presence of fixed effects, we use the Honoré (1992) least absolute deviations Tobit estimator, which is both consistent and asymptotically normal under suitable regularity conditions and assumes neither a particular parametric form nor homoskedasticity. For simplicity, we report only the level results in this chapter, because there are no crucial differences in the estimation results between the two methods.[8]

---

5. For example, Thomas (1990, 1994) finds that maternal education and nonlabor income have a bigger impact on the height of a daughter, relative to a son, and that paternal education has a bigger impact on a son, relative to a daughter.

6. Families with at least two children are included so that birth order and sex dummies are relevant in the family fixed-effects specification. The fixed-effects procedure eliminates selectivity bias because family size, which affects selection into the sample, is a family-specific variable (Pitt and Rosenzweig 1990).

7. That is, the observed transfer, T_{ij}, to child i in family j would be given by $T_{ij} = t_j + \beta X_{ij} + u_{ij}$, where the family-specific effect is a dummy variable, t_j, which is taken to be constant for a family (Hsiao 1986).

8. Since the dependent variable is censored in the land transfers equations, we used a fixed-effects Tobit estimator, because Honoré (1992) has shown that the ordinary Tobit estimator is inconsistent in the presence of fixed effects. This trimmed least-absolute-deviations estimator is preferred because it is both consistent and asymptotically normal under suitable regularity conditions and assumes neither a particular parametric form nor homoskedasticity.

Determinants of Land Inheritance and Schooling
Investments in the Respondents' Generation

Table 9.1 presents Tobit regression results on the determinants of land transfers and years of schooling for respondents and their siblings. We analyze four categories of land transfers: "permanent" transfers, consisting of the sum of inherited and gift land, inherited land, gift land, and "temporary" transfers or allocated land. Technically, allocated land should not be considered as a permanent intergenerational transfer, although land rights can be strengthened on such land through tree planting. We include allocated land in the discussion to illustrate the contrast in transfer patterns between land with strong and weak land rights.

The daughter dummy is negative and significant in the gift and allocated land regressions. Although it may seem that daughters may claim use rights on food crop fields through allocation from their matrilineal families, this method of transfer is biased "socially" against women. Thus, regardless of land use type, women are disadvantaged in land transfers. The non-Akan dummy is negative and significant in the permanent land transfer equation, reflecting greater difficulty of access to land by non-Akans, who tend to be migrants to the area. The interaction term between the daughter and non-Akan dummies is insignificant, suggesting the absence of stronger social discrimination against women in non-Akan communities.[9] As expected, half-siblings appear disadvantaged in land receipts. Interestingly, the number of brothers exerts a negative influence on all land received, whereas the number of sisters has a positive effect on gift land and on allocated land. This suggests that brothers, rather than sisters, compete for the family's land resources; this is consistent with other findings for Ghana on sibling rivalry (Garg and Morduch 1998a, 1998b; Filmer 1999). Although the positive effect of the number of sisters on gift land is not unexpected, it is difficult to interpret the positive effect on allocated land. Larger sizes of land owned by the father are positively associated with larger receipts of all land and inherited land by children. Judging from the negative and significant coefficient on the interaction term between the daughter dummy and father's land in the inheritance regression, as well as in the total permanent land transfer regression, sons seem to be favored, relative to daughters, by their father when he owns more land.

We pay special attention to the gift equation because gift transfers can be considered to be an institutional innovation, which makes it possible to transfer land to desired heirs. Gift transfers are less common among non-Akans, since there is no incentive to use inter vivos transfers to prevent one's wealth

---

9. The interaction term between the daughter dummy and the non-Akan dummy was not included in the gift land regression owing to nonconvergence. Upon examination of the data, we found that the incidence of gift transfers among non-Akans was so low that there were hardly any significant variations.

from being absorbed by the matriclan at the expense of one's own children. Gifts also seem to have become more prevalent over time, as indicated by the positive coefficient on birth year, which outweighs the negative effect of its squared term. Father's land is positively associated with gift transfers, whereas mother's land has a negative effect, possibly because the matriclan still has claims on her land. It may well be that the fathers, who can more easily receive permission to transfer land as gifts from their relatives, are more likely than the mothers to plant trees. It is worth emphasizing that the interaction terms between the daughter dummy and parental landownership are insignificant, which indicates the absence of parental discrimination against daughters with respect to gift transfers.

Gender disparities are more obvious in the schooling equation, where the daughter dummy is negative and highly significant. It is likely that daughters are subject to social discrimination in both land transfers and schooling investments. Schooling attainment does improve through time at a decelerating rate, as shown by the coefficients on birth year and its square. Both father's land and schooling exert a positive influence on child schooling completion, whereas mother's schooling has no effect. This is probably the result of the extremely low levels of schooling among women of this generation. The number of sisters has a positive and significant effect on own schooling attainment, a result consistent with those of Garg and Morduch (1998b) for Ghana.[10] To the extent that parental landownership and schooling represent parental wealth, the absence of significant effects of the interaction terms between the daughter dummy and parental land or schooling indicates the absence of parental discrimination associated with their wealth.

F-tests on coefficients suggest that the effects of paternal and maternal schooling are significantly different from each other in the inheritance and schooling equations, and that the coefficients on parental land are also different from each other in the total land and inheritance equations. This leads us to reject the unitary model of household behavior in Ghana; this is consistent with Doss's (1996a) findings.

Results from the family fixed-effects estimates, which are not shown here, are consistent with those in Table 9.1.[11] For example, even if family-level un-

---

10. Garg and Morduch (1998a) find predicted improvements of as much as 40 percent in anthropometric measures of children in Ghana when shifting from a scenario where all siblings are brothers to one in which all are sisters. Garg and Morduch (1998b) also find that predicted enrollments in secondary school are increased by more than 50 percent when shifting from an all-brothers to an all-sisters scenario, but they find negligible impacts on primary school enrollments. Filmer (1999) finds that the number of other males in the household reduces girls' years of schooling, but the number of other females does not affect boys' years of schooling.

11. The estimation sample for the fixed-effects estimates consists of families that report making the particular type of transfer to at least one child or in which at least one child has attended school.

TABLE 9.1 Determinants of schooling, land inheritance, and family land allocation among respondents and siblings: Tobit estimates

Variables	Inherited + gift land		Inherited land		Gift land		Allocated land		Schooling	
	Coefficient	t-statistic	Coefficient	t-statistic	Coefficient	t-statistic	Coefficient	t-statistic	Coefficient	t-statistic
Daughter dummy	-0.76	-1.17	0.36	0.48	-2.47	-3.44**	-2.95	-3.52**	-4.96	-7.49**
Non-Akan dummy	-2.55	-3.13**	-0.94	-1.01	-6.79	-5.67**	-1.44	-1.50	-1.16	-1.50
Daughter × non-Akan	0.99	0.95	0.38	0.33	n.a.	n.a.	-0.03	-0.02	-0.26	-0.24
Birth year	0.27	0.08	-4.42	-1.10	16.04	3.38**	1.86	0.44	27.18	6.68**
(Birth year/1,000) squared	-70.45	-0.08	1,126.33	1.09	-4096.50	-3.36**	-471.83	-0.43	-6,920.11	-6.62**
Half-sibling dummy	-1.92	-3.89**	-1.20	-2.06*	-2.90	-4.91**	-1.64	-2.81**	0.41	0.88
Number of brothers	-0.29	-2.91**	-0.06	-0.53	-0.57	-4.88**	0.05	0.39	-0.13	-1.27
Number of sisters	0.20	1.92	-0.07	-0.58	0.39	3.07**	0.27	2.25*	0.50	4.82**
Eldest dummy	0.52	0.76	0.56	0.69	0.66	0.87	0.47	0.57	0.45	0.63
Youngest dummy	-0.95	-1.27	-0.59	-0.68	-0.94	-1.13	0.12	0.14	-0.12	-0.17
Father's schooling	-0.02	-0.16	-0.13	-0.97	0.07	0.69	-0.08	-0.84	0.27	3.17**
Mother's schooling	-0.48	-2.00*	-1.81	-2.84**	-0.18	-0.79	0.06	0.29	-0.27	-1.37
Father's land	0.16	8.65**	0.16	7.41**	0.06	2.82**	-0.04	-1.36	0.06	2.91**
Mother's land	-0.16	-1.93	-0.08	-0.93	-0.40	-2.50*	0.10	1.22	0.04	0.61
Daughter × father's schooling	0.02	0.15	-0.05	-0.22	0.15	0.92	0.38	2.30*	0.05	0.38
Daughter × mother's schooling	-0.01	-0.02	1.21	1.37	-0.40	-0.80	-0.41	-0.84	0.46	1.29
Daughter × father's land	-0.09	-2.60*	-0.13	-2.97**	0.02	0.56	0.04	0.69	-0.02	-0.50
Daughter × mother's land	0.14	1.15	0.07	0.51	0.31	1.54	-0.10	-0.67	0.01	0.11
Constant	-261.45	-0.08	4,321.36	1.11	-15,694.96	-3.39**	-1,845.01	-0.44	-26,691.73	-6.73**

F-tests "son effects" (p-value)									
Father's schooling = mother's schooling	2.39	(.12)	6.24	(.01)**	0.75	(.39)	0.29	(.59)	4.85	(.03)*
Father's land = mother's land	13.75	(.00)**	6.86	(.01)**	7.79	(.01)**	2.28	(.13)	0.08	(.78)
F-tests "daughters relative to sons" (p-value)									
Daughter × father's schooling = daughter × mother's schooling	0.00	(.95)	1.71	(.19)	0.88	(.35)	1.88	(.17)	0.84	(.36)
Daughter × father's land = daughter × mother's land	3.11	0.08	1.77	0.18	1.78	0.18	0.61	0.43	0.07	0.79
F-tests "daughter effects" (p-value)									
Schooling plus interaction terms equal	1.01	(.32)	0.38	(.54)	2.36	(.13)	1.56	(.21)	0.12	(.73)
Land plus interaction terms equal	0.67	(.41)	0.15	(.70)	1.31	(.25)	0.00	(1.00)	0.01	(.91)
Number of observations	1,270		1,270		1,270		1,270		1,270	
χ^2 statistic	191.25		196.10		237.91		133.94		465.60	
p-value	.00		.00		.00		.00		.00	
Number of censored observations	656		830		1,038		1,073		552	
Number of uncensored observations	614		440		232		197		718	

NOTES: Individuals who lived to at least age 21, whether living or dead at time of interview, are included. Village dummies are included but coefficients are not reported.
* indicates significance at the 5 percent level; ** at the 1 percent level.

observables are controlled for, we still observe that daughters do worse in permanent land transfer only with respect to gifts. Half-siblings also fare worse generally with respect to permanent land transfers. However, none of the coefficients in the allocated land equation is significant in the fixed-effects specification, perhaps because decisions on land allocations are made not by the biological parents but by the extended family. Moreover, slightly stronger indications of parental gender preference emerge in the inherited land equation. Mothers with more land and schooling seem to favor daughters in land inheritance. This type of land transfer is possible, because land owned by mothers is often land that they have received as a gift and for which they have strong transfer rights. Fathers with more land favor sons, which is consistent with other studies on parental gender preference (Thomas 1994).[12] The results discussed above provide additional evidence against the unitary model of the household. Although discrimination against daughters in land transfers does not seem pervasive, daughters are clearly disadvantaged with respect to schooling attainment. We return to an analysis of changes in total gender discrimination after completing the analysis of intergenerational transfers to the children's generation.

Summary of Findings

1. Daughters receive significantly less gift and allocated land, even if they may claim use rights on food crop fields from their matrilineal families. Brothers, rather than sisters, compete for the family's land resources.
2. Although larger sizes of land owned by the father increase transfers to all children, sons are favored in land inheritance when the father owns more land.
3. Gift transfers are more prevalent among Akans, and seem to have increased through time. There is no parental discrimination against daughters with respect to gift transfers.

Determinants of Wealth Transfer in the Children's Generation

Readers who are not interested in the technical details of statistical estimation may proceed directly to the "Summary of Findings" at the end of this section on page 212.

We now examine potential bequest and schooling decisions by respondents and their wives. Table 9.2 shows Tobit estimates of the determinants of expected land transfer and schooling of the respondent's children, disaggregated by source. This type of land transfer corresponds loosely to the "permanent" land transfer category in the previous generation, since respondents no longer dis-

---

12. Thomas (1994) finds that in three countries—the United States, Brazil, and Ghana—the education level of the mother has a larger effect on a daughter's height, and the education of the father has a larger effect on a son's height.

tinguish between "inheritance" and "gifts" in their plans to transfer land to their children. Temporarily allocated family land is not included in the analysis because there is no long-term plan for such short-term, temporary land transfers. Nor did we include land transfer from relatives, because it is not in practice feasible to obtain data on proposed transfers from a large number of relatives. Thus, social discrimination is expected to appear, to the extent that parental land will be transferred to other members of the extended family. Although the omission of the data on land transfer from relatives may impart some bias in our regression analysis, we believe that our data-collection methodology will be useful to examine possible changes in gender differences in land transfers from parents to their children. The sample is restricted to respondents' children who are aged 7 years and over and who were alive at the time of the survey.

We find that daughters are clearly disadvantaged with respect to proposed bestowals of land from both parents. Transfers to daughters from their fathers appear to be smaller in non-Akan households, judging from the negative and significant coefficient on the interaction term between the daughter and Akan dummies. This is consistent with our contention that the evolution of the land tenure system among Akans favors wives and daughters. The number of brothers has negative and significant coefficients, suggesting that brothers continue to compete for the family's land, but the number of sisters does not seem to have such an effect. These results are consistent with the tradition of matrilineal inheritance. The negative effect of being a daughter is counteracted by the positive effects of the interaction term with father's schooling and mother's land, although this result is not robust to the inclusion of fixed effects (see below). In other words, there seems to be some discrimination by less educated fathers and mothers with less land relative to their more endowed counterparts. It seems clear, however, that there is less parental discrimination against daughters in the children's generation.

F-tests on coefficients show that the coefficients on parents' land and their interaction with the daughter dummy are significantly different from each other in the equation for land from the father. Recall that the test for the equality of the interaction terms with child gender is whether parents treat daughters differently than sons. As far as land from the father is concerned, mothers and fathers have very different preferences regarding bestowals on daughters relative to sons: whereas fathers with more land do not significantly discriminate against girls, mothers with more land strongly favor girls. The rejection of the unitary model is likely to be stronger for land coming from the father, in part because fathers are the most important source of land and thus it is more likely that parents would be bargaining over this significant source of land rather than the smaller amounts coming from the mother. The coefficients on father's and mother's schooling are also significantly different from each other in the equation for land from both parents. These results indicate that the unitary model of the household can be rejected as far as land bestowal decisions are concerned.

TABLE 9.2 Determinants of expected land transfers to and schooling of respondents' children: Tobit estimates

| | Levels estimates | | | | | | | |
| | Land from father | | Land from mother | | Land from both parents | | Years of schooling | |
Variables	Coefficient	t-statistic	Coefficient	t-statistic	Coefficient	t-statistic	Coefficient	t-statistic
Daughter dummy	-0.327	-1.700	-0.067	-0.370	-0.466	-2.460*	-2.130	-3.480**
Non-Akan dummy	0.353	1.580	-0.334	-1.590	-0.149	-0.800	-0.538	-0.730
Daughter × non-Akan	-0.824	-3.040**	0.267	1.110			-0.066	-0.070
Age	0.007	0.270	0.025	1.170	0.018	0.650	0.801	9.790**
Age squared	0.000	0.770	0.000	-0.910	0.000	0.330	-0.013	-7.840**
Number of brothers	-0.055	-1.540	-0.083	-2.720**	-0.110	-2.860**	0.076	0.650
Number of sisters	-0.023	-0.740	0.008	0.280	-0.016	-0.480	-0.092	-0.910
Father's schooling	-0.060	-3.440**	-0.001	-0.080	-0.076	-4.000**	-0.030	-0.540
Mother's schooling	-0.004	-0.190	0.000	0.030	-0.002	-0.110	-0.028	-0.450
Father's land	0.016	2.640**	0.007	0.830	0.017	2.570*	0.025	1.240
Mother's land	-0.001	-0.030	0.026	0.950	0.006	0.160	0.049	0.410
Daughter × father's schooling	0.050	2.100*	0.013	0.630	0.061	2.390*	0.102	1.340
Daughter × mother's schooling	-0.029	-1.070	0.013	0.600	-0.025	-0.860	0.087	1.010
Daughter × father's land	-0.006	-0.750	0.000	0.020	-0.005	-0.590	-0.006	-0.230
Daughter × mother's land	0.092	2.090*	0.005	0.160	0.062	1.330	-0.144	-0.960
Constant	0.738	2.240*	-0.263	-0.950	1.083	3.020*	-3.348	-3.120*

F-tests "son effects" (p-value)

Father's schooling = mother's schooling	3.35 (.07)	0.00 (.95)	4.88 (.03)*	0.00 (.98)
Father's land = mother's land	0.21 (.65)	0.34 (.56)	0.07 (.79)	0.04 (.85)

F-tests "daughters relative to sons" (p-value)

Daughter × father's schooling = daughter × mother's schooling	3.37 (.07)	0.00 (.98)	3.47 (.06)	0.01 (.91)
Daughter × father's land = daughter × mother's land	4.31 (.04)*	0.02 (.90)	1.79 (.18)	0.73 (.39)

F-tests "daughter effects" (p-value)

Schooling plus interaction terms equal	0.50 (.48)	0.01 (.93)	0.14 (.71)	0.02 (.90)
Land plus interaction terms equal	5.70 (.02)*	0.51 (.48)	2.36 (.13)	0.96 (.33)

Number of observations	509	506	506	513
χ^2 statistic	175.02	57.2	150.34	216.86
p-value	.00	.00	.00	.00
Number of censored observations	92	373	63	54
Number of uncensored observations	417	133	443	459

NOTES: Living children aged 7 years and over are analyzed. Village dummies are included but coefficients are not reported. * indicates significance at the 5 percent level; ** at the 1 percent level.

The most striking result from the fixed-effects estimates (not reported here) is the insignificance of the interaction terms between the daughter dummy and parental wealth variables. Such results support the hypothesis that parents are egalitarian with respect to the transfer of their own wealth. The results also show that daughters within the Akan ethnic group are no longer subject to social discrimination in land transfers but they still suffer with respect to schooling, suggesting that different social factors affect land transfers and schooling investments. The results indicate in addition that the discrimination in land transfers against daughters persists in non-Akan families, although the coefficients are weakly significant.

Finally, we turn to the determinants of schooling investments in children aged 7 years and over. To take into account younger children's incomplete schooling decisions, we control for the correlation between age and schooling completion by including linear and quadratic terms in child age. We deal with censoring in schooling attainment by using a Tobit estimator, since a non-negligible proportion of children have never attended school.[13] Levels estimates of schooling attainment point to gender disparities in schooling: girls do worse than boys in terms of years of schooling. This result is consistent with the fixed-effects estimates: daughters consistently get fewer years of schooling compared with their brothers. However, the coefficient on the daughter dummy is much smaller in the regression of the children's generation than in the respondents' generation, indicating the declining gender gap in schooling over the two generations.

Summary of Findings

1. Daughters in the children's generation continue to be disadvantaged with respect to land bestowals, especially in non-Akan households. However, it appears that the Akan inheritance system has evolved to be less discriminatory against girls in the younger generation, even though some discrimination persists.
2. There is no significant parental discrimination against girls in land transfers in the children's generation.
3. Girls continue to be worse off with respect to schooling, although the gender gap has narrowed.

Changing Patterns of Gender Discrimination

To test whether patterns of overall gender discrimination have changed across generations rigorously, we examine changes in the total discrimination effect, which consists of the sum of social and parental discrimination. We examine the sources of discrimination by differentiating the estimated transfer equation

---

13. In this sample, 11 percent of children aged 7 years and older had never attended school.

with respect to the daughter dummy, evaluating the interaction terms at the means for the parental resource variables, and testing whether the total effect is equal to zero. Using the estimation results shown in Tables 9.1 and 9.2, we present the results separately for each type of transfer and for each generation in Tables 9.3 and 9.4.

In the respondents' generation, there is significant bias against women in total land transfer through inheritance and gift among families of Akan ethnicity (Table 9.3). This is largely owing to the strong bias against women in gift transfers, which arises primarily from strong social discrimination (see Table 9.1). In contrast, total discrimination in land transfers among non-Akans can be found only for gift transfers, which may be the result of the relatively small sample size (see Table 8.8). Strong gender bias is observed in schooling for both ethnic groups. This can be attributed primarily to strong social discrimination against daughters, according to the estimation results in Table 9.1.

In the generation of the respondents' children (Table 9.4), it is remarkable to find no significant discrimination against females among Akans in land transfers, despite the significantly negative effect of the daughter dummy in the total land transfer regressions reported in Table 9.2. However, we now clearly observe strong total discrimination among non-Akans with respect to land from the father. It may well be that social discrimination against women persists in non-Akan patrilineal communities, where men generally dominate not only landownership but also decisions about farming and household affairs. Lastly, it must be pointed out that total discrimination against daughters persists in schooling for both Akans and non-Akans. Yet, it is important to note that F-values are much smaller for the children's generation than for the respondents' generation, which reflects the declining gender gap in schooling over time.

The persistence of gender discrimination in schooling is consistent with Filmer's (1999) findings using a large nationally representative dataset from Ghana. He finds that parents tend to compensate for girls' innate cognitive and health endowments by seeking more preventive care for sicklier daughters, but providing less schooling for girls with higher cognitive endowments. In contrast, boys' cognitive endowments are reinforced with more schooling and preventive care. Since the marginal biological returns to investment are constant across genders, Filmer argues that the greater investment in boys is a response to higher pecuniary returns to males in the Ghanaian economy.

Summary of Findings

1. There is strong discrimination against daughters in gift and schooling for both Akans and non-Akans in the respondents' generation. However, discrimination with respect to land transfers has disappeared among Akans in the children's generation.
2. Discrimination against girls in schooling investments persists in the children's generation, although it becomes weaker.

TABLE 9.3 Tests for gender discrimination in Ghana: Respondents' generation

Total gender effects	Inherited + gift		Inherited land		Gift		Schooling	
	F-value	p-value	F-value	p-value	F-value	p-value	F-value	p-value
For Akans	7.35	.01**	0.47	.49	8.15	.00**	99.43	.00**
For non-Akans	0.26	.61	0.00	.96	12.60	.00**	29.20	.00**

NOTES: Gender effects are evaluated at means of respective ethnic groups for Akans and non-Akans. Coefficients from levels regressions are used. * indicates significance at the 5 percent level; ** at the 1 percent level.

TABLE 9.4 Tests for gender discrimination in Ghana: Children's generation

Total gender effects	Land from father		Land from mother		Land from both		Schooling	
	F-value	p-value	F-value	p-value	F-value	p-value	F-value	p-value
For Akans	0.99	.32	0.63	.43	2.12	.15	9.88	.00**
For non-Akans	12.67	.00**	1.99	.16	0.90	.34	5.99	.01**

NOTES: Gender effects are evaluated at means of respective ethnic groups for Akans and non-Akans. Coefficients from levels regressions are used. * indicates significance at the 5 percent level; ** at the 1 percent level.

Determinants of Household Income and Expenditures

Readers who are not interested in the technical details of statistical estimation may proceed directly to the "Summary of Findings" at the end of this section on page 223.

Estimation of Agricultural Income Functions

Agricultural income is obtained from two sources: mature cocoa and food crop cultivation on young cocoa and pure food crop fields. Because of technical differences in the growing cycle of young cocoa and mature cocoa (discussed in Chapter 8), most importantly the intercropping of young cocoa with food crops, we estimate agricultural income functions separately for mature cocoa and food crop cultivation. We present agricultural income regressions for mature cocoa in Table 9.5, using both levels and fixed-effects estimates. In addition to the land tenure dummies, characteristics of the parcel at acquisition, and current field characteristics found in the tree-planting and fallow choice regressions, we include the age of trees and the number of kola, oil palm, and other trees on the parcel. Note that generally only a small number of trees are grown on cocoa fields and that our income data do not include income from other trees; this can safely be assumed to be marginal according to our own observations. It is possible that the presence of other trees may affect labor use, as well as income from cocoa, if overcrowding causes competition among different tree species.

According to the estimation results in Table 9.5, no land tenure variables are significant in the cocoa income functions. This finding is robust to the choice of estimation method and is supported by a joint test of the significance of the land tenure dummies. These results support the hypothesis that the management intensity of cocoa fields tends to be equalized owing to the establishment of secure land rights after tree planting, regardless of the manner of land acquisition. This is consistent with the findings reported in Chapter 6 for Sumatra and in a recent study of commercial tree planting in Uganda (Place and Otsuka 2002). Although it appears that net revenue is lower on woman-owned parcels, this finding is not robust to the inclusion of household fixed effects.

We perform a similar analysis for food crop production on young cocoa and pure crop fields. According to Table 8.7, gross revenue, as well as income, from pure food crop fields is much higher than that from mixed-crop fields, except in the first two years of cocoa cultivation. The relatively high income from young cocoa fields clearly demonstrates the advantage of cocoa and food intercropping. Paid-out costs and labor hours, however, are much higher in the initial year of cocoa cultivation, owing to the high labor requirement of establishing cocoa fields. Although total labor input and net revenue per hectare are higher in pure food cultivation than in cocoa cultivation (see Tables 8.6 and 8.7), the intensity of cultivation is much higher in cocoa cultivation.

TABLE 9.5 Determinants of agricultural income per hectare from mature cocoa production at the field level

Variables	Levels regressions with robust standard errors		Fixed-effects estimates	
	Coefficient	t-statistic	Coefficient	t-statistic
Current field characteristics				
Distance to field	−16.24	−1.18	−21.57	−0.47
Field size (hectares)	−51.19	−2.53*	3.77	0.08
Years since acquisition	−11.39	−0.92	68.22	2.39*
Years since acquisition squared	0.26	1.25	−1.14	−1.88
Woman-owned field	−124.49	−2.02*	−65.29	−0.51
Schooling of field owner	−9.14	−0.49	−22.10	−0.57
Number of kola trees per hectare	1.71	0.56	16.33	1.27
Number of oil palm trees per hectare	1.31	0.53	−2.64	−0.11
Number of other trees per hectare	17.48	1.55	22.40	1.27
Characteristics of parcel at acquisition				
Dummy for forest	−2.76	−0.04	−430.65	−1.84
Dummy for cocoa	153.50	1.36	573.55	2.27*
Tree characteristics				
Amazonia dummy	36.94	0.41	−278.16	−0.93
Hybrid dummy	34.45	0.29	−209.98	−0.52
Average age of trees	−0.63	−0.05	−13.19	−0.50
Age of trees squared	−0.13	−0.43	0.07	0.13
Land tenure dummies				
Allocated and matrilineal	91.56	0.52	243.14	0.49
Land received as gift	100.71	0.52	350.82	0.83
Patrilineal gift	57.10	0.17	420.89	0.60
Appropriated village land	25.58	0.14	734.71	1.29
Purchased village land	106.36	0.51	92.86	0.17
Privately purchased	−187.38	−0.58	[Dropped]	
Rented in	−75.93	−0.48	369.99	0.84
Ownership through renting	−108.17	−0.52	853.41	1.56
Caretaker	−241.42	−1.72	−36.27	−0.07
Household characteristics				
Gender of head (1 = male)	−178.76	−1.27		
Age of head (years)	−6.88	−1.83		
Schooling of head (years)	−6.24	−0.38		
Patrilineal household	108.92	1.16		
Total landholdings (hectares)	10.94	1.46		
Number of adult males in household[a]	30.09	1.32		
Number of adult females in household[a]	−6.36	−0.23		

(continued)

TABLE 9.5 *Continued*

	Levels regressions with robust standard errors		Fixed-effects estimates	
Variables	Coefficient	*t*-statistic	Coefficient	*t*-statistic
Constant	937.83	3.39**	−19.81	−0.03
R^2	.23			
F-test (*p*-value)			1.25	(.28)
F-test: Land tenure dummies = 0 (*p*-value)	1.35	(.22)	0.85	(.57)
Breusch–Pagan Lagrange multiplier test (*p*-value)			1.92	(.17)
Hausman specification test (*p*-value)			21.46	(.55)
Number of observations	241		112	

NOTES: Dummies for allocated patrilineal land, borrowing, and inherited patrilineal land were dropped owing to collinearity with the fixed effects. * indicates significance at the 5 percent level; ** at the 1 percent level.

[a] Adults comprise those aged 15–65 years and those older than 65 who list their main occupation as farming.

In order to identify the effects of land tenure institutions on income and total labor use in young cocoa and pure food crop fields, we estimated agricultural income functions per hectare using levels estimates and household-level fixed-effects and random-effects models. Again, fixed effects are found to be the preferred specification.[14] Because cocoa is intercropped with a variety of food crops in different combinations, we included the proportion of area planted to each of the food crops present in the field (for example, the proportion devoted to cocoyam in 1997) as well as their interactions with a dummy variable indicating that young cocoa is grown in the field. We also included dummy variables for the age of the cocoa trees, with trees less than 1 year old as the reference category. Since 34 percent of the sampled food crop fields have a female cultivator other than the male or female manager, we include a dummy variable for the presence of another female cultivator or field manager.

The results, which are reported in Table 9.6, are very similar to those for mature cocoa fields. Income per hectare is not significantly different in fields under different land tenure regimes, and we cannot reject the hypothesis that the land tenure effects are jointly equal to zero. This suggests that once the household's "stock" of land under different land tenure institutions is controlled

---

14. Although Breusch–Pagan Lagrange multiplier tests show that unobserved heterogeneity is important, in the net revenue regressions the random-effects estimate $\sigma_u = 0$ degenerates to pooled OLS, making the Hausman test inappropriate. For the labor use regressions, the Hausman test indicates that fixed effects is the preferred specification. We thus present the fixed-effects results.

TABLE 9.6 Determinants of agricultural income per hectare from young cocoa and pure food crop fields

Variables	Levels estimates		Fixed-effects estimates	
	Coefficient	t-statistic	Coefficient	t-statistic
Current field characteristics				
One-year-old cocoa dummy	127.24	1.02	300.39	1.01
Two-year-old cocoa dummy	193.93	1.23	−136.44	−0.42
Three-year-old cocoa dummy	33.42	0.23	25.45	0.06
Four-year-old cocoa dummy	−41.14	−0.28	160.40	0.45
Distance to field	18.91	0.66	2.31	0.02
Field size (hectares)	464.68	1.12	1006.42	0.84
Years since acquisition	−11.26	−1.75	−20.08	−0.70
Years since acquisition squared	0.21	1.91	0.63	1.11
Woman-owned field	59.06	0.66	47.75	0.24
Schooling of field owner	−4.89	−0.22	−37.45	−0.52
Presence of other female cultivator	84.30	1.03	−155.15	−0.49
Number of kola trees per hectare	−2.00	−0.65	−14.04	−1.58
Number of oil palm trees per hectare	0.56	0.22	−1.25	−0.36
Number of other trees per hectare	−4.57	−0.83	−11.39	−0.73
Characteristics of parcel at acquisition				
Dummy for forest	−75.90	−0.93	476.49	0.64
Dummy for cocoa	−103.09	−1.33	166.40	0.34
Land tenure dummies				
Allocated and patrilineal	−4.03	−0.01	−512.29	−0.32
Inherited and patrilineal	−357.59	−1.83	−923.43	−0.76
Allocated and matrilineal	−232.70	−1.93	−553.05	−0.70
Land received as gift	−83.17	−0.73	−314.59	−0.38
Patrilineal gift	−218.81	−1.38	478.81	0.60
Appropriated village land	−39.54	−0.23	−2248.33	−1.38
Purchased village land	323.78	1.86	638.73	0.49
Privately purchased	−231.00	−1.52	−35.54	−0.04
Rented in	−79.09	−0.64	−120.39	−0.14
Ownership through renting	19.72	0.09	[Dropped]	
Caretaker	222.81	0.64	[Dropped]	
Borrowed from nonrelatives	134.77	0.73	−175.19	−0.20
Household characteristics				
Gender of head (1 = male)	−0.55	−0.19		
Age of head (years)	162.72	0.87		
Schooling of head (years)	−0.76	−0.03		
Total landholdings (hectares)	−3.74	−1.49		
Patrilineal household	6.68	0.06		
Number of adult males in household[a]	11.24	0.48		

(continued)

TABLE 9.6 *Continued*

Variables	Levels estimates		Fixed-effects estimates	
	Coefficient	*t*-statistic	Coefficient	*t*-statistic
Number of adult females in household[a]	−7.25	−0.29		
Constant	480.73	2.04**	873.25	0.85
R^2	.32			
F-test (*p*-value)			0.94	(.59)
F-test: Land tenure dummies = 0 (*p*-value)	3.80	(.00)**	0.53	(.88)
Breusch–Pagan Lagrange multiplier test (*p*-value)			2.86	(.09)
Hausman specification test (*p*-value)			Not estimated[b]	
Number of observations	273		154	

NOTES: Dummies for allocated patrilineal land, borrowing, and inherited patrilineal land were dropped owing to collinearity with the fixed effects. * indicates significance at the 5 percent level; ** at the 1 percent level.

[a] Adults comprise those aged 15–65 years and those older than 65 who list their main occupation as farming.

[b] The estimate of $\sigma_u = 0$, the random-effects estimator, degenerated to pooled OLS, so the Hausman test is not valid.

for—as in the fixed-effects estimates—profitability across plots is equalized within the household. These findings are consistent with those of Place and Hazell (1993), Place and Otsuka (2001b), and Suyanto, Tomich, and Otsuka (2001a, 2001b).[15] There are no significant differences in income per hectare depending on whether or not a field is managed by a woman, which indicates that the transfer of land to women through gifts has improved gender equity without sacrificing production efficiency.

Estimation of Per Capita Expenditure Functions

We would ideally want to examine the effect of different landownership and schooling investments on total household income, but we do not have complete income data covering both agricultural and nonfarm income sources. Our data refer only to income from farm production of mature cocoa and from young co-

---

15. Although unreported in this study, the factors that significantly affect labor use are found to be the tree age dummies. Relative to trees less than 1 year old (the excluded category), labor use per hectare in succeeding years is significantly less. Given that a major proportion of labor input into young cocoa cultivation is provided by women and children, it is not surprising that gift transactions have evolved to increase their incentive to provide labor in establishing cocoa.

coa and food crops. Thus, we use household expenditure as our dependent variable because it is a good proxy for household permanent income. We use expenditure per capita to adjust for possible effects of household size. To ensure that the estimation sample corresponds closely to that used in the inheritance regressions, we restrict the estimation sample to households with one male head and one coresident wife. Regression results are presented in Table 9.7.

Land resources are a positive and significant determinant of per capita expenditure; the estimated coefficient of 0.25 implies that a 1 percent increase in total cultivated land results in a 0.25 percent increase in per capita expenditure, suggesting that family-owned resources other than land significantly contribute to household income. The ratio of cocoa land in the household's total landholdings is also positive and significant. This is expected because cocoa land brings in more income than food crop land. As may be expected, household size has a negative and significant effect on per capita expenditure. The average years of schooling of male working members contribute positively and significantly to expenditures per capita, reflecting considerable returns to male education in these sites. Considering that schooling does not have significant effects on agricultural incomes (see Tables 9.5 and 9.6), this result suggests that men's schooling significantly affects their nonfarm earnings. However, the coefficient on the average years of schooling of female working members is negative, though insignificant, which strongly indicates that returns to female education are low, possibly owing to social discrimination in nonfarm jobs. None of the dummies for the age composition of the labor force is significant. In addition, tenants have lower per capita expenditures than pure owners, although this result is significant only at the 10 percent level.

*Implications of the Distribution of Land and Education
between Men and Women*

To investigate whether or not a redistribution of land and human capital would have significant effects on male and female agricultural incomes as well as on household per capita expenditures, we conducted several simulation exercises using the coefficients estimated from the agricultural income and per capita expenditure functions (Table 9.8). First, we predicted the baseline agricultural income of a "typical" household for mature cocoa and food cultivation, using the coefficients from the levels estimates in Tables 9.5 and 9.6 and the average values of the existing explanatory variables for male and female field managers. The baseline scenario shows that males earn significantly higher agricultural incomes from both mature and young cocoa; this is mostly owing to the larger areas cultivated rather than to differences in agricultural income per hectare. It is also clear from the large difference between total agricultural income and household expenditure that households in our Ghana sites earn a considerable amount of nonfarm income, even though we failed to collect nonfarm income data. Such large differences may also be explained partly by negative savings.

TABLE 9.7 Determinants of log per capita expenditures in Ghana

Variables	Coefficients
Constant	14.39**
	(44.09)
Log farm size	0.25**
	(3.98)
Ratio of cocoa area	0.004*
	(2.05)
Log household size	−0.92**
	(−9.54)
Ratio of female workers	−0.12
	(−0.36)
Average years of schooling of	
Male working members	0.02*
	(2.55)
Female working members	−0.00
	(0.10)
Ratio of working members	
Aged 26–35	0.13
	(0.97)
Aged 36–45	0.02
	(0.14)
Aged 46–55	0.20
	(0.95)
Aged 56–65	−0.30
	(−0.78)
Akan dummy	−0.13
	(−1.22)
Tenant dummy	−0.28
	(−1.69)
Caretaker dummy	−0.09
	(−0.57)
Owner–tenant dummy	−0.07
	(−0.76)
Owner–caretaker dummy	−0.16
	(−1.27)
Owner–caretaker–tenant dummy	−0.06
	(−0.50)
R^2	.46
F-statistic (p-value)	6.73 (.00)**
Number of observations	145

NOTES: Numbers in parentheses are asymptotic t-statistics; * indicates significance at the 5 percent level; ** at the 1 percent level, two-tailed t-test.

TABLE 9.8 Simulation of the effects of changing the distribution of land and schooling between men and women in Ghana

				Difference from baseline	
	Men	Women	Difference	Men	Women
Baseline (1,000 cedis)					
Net income from young cocoa and food crops	506.76	260.83	245.93*		
	(55.17)	(62.39)	(117.827)		
Net income from mature cocoa	1,678.86	604.19	1,074.67**		
	(171.36)	(84.38)	(380.06)		
Total household expenditures		4,095.16			
		(9,045.00)			
Effect of giving same education to men and women					
Net income from young cocoa and food crops	510.30	235.92	274.38*	3.54	−24.90
	(55.07)	(63.23)	(117.71)	(51.50)	(35.64)
Net income from mature cocoa	1,678.08	534.41	1,143.67**	−0.78	−69.78
	(176.86)	(73.84)	(391.71)	(270.0)	(81.82)
Total household expenditures		3,870.95			−224.21
		(771.46)			(462.54)
Effect of giving same land to men and women					
Net income from young cocoa and food crops	386.46	419.83	−33.36	−120.29	159.00
	(26.56)	(43.64)	(58.74)	(730.81)	(407.97)
Net income from mature cocoa	852.10	608.82	243.28**	−826.76	4.63
	(27.89)	(51.85)	(65.83)	(2,185.53)	(491.90)
Effect of giving same land and education to men and women					
Net income from young cocoa and food crops	389.43	405.93	−16.50	−117.33	145.10
	(26.60)	(44.00)	(58.86)	(731.54)	(410.46)
Net income from mature cocoa	860.88	538.66	322.22**	−817.98	−65.53
	(26.86)	(47.94)	(63.09)	(2,187.21)	(499.45)

NOTES: Numbers in parentheses are standard errors. * indicates significance at the 5 percent level; ** at the 1 percent level. The exchange rate was US$1 = 2050 cedis.

In the first counterfactual simulation, we provide both male and female field managers with the same level of schooling as the sample average. We find that this increases male income and decreases female income (though the changes in male and female incomes are insignificant), widening the gender gap in agricultural incomes. This is the result of the low or even negative returns to female education in agriculture. In the second scenario, we examine the possibility of giving male and female field managers the same area of land as the sample average in both young and mature cocoa. This redistribution of land reduces male agricultural incomes and increases female agricultural incomes, particularly in young cocoa and food crop production, although male incomes from mature cocoa still exceed those of females. Finally, we give both male and female field managers the sample averages of years of schooling and land. This simulation yields results midway between the first and second simulations—incomes decrease for males and increase for females, but not as much as in the previous simulations.

Although the changes in male and female incomes from the baseline situation are insignificant, the direction of change gives us clues to the possible direction of response to policy interventions in land and schooling. It is clear that increasing the amount of land resources that women control is a more effective way of increasing women's agricultural incomes. This is partly because of the large disparity in access to land within the household. However, increasing women's education does not have positive effects on agricultural income, partly because agriculture has low returns to schooling (Jolliffe 1998). Would increasing women's education have beneficial effects on household per capita expenditures? We also simulate the effect of giving men and women the same levels of schooling as the sample average, and find that it decreases per capita expenditure, owing in part to the negative returns to female education in the per capita expenditure function. This suggests that attempts to increase female education will be stymied by the barriers that women may face in both agricultural production and nonfarm employment.

Summary of Findings

1. Land tenure institutions do not have a significant effect on agricultural incomes from either mature cocoa or young cocoa intercropped with food. Although female field managers may obtain lower incomes per hectare in mature cocoa, this result is not robust to the inclusion of unobserved family characteristics. Agricultural incomes per hectare from young cocoa and food crops are not significantly different for male and female field managers. However, owing to the larger areas cultivated by males, men obtain larger absolute amounts of agricultural incomes than do women.

2. Land is an important determinant of per capita expenditures, and the share devoted to cocoa also positively affects the household's permanent income. However, only the schooling of males has a positive impact on per

capita expenditures, indicating the possibility of discrimination against females in local labor markets.

3. Simulations of counterfactual redistribution of land and education between men and women show that giving women and men the same land-holdings as the sample average—equalizing the distribution of land between men and women—increases women's agricultural incomes. Giving the same level of schooling as the sample average decreases women's agricultural incomes, owing to the low returns to female education in agriculture and possible discrimination against women in the nonfarm labor market. This suggests that attempts to increase women's education must be accompanied by reforms to remove barriers to women's employment.

Summary and Conclusions

The estimated per capita expenditure functions show that the size of land owned and the share devoted to cocoa are important determinants of household permanent income. It is also important to emphasize that only male education, and not female education, positively affects per capita expenditures. This indicates that returns to women's education are low in agriculture, but it also highlights the possibility that discrimination against women in nonfarm employment may be an important constraint on increasing women's education in rural areas. This conjecture is consistent with the finding from agricultural income functions for mature and young cocoa intercropped with food that, once family-level unobservables are considered, there are no significant differences in agricultural incomes between male and female parcel managers. Indeed, larger areas of land are less intensively cultivated, so agricultural income per hectare declines with field size. However, males cultivate larger areas of land, so males earn higher agricultural incomes than women do. Thus, because of the low returns to female education in rural areas, increasing the areas of land cultivated by women is key to increasing women's income in rural Ghana. Increasing women's education will yield greater returns only if barriers to women's employment in the nonfarm sector are eliminated.

Parents have also been changing the allocation of land transfers and schooling between sons and daughters over time. Whereas there used to be strong discrimination against daughters in gifts of land and years of schooling for both Akans and non-Akans in the respondents' generation, discrimination with respect to land transfers has disappeared among Akans in the children's generation. We attribute this change to the increase in the demand for female labor in cocoa cultivation. There is no doubt that the increase in the land area cultivated by women significantly contributed to increases in women's agricultural incomes.

Discrimination against girls in schooling investments has weakened between the respondent and child generations. The gender gap in schooling, although it exists, is beginning to narrow, but in all likelihood the sustainability of such efforts will depend on complementary reforms in labor markets.

Our results show that parental transfer decisions, although basically egalitarian, do not support the unitary model of household behavior. Fathers and mothers have different preferences in wealth transfers depending upon the resources they brought into marriage. This indicates that the collective model of household behavior is relevant in rural Ghana. Even if parents are egalitarian, however, social discrimination against women is a force that needs to be addressed in formulating interventions to improve women's welfare in Ghana.

10 Inter- and Intrahousehold Equity in Ghana

In our Ghana sites, area of cultivated land and the share of cocoa area are both important determinants of agricultural incomes and total expenditure per capita. As in Sumatra, land tenure institutions in these customary land tenure areas have been evolving toward individualized ownership systems, which would have contributed improvements in the management efficiency of land and tree resources. What are the consequences for income distribution among rural households of such evolutionary changes in land tenure institutions? The first objective of this chapter is to explore interhousehold inequality in the distribution of land and consumption expenditures, the latter being a proxy for permanent income of households.

We postulated that parents have egalitarian motives for the transfer of wealth to their sons and daughters. This hypothesis was generally supported by the analysis of land inheritance and schooling investments conducted in Chapter 9, although social discrimination continues to be an important issue for non-Akans, and less educated fathers and mothers with less land tend to discriminate against daughters in land transfers relative to their better endowed counterparts. We now test the same basic hypothesis using the analysis of current expenditure patterns. Thus, the second purpose of this chapter is to assess statistically whether there is a significant gender bias in the intrahousehold distribution of consumption expenditures among family members. As in the Sumatra and Philippine cases, we also examine the validity of the unitary model of household decisionmaking with respect to expenditure allocations.

This chapter has three main sections. The first explores the structure of interhousehold landownership and consumption expenditure inequalities among sample households by applying the Gini decomposition analysis formulated in the Philippine study. The second section identifies the determinants of consumption expenditure shares statistically. The last section provides the summary and conclusions.

Landownership Inequality among Households

Because access to land resources is a major determinant of household income in rural communities, the distribution of land will be an important determinant of household income distribution. In this section, we examine the distribution of operational landholdings and consumption expenditures, rather than income, because we did not collect income data from sources other than cocoa and food crop cultivation. Moreover, consumption expenditures are a good proxy for the household's permanent income.

The evolution of customary land tenure institutions toward individualized ownership systems may lead to an inequitable distribution of landholdings. This is because customary land tenure institutions are designed to achieve the equitable allocation of land among a large number of extended family members by transferring family land. In order to quantify the relative contribution of land under different tenure categories to the overall inequality of land distribution, we apply a decomposition analysis of the Gini measure of landholding inequality as developed by Fei, Ranis, and Kuo (1978) and Pyatt, Chen, and Fei (1980) for household data (see Chapter 4 for details).

The Gini decomposition formula is given by

$$G(Y) = \Sigma s_i PG(Y_i),$$

where $G(Y)$ equals the Gini ratio of total operational landholdings; Y_i pertains to landholdings of the ith tenure type; s_i equals the average share of the ith type of land; and $PG(Y_i)$ equals the pseudo-Gini of landholding inequality. If $PG(Y_i)$ is greater (smaller) than $G(Y)$, distribution of ith type of landholding is less (more) equitable than the average, thereby contributing to the expansion (contraction) of inequality in the overall landholding distribution. Results of the computations using household data on operational landholdings are shown in Table 10.1.

The overall Gini ratio is 0.34, which is relatively small by international standards and indicates the relatively egalitarian distribution of operational holdings. Compared with the overall Gini ratio, the pseudo-Gini coefficient is particularly small for allocated family land, which strongly suggests that traditional egalitarian motives prevail in the decision to allocate family land. In contrast, inheritance is inequality increasing and gifts have a neutral effect on land distribution. It may well be that land-abundant households maintain traditional inheritance practices. Using retrospective data on land acquisition, Quisumbing et al. (2001a) find that the prevalence of family land allocation and gifts has increased, whereas that of inheritance has decreased, over time. Therefore, in all likelihood, these changes in customary land tenure institutions from inheritance to family allocation and gifts have improved the equality of land distribution.

Appropriation and purchase of village forestland were possible only for older indigenes and early migrants, contributing to the inequality of land distribution. Not surprisingly, private land purchase also contributes to landholding inequality. It is more remarkable to find that the pseudo-Gini ratio of current renting, which accounts for 19 percent of operational land area, is small. As was mentioned in Chapter 8, renting in the form of share tenancy is impor-

TABLE 10.1 Overall Gini ratio of operational landholdings and contribution by land component in Ghana

Land tenure type	Land share (percent)	Pseudo-Gini
Allocated family land	11	0.25
Inherited family land	4	0.82
Appropriated village forestland	12	0.66
Purchased village forestland	4	0.75
Received as gift	37	0.35
Privately purchased	2	0.59
Acquired through renting	2	0.35
Currently renting	20	0.15
Borrowing from non-relatives	8	−0.08
All landholdings	100	0.34[a]

[a] Identical to the overall Gini ratio.

tant for migrant workers in our study sites (Robertson 1982; Boadu 1992). Also noteworthy is the negative pseudo-Gini ratio of temporary borrowing from nonrelatives with no payment of explicit fees. It is clear that renting and borrowing significantly contribute to the equalization of operational holdings by reallocating land use rights from land-rich to land-poor households. The importance of land renting for equity is also emphasized in a recent survey of land market literature by Otsuka (2002).

Consumption expenditures are even more equally distributed among households than operational holdings, with a Gini coefficient of only 0.28 for both Akan and non-Akan households (see the last line in Table 10.2 below). This indicates that nonfarm incomes from nonagricultural labor markets and entrepreneurial activity, together with remittances, have an income-equalizing effect.

To conclude, there is no indication in our Ghana sites that the evolution of customary land tenure institutions results in a highly skewed distribution of operational landholdings. This is in marked contrast to the Sumatra case, where the privatization of land tenure institutions is associated with increased inequality. The contrast between the Ghana and Sumatra cases is probably the result of land scarcity in Sumatra relative to Ghana. Communal land tenure systems tend to distribute land relatively equitably across households. In land-abundant situations, this is accomplished mainly through land clearing and inheritance acquisition methods. Similarly, the development of land rental markets through the privatization of communal systems typically does not lead to land concentration, since renting is undertaken mainly by migrants and by households with poor access to both inherited and gift land. As in Sumatra and elsewhere in Asia, renting is equity enhancing in the allocation of land. Since the scarcity of land will contine to increase in Ghana, renting will play an increasingly important role in the efficient and equitable allocation of land.

The effect of land sales markets tends to be equity reducing in both Ghana and Sumatra. Because Ghana still has a relatively land-abundant situation, privately purchased land accounts for a small portion of cultivated land.

Summary of Findings

1. The distribution of operational holdings is relatively egalitarian. Whereas inheritance tends to increase inequality, the growing prevalence of family allocations and gifts has tended to reduce interhousehold inequality in operational holdings. The appropriation and purchase of village forestland and private land purchase also contribute to inequality, but are counteracted by land rental agreements and borrowing from nonrelatives. Land rental markets thus contribute to the equalization of operational holdings by reallocating land from land-rich to land-poor households.
2. The distribution of consumption expenditures is even more equal than that of operational holdings. This suggests that nonfarm incomes, from the nonagricultural labor market and own-account activity as well as from remittances, have an equalizing effect on income distribution.
3. Despite the relative abundance of land in Ghana, land rental markets play an important role in the equitable allocation of operational landholdings, as they do in the more land-scarce situation in Sumatra.

Determinants of Consumption Expenditure Shares

Specification of Estimated Functions

Readers who are not interested in the technical details of statistical estimation can proceed directly to the "Summary of Findings" at the end of this section on page 233.

As in the Philippine and Sumatra studies, we now examine the allocation of expenditures within the household. We focus on identifying whether some expenditure items are geared toward certain demographic categories. The expenditure shares regressions also provide an additional test of the unitary or the collective household model. This is especially relevant in Ghana, where household financial management can be described as "separate purses." Another important question is whether household expenditures, which are determined essentially by parents, are equitable within a household.

Censoring of the dependent variable is not severe in our Ghana sites, so that we were able to estimate the expenditure shares equations using two-stage least squares (2SLS) with per capita expenditure treated as endogenous.[1] Instruments for per capita expenditure included the log of owned land, the ratio

---

1. We first attempted to estimate the equations as Tobits, for comparability with the Philippine and Sumatra cases, but the degree of censoring was so minimal that the results were more consistent with theoretical expectations using the 2SLS estimates.

of cocoa area to the total, the ratio of female working members, the average years of schooling of male and female working members, respectively, and the ratios of working members in four age categories (26–35 years, 36–45 years, 46–55 years, and 56–65 years). The first-stage regression on log per capita expenditure (ln *PCE*), estimated using ordinary least squares (OLS), is presented in Table 9.7 and was discussed in Chapter 9.

In the second-stage regression, we estimate a series of expenditure share functions, specified as

$$
\begin{aligned}
\mathbf{W} = \gamma_0 &+ \gamma_1 \ln PCE^* + \gamma_2 \ln \text{household size} \\
&+ \gamma_3 \ln \text{father's schooling} \\
&+ \gamma_4 \ln \text{mother's schooling} \\
&+ \gamma_5 (\text{father's land at marriage})^{\frac{1}{2}} \\
&+ \gamma_6 (\text{mother's land at marriage})^{\frac{1}{2}} \\
&+ \sum_{i=7}^{15} \gamma \, (\text{proportion in each gender/age group category}) \\
&+ \Sigma\gamma_{16} (\text{Akan household dummy}) + \gamma, \quad\quad (10.1)
\end{aligned}
$$

where $\mathbf{W}$ is a vector of expenditure shares, γ are parameters, and θ is an error term.

Household size is expected to capture the effect of the strength of size economies or diseconomies in household consumption expenditures. We use the data on land areas received at marriage and schooling of fathers and mothers as indicators of spouses' exogenously determined bargaining power, because both human and physical asset ownership critically determine spouses' potential income earnings. We test the unitary versus the collective model of the household by testing whether the coefficients on husband's and wife's human and physical capital are significantly different from each other, after controlling for the effects of per capita household expenditures.

Given the levels of household income (as proxied by per capita expenditure), the difference between the husband's and wife's asset effects should be equal to zero if the unitary model holds in a dynamic framework. Our demographic groupings are males and females separately in age brackets 0–5, 6–9, 10–19, and 20–65, using males in age bracket 20–65 as the control category. We also include a dummy variable for Akan households.

The regressions were based on a subsample of monogamous households with complete information on assets at marriage for both husband and wife; these account for only 56 percent of our sample households.[2] We used this sub-

---

2. Out of 265 households, 29 were female headed with no husband present and 25 were male headed without a wife present. There were 23 households with two wives. Restricting the sample to male-headed households with only one wife reduced the sample size to 188. Further restrictions

sample because we needed to have data on assets at marriage, which can be considered as exogenous for current expenditure decisions. It can be argued that this sample selection criterion creates biases because the subsample of intact couples is not representative of the population. This criterion, however, is common in studies that test the unitary versus the collective model by examining differences in coefficients between spouses, because one needs information on both spouses. To the extent that households where disagreement is strongest are more likely to split, however, they will be less likely to be represented in the subsamples we examine. Hence the likely effect of any resulting selection bias is toward a failure to reject the unitary model, making the strategy adopted here a conservative one.

Data on Expenditure Shares

We divide household expenditure items into food, health, education, clothing, alcohol and tobacco, and other (Table 10.2). Households in western Ghana are poorer than those in our Philippine and Sumatra sites, and they allocate a larger proportion of total expenditures to food (about 64 percent). The education budget share is less than 2 percent of the total because our data on educational expenditures include only direct costs, such as school fees and costs of textbooks and other school supplies (but not cost of time), which are low owing to public provision of primary education. Other expenditures, which include consumer durables, transportation, and recreation, comprise about a quarter of the total.

An important issue here is how expenditures in each category are affected by the age and gender composition of the household. We examine this issue in the next subsection.

Estimation Results

The regression results of the expenditure shares functions are shown in Table 10.3. We include food, health, schooling, child clothing, and alcohol and tobacco (which are grouped separately because they are commonly considered to be "adult goods" in expenditure analyses). According to the estimation results, the share of food in total expenditure tends to decline with an increase in PCE, consistent with Engel's law. Expenditures on health, child clothing, and alcohol and tobacco also decline with an increase in PCE, but these coefficients, although negative, are insignificant. Larger households do not have a significantly lower food share, suggesting that economies of scale in food consumption are not significant.

The effects on expenditure shares of father's and mother's schooling and land at marriage are not significant, except in two cases. Father's schooling has a positive and significant effect on the expenditure share of child clothing, and

---

to couples for whom we had complete information on assets at marriage, land tenure, and consumption expenditures reduced the sample size to 145.

TABLE 10.2 Expenditure shares, by ethnic group, in Ghana

	Akan	Non-Akan	All
Expenditure items (percent)			
Food	64.5	62.6	64.2
Health	2.6	2.8	2.6
Education	1.9	1.8	1.9
Clothing	6.7	6.3	6.6
Tobacco and alcohol	1.9	1.1	1.8
Other	22.4	25.4	22.9
Total	100.0	100.0	100.0
Total consumption expenditure			
(thousand cedis/year)	4,045.17	4,360.32	4,095.16
Per capita consumption expenditure			
(thousand cedis/year)	998.17	811.13	966.02
Gini coefficient of inequality	0.28	0.28	0.28

NOTE: The exchange rate was approximately US$ = 2,050 cedis.

father's land decreases the expenditure share on education. The general insignificance of the coefficients on parental characteristics suggests that, once per capita expenditures are controlled for, parental characteristics do not have any additional explanatory power. In short, parents are egalitarian, which is largely consistent with the gradual disappearance of parental discrimination against daughters in the transfer of land and schooling investments observed in Chapter 9. Note, however, that this finding must be viewed with caution because we used a small subsample of intact, monogamous households.

We examine the validity of the unitary model of household behavior in western Ghana by testing whether the coefficients on father's and mother's schooling and the coefficients on father's and mother's landholdings are the same. Controlling for per capita expenditures (a proxy for permanent income), if the coefficients on father's and mother's characteristics are not significantly different, we cannot reject the unitary model in favor of the collective model. Equality of coefficients suggests that human and physical assets brought into marriage by mothers and fathers have equal effects on consumption expenditures. The F-statistics shown in the bottom panel of Table 10.3 are all below the critical values at the 5 percent level of significance, which means that father's and mother's schooling and father's and mother's landholdings have the same effects on the expenditure shares. Thus, the unitary model cannot be rejected with respect to decisions on budget shares.[3]

---

3. However, as we have seen in Chapter 9, father's and mother's schooling and landholdings have different effects on land inheritance and schooling attainment. In this case, the collective model of the household—a model in which household members have different preferences—seems

In general, the shares of household members in different age/sex categories do not significantly affect the budget shares devoted to health, education,
and adult goods (alcohol and tobacco). However, having males aged 0–5 years
and 6–9 years, as well as females aged 0–5 years and 10–19 years, increases
the budget share of clothing. Food expenditures appear to be lower in households with older females, a result that may suggest some age- and gender-
related discrimination. Thus, while there is little evidence to indicate that males
and females of the same age brackets differentially affect expenditure patterns,
it is possible that older women may be a vulnerable demographic category.

Summary of Findings

1. In general, the shares of household members in different age/sex categories
    do not significantly affect the shares of expenditures on food, housing, child
    clothing, schooling, and tobacco. The only exception worth noting is the
    lower food share in households with older females. Thus, we may safely
    conclude that household expenditure allocation tends to be egalitarian,
    which implies the absence of parental discrimination against particular chil-
    dren in the household in western Ghana.
2. The unitary model of the household—a model in which individuals within
    the household share the same preference or there is a single decisionmaker
    who decides for all—cannot be rejected in the case of expenditure alloca-
    tions in Ghana.

Summary and Conclusions

The first objective of this chapter was to assess whether the evolution of land
tenure institutions has increased interhousehold inequality in the distribution of
land and expenditures. We found that both the evolution of the inheritance system away from pure inheritance toward family allocations and gifts has increased the equality of operational holdings. Moreover, the rise of land rental
markets has contributed to greater equality by facilitating the transfer of land
from land-rich to land-poor households. Household expenditures are also more
equally distributed than operational holdings, indicating that nonfarm incomes
may have an equalizing and compensating effect.

The second objective was to assess whether there is significant bias in
intrahousehold allocation of expenditures among male and female family
members. We found that none of the ratios of male and female members falling

---

to apply. This result is very similar to what we found in Chapter 7. Whereas parents may agree
on the overall allocation of household resources to large expenditure categories, they may disagree on long-term schooling decisions for particular individuals and such major decisions as
land transfers. Thus, tests of the unitary model using household-level data may be weaker because they do not reveal parental preferences as closely as individual-level data do.

TABLE 10.3 Determinants of expenditure shares in Ghana: Two-stage least squares estimates

Variables	Food		Health		Education		Child clothing		Alcohol and tobacco	
	Coefficient	t-statistic	Coefficient	t-statistic	Coefficient	t-statistic	Coefficient	t-statistic	Coefficient	t-statistic
Ln per capita expenditure[a]	-11.69	-3.93**	-1.22	-1.30	0.66	0.96	-0.16	-0.46	-1.25	-1.61
Ln household size	1.08	0.14	-2.58	-1.17	1.79	1.02	-1.96	-1.46	-0.71	-0.30
Ln father's schooling	-1.82	-1.59	0.54	1.88	0.17	0.66	0.38	2.21*	0.09	0.26
Ln mother's schooling	-0.14	-0.15	-0.09	-0.24	-0.30	-1.27	0.17	1.08	-0.16	-0.50
Square root of father's land at marriage	0.07	0.10	-0.03	-0.15	-0.29	-1.95	0.11	1.08	-0.25	-1.18
Square root of mother's land at marriage	0.39	0.21	-0.10	-0.20	-0.40	-1.32	-0.21	-0.68	0.40	0.95
Proportion of household members										
Males aged 0–5	-2.21	-1.24	0.12	0.31	-0.29	-0.66	0.97	3.05**	-0.15	-0.31
Males aged 6–9	-2.03	-1.01	0.53	0.89	-0.09	-0.17	1.06	2.78**	-0.54	-0.81
Males aged 10–19	-3.43	-1.85	0.41	0.74	0.78	1.54	0.65	1.56	0.75	1.41
Males aged 65+	3.44	0.51	-1.00	-0.75	0.19	0.32	1.65	1.54	-0.84	-0.66
Females aged 0–5	-0.26	-0.14	0.18	0.34	-0.86	-0.71	0.65	1.97*	-0.58	-1.16

Females aged 6–9	-0.96	-0.47	-0.59	-1.16	-0.20	-0.39	0.51	1.65	0.12	0.22
Females aged 10–19	-2.56	-1.44	0.29	0.53	0.45	0.77	0.84	2.36**	-0.22	-0.35
Females aged 20–64	-0.06	-0.02	0.23	0.46	-0.21	-0.48	-0.11	-0.28	0.08	0.11
Females aged 65+	-14.69	-3.32**	2.25	1.27	1.18	0.93	1.01	1.11	-0.94	-0.90
Akan household dummy	-1.44	-0.49	-0.76	-0.47	0.76	1.48	-0.45	-0.84	0.91	1.75
Constant	230.93	5.35**	22.50	1.43	-10.70	-1.07	4.96	0.92	19.73	1.74
F	3.98		0.79		2.58		3.10		0.85	
p-value	.00**		.70		.00**		.00**		.62	
Number of observations	145		145		145		145		145	
F-tests on coefficients (p-values)										
Father's schooling = mother's schooling	1.06	(.31)	1.27	(.26)	1.28	(.26)	0.76	(.38)	0.22	(.64)
Father's land = mother's land	0.02	(.89)	0.01	(.91)	0.09	(.77)	0.82	(.37)	1.29	(.26)

NOTES: * indicates significance at the 5 percent level; ** at the 1 percent level.
a Endogenous regressor. Instruments include log of cultivated land, ratio of female working members (aged 15–65), average male schooling, average female schooling, ratio of working members aged 26–35, 36–45, 46–55, and 56–65, and five land tenure dummies.

into the same age categories have significantly different impacts on the expenditure shares, with one exception. Based on the expenditure shares regressions, one cannot reject the hypothesis that Ghanaian households are egalitarian, but this finding must be taken with caution because we used a small subsample of intact, monogamous households. The issue of egalitarian household allocations needs to be revisited in further work that is not restricted to a specific household structure.

The last objective was to test whether the unitary household model applies to households in western Ghana. We did not find significant differences between the coefficients on parental schooling or landholdings. Again, for the subsample of intact households, our results do not lead us to reject the unitary model so far as household expenditures are concerned. Although households that have remained intact are those that have arrived at a more "unitary" way of making household decisions, this conclusion is markedly different from the strong rejection of the unitary model in the analysis of land inheritance and schooling investments between sons and daughters. It is possible that parents have markedly different preferences for long-term decisions on wealth transfers, which are usually to specific individuals, but not for short-term decisions on broad categories of household expenditures. Indeed, disagreements are more likely to arise over wealth transfers, because they involve a significant outflow of wealth (whether at one time or over a long period, as in educational expenditures) and there is a lot of uncertainty regarding returns to long-term investments. Given the magnitude and uncertainty surrounding such transfers, it is no surprise that husbands' and wives' different perceptions and preferences would be reflected in bargaining over transfer decisions.

11 Conclusion: Summary and Policy Implications

This study has hypothesized that parents have egalitarian and efficiency-oriented motives in transferring wealth to their children through land inheritance and schooling investment—the two major forms of wealth transfer in rural areas of developing countries. Using household surveys in the Philippines, Sumatra, and Ghana, we have tested the empirical hypothesis that parents bequeath their wealth to their sons and daughters in accordance with their comparative advantages in lowland and upland farming and in nonfarm jobs. Therefore, if sons and daughters have comparative advantages in lowland farming and nonfarming activities, respectively, we expect sons to receive larger areas of farm land, whereas daughters receive more schooling, since schooling is particularly important in nonfarm jobs.

Parents' egalitarian bequest motives, however, do not assure that "equal" outcomes between men and women will prevail in terms of lifetime or permanent income. This is because women can be subject to social discrimination in land inheritance and schooling investments. If such discrimination exists, the opportunity set of incomes of all family members combined will be skewed against women. As a result, even though parents may be basically egalitarian or their indifference curves may be symmetrical with respect to sons' and daughters' lifetime income, parents would rationally favor sons in their transfers of wealth. In order to substantiate such arguments, we tested the hypotheses that the presence of parental discrimination can be revealed in the significant gender-specific effects of parents' resources at marriage on the intergenerational transfer of land and schooling investments (as measured by the coefficients on the interaction terms with child gender), and that social discrimination will be reflected in the significant coefficients on the gender dummy, independently from parental wealth ownership.

In the first section of this final chapter, we summarize the results of our analyses of the determinants of land inheritance and schooling investment, and the overall effects of wealth transfers on children's lifetime or permanent income by gender. We also examine the relative validity of unitary versus collective models of household decisionmaking. The second section discusses the major remaining research issues in the analysis of intergenerational wealth transfers. We outline the policy implications of our study in the final section of the chapter.

Summary of Results

Land Inheritance

If land bequest decisions are made in accordance with the comparative advantages of sons and daughters in farming, land will be bequeathed to men and women according to their relative specialization in farm work. As summarized in Table 11.1, in the Philippines, where farming is much more intensive in male labor, men inherit more land than women in both the respondents' and the children's generations. Supportive evidence was also obtained from Sumatra, where matrilineal inheritance has traditionally been practiced, in which mothers bequeath land to their daughters. In Kerinci, where both men and women work more or less equally on lowland paddy fields and upland agroforestry fields, men and women currently inherit both types of land roughly equally. In Bungo Tebo, where men work primarily on rubber agroforest and women specialize in lowland paddy production, men inherit rubber fields and women inherit paddy fields. Furthermore, in Ghana where uterine matrilineal inheritance has traditionally been practiced—in which the property of a deceased man is transferred immediately or eventually to his sister's sons—wives and daughters began to acquire landownership through gifts from the husband or father, provided that they help establish cocoa agroforests. It is not mere coincidence that, at present, women contribute about 30 percent of the labor input in cocoa farming (see Table 8.6) and own nearly 30 percent of cocoa land.[1] Evidence from our study sites supports the hypothesis that the relative importance of men's and women's labor inputs is an important determinant of the land transfers to men and women.

This does not imply, however, that women have never been discriminated against in intergenerational land transfers. In Ghana, social discrimination against women persists, though it has been weakened considerably over time. There is also parental discrimination against daughters in land transfers. In Ghana, for example, fathers tend to transfer smaller areas of their land to their daughters in the respondents' generation (Table 9.1). In contrast, there are cases of land transfers from the parents' to the respondents' generation in which mothers who own large land areas transfer their land preferentially to their daughters (see Table 3.1 for the case of the Philippines and Table 6.2 for the case of Bungo

---

1. In the respondents' generation, females own close to 1 hectare of land, whereas males own a little over 2 hectares (Table 8.9). The female share of owned land is 28 percent for Akans and 25 percent for non-Akans.

TABLE 11.1 Summary of results: Gender equity in intergenerational land transfers and schooling investment

	Philippines	Sumatra		Ghana
		Kerinci	Bungo Tebo	
Land inheritance				
Parents to respondents	Men	Equal	Equal/ Women[a]	Men
Respondents to children	Men	n.a.	n.a.	Men
Schooling				
Parents[b]	Men	Men	Men	Men
Respondents	Equal	Equal	Men	Men
Children	Women/ Equal[c]	Equal	Equal	Men
Overall effects of land and schooling on income[d]	Equal	Equal	Equal/ Men[e]	Men

NOTES: "Men" implies that men are favored, whereas "Women" means that women are favored. "Equal" signifies the absence of a statistically significant gender difference. n.a. means data are not available.

[a] Equal or slightly in favor of women.

[b] Based on descriptive statistics rather than the results of econometric analyses.

[c] Daughters over 20 years of age are favored, whereas younger school-aged children of 13–20 years are equally treated.

[d] Except in the case of the Philippines, consumption expenditure is used as a proxy for permanent income.

[e] Equal or slightly in favor of men.

Tebo in Sumatra). There are a few other instances of parental landownership and schooling being positively associated with gender discrimination against daughters. An important observation, however, is that only a small number of significantly discriminatory effects are obtained in land transfers from parents to respondents. Needless to say, the absence of statistical significance does not imply the absence of discrimination against daughters; rather, the statistical evidence does not support the persistence and universal presence of gender discrimination. Furthermore, there is almost no evidence of gender-related parental discrimination in land transfers from respondents to their children, even if husband's and wife's characteristics may have different effects.

Thus it seems reasonable to conclude that there was "weak" parental discrimination in the respondents' generation, but this is less in the present generation. Considering the presence of and changes in social discrimination over time, these conclusions are generally consistent with the hypothesis of parents' egalitarian land transfer motives.

Schooling Investments

Land inheritance (including gifts in Ghana) and schooling investments can be considered to be alternative forms of intergenerational wealth transfers. It may therefore be misleading to analyze land transfers and schooling investment independently. This argument is clearly supported by the Philippine case study, where sons inherit more land but daughters receive more schooling for the generation of older children above 20 years (see the summary results in Table 11.1). This finding strongly indicates that land inheritance and schooling are close substitutes. It is also important to point out that schooling may be increasing in importance in the Philippines: younger sons and daughters currently receive almost equal levels of schooling, despite larger expected land transfers to sons.

However, evidence of a complementary relationship between land inheritance and schooling was not found in the Sumatra and Ghana studies. Roughly speaking, in both our sites in Sumatra, Indonesia, men and women are treated equally in land inheritance and schooling investments in the respondents' and children's generations. In Ghana, in contrast, women are disfavored in both land transfers and schooling, though this gender bias has been appreciably reduced over time. We conjecture that we obtained these different results because, in the Philippines, women work primarily in nonfarm jobs, where educated women and men are equally treated; in the other two sites, both men and women work mostly on farms.

In all three study sites, the evidence of parental discrimination against daughters in schooling investments is either weak or nonexistent in the respondents' and children's generations. The lower level of female schooling in Ghana seems to be attributable to social discrimination against females or "autonomous" parental discrimination independently from their wealth ownership, but not to parental discrimination associated with wealth ownership. Thus, in schooling, too, the hypothesis of egalitarian bequest motives cannot be denied empirically.

Overall Effects of Wealth Transfers on Men's and Women's Income

We are interested in the consequences of gender differences in land inheritance and schooling investments for the lifetime or permanent incomes of men and women. In order to analyze this issue, we assessed the effects of schooling and the gender composition of household members on incomes from agricultural production and on household expenditure (which is used as a proxy for permanent income). Our results are summarized in Table 11.2, and several important observations can be made.

First, schooling is not an important determinant of agricultural income, whether it comes from food crop or tree crop farming. The same conclusions are obtained from the profit function estimation for rice farming in the Philippines (Estudillo and Otsuka 1999, 2001; Estudillo, Quisumbing, and Otsuka

TABLE 11.2 Summary of results: Effects of schooling and gender composition of family labor on agricultural income and household expenditure

		Sumatra		
	Philippines	Kerinci	Bungo Tebo	Ghana
Food crop cultivation				
Schooling	No	No	No	No
Gender composition	No[a]	No[a]	No[a]	No[b]
Tree crop cultivation				
Schooling	n.a.	No[c]	No	No
Gender composition	n.a.	No[a]	No[a]	No[b]
Per capita expenditure				
Men's schooling	No	Yes[d]	Yes[d]	Yes
Women's schooling	Yes			No
Gender composition	No[e]	No[a]	No[a]	No[a]

NOTES: "No" implies no significant effect, whereas "Yes" means significant and positive effect. n.a. means not applicable.

[a] Gender composition is measured by the ratio of female workers.

[b] Gender composition is measured by the gender dummy of either field manager or owner.

[c] Regression coefficient in the income regression is negative and significant probably because educated family members work in nonfarm sectors.

[d] No distinction was made between men's and women's schooling.

[e] Gender composition is measured by the ratios of household members in different age/sex categories.

2001a), rice and tree crop farming in Sumatra (Suyanto, Tomich, and Otsuka 2001a, 2001b), coffee farming in Uganda (Place and Otsuka 2001a), and maize and tobacco farming in Malawi (Place and Otsuka 2001b). This is also supported by the majority of the existing literature (for example, Jolliffe 1998; Fafchamps and Quisumbing 1999), although there are a few exceptions (Foster and Rosenzweig 1996; Yang 1997). Thus, we should not expect increased schooling to have significantly positive effects on agricultural incomes and efficiency, unless technological changes enhance returns to schooling by creating significant disequilibria, as argued by Schultz (1975).

Second, women's schooling, but not men's schooling, has positive and significant effects on per capita household expenditures in the Philippines, whereas the opposite relation holds in Ghana. The former finding is consistent with our argument that women are more educated in the Philippines and tend to work in nonfarm jobs, where returns to schooling are higher. The latter finding, in contrast, suggests that women are discriminated against in nonfarm labor markets in Ghana; this, in turn, is likely to discourage investment in daughters' schooling.

Third, gender composition has no significant effect in any of the cases examined in Table 11.2. This finding implies that men's and women's contributions to food crop income, tree crop income, and permanent household income are equalized at the margin. Aside from the possible discrimination against educated women in nonfarm jobs in Ghana, the gender bias in income-earning activities seems minimal.

Based on these results and the estimation results on the effects of farm land on household incomes, we estimated the lifetime or permanent incomes of men and women. The results are summarized in the last row of Table 11.1. In the Philippines, the smaller farm income of daughters owing to their smaller area of inherited paddy land is almost exactly compensated for by their larger nonfarm incomes owing to their higher schooling attainments. In both the Sumatra sites, sons' and daughters' incomes are largely equalized, reflecting the rough equality of agricultural land inheritance and of level of schooling between sons and daughters. In the case of Ghana, however, women's income is significantly lower than men's. This persistent and significant income gap can be attributed largely to social discrimination against females in land transfers and schooling. Declining trends in such discrimination over generations in Ghana, however, are encouraging. To conclude, as far as our study sites are concerned, men's and women's long-term incomes tend to be equalized, unless there is significant social discrimination against women.

Unitary versus Collective Household Models

One of the objectives of this study was to test the validity of the unitary and the collective models of household behavior. We used various tests of the collective model: (1) a test of the equality of husband and wife land coefficients; (2) a test of the equality of husband and wife schooling coefficients; and (3) a test of the equality of the interaction terms of child gender with parental land and schooling variables. Table 11.3 presents a summary of the findings from each of the country studies.

Our results show that the unitary model is overwhelmingly rejected for the land inheritance equation, whether for the respondents' generation or the children's generation. This suggests that parents do not have the same preferences regarding transfers to their children, and that the physical and human capital brought to marriage by parents affect decisions regarding land transfers. The variables that affect land transfers most significantly are a parent's own landholdings: in general, sons tend to benefit when their fathers have more land, whereas daughters benefit from mothers' land.

We also reject the unitary model for schooling decisions. In the case of the Philippines, parents' schooling levels have differential effects depending on the gender of the child in both the respondents' and children's generations. In Sumatra, interestingly enough, different types of land have differential effects depending on the gender of the child. In Kerinci, in the respondents' genera-

TABLE 11.3 Summary of results: Tests of the unitary versus the collective model of household decisionmaking

		Sumatra		
	Philippines	Kerinci	Bungo Tebo	Ghana
Land inheritance				
Parents to respondents	Collective	Collective[a]	Collective[b]	Collective
Respondents to children	Collective	n.a.	Collective	
Schooling				
Respondents	Collective	Collective	Collective	Collective
Children	Collective	Collective	Collective	Unitary
Expenditure shares	Unitary		Unitary[c]	Unitary

NOTE: n.a. means not available.

[a] Unitary model rejected for paddy and agroforestry land.

[b] Unitary model rejected for agroforestry and bush-fallow land.

[c] Expenditure shares were estimated on the pooled Kerinci and Bungo Tebo samples.

tion, sons complete more years in school when fathers have more paddy land, and daughters do better in school when fathers have more agroforestry and bush-fallow land. This is probably because fathers prefer to transfer agroforestry and bush-fallow land to sons, and they compensate daughters with more schooling. In Bungo Tebo, on the other hand, daughters do better in school if their mothers have more bush-fallow holdings. Only in the case of the children's generation in Ghana is the unitary model accepted.

However, we do not reject the unitary model in expenditure allocations. In the expenditure shares regressions, none of the parental asset variables are significantly different from each other. This could indicate that parents have the same preferences when making allocations to broad expenditure categories, but may have different preferences when deciding on more substantial transfers of schooling and land to their children. It could also suggest that parents may have the same preferences on short-run decisions but not on longer-run decisions. Nevertheless, our results also show that, even if the unitary model is rejected, parents have egalitarian motives toward their sons and daughters.

Remaining Issues

A major question is how far our conclusions can be generalized. We have to emphasize here that the traditional inheritance systems in our sites—the Philippines' bilateral system, Sumatra's matrilineal system, and Ghana's uterine matrilineal system—are relatively unusual. Although we do not have relevant information on the prevalence of these inheritance systems in developing countries as a whole, it is probably true that the patrilineal inheritance system, in which land is bequeathed from a father to his sons, is more dominant. In the case of the three inheritance systems we have studied, women have both interests in and influence on land inheritance in one way or another. Thus, men and women negotiate to whom particular pieces of land should be transferred. In patrilineal communities, in contrast, women are often excluded from land inheritance decisions altogether, because it is usually a small number of men who have interests in and decisionmaking authority over the inheritance of family land. The persistence of discrimination again women is observed in our Ghana sites among non-Akans, who practice patrilineal inheritance. Micro-level studies in South Asia show significant pro-male bias in patrilineal societies: women have less access to land (Agarwal 1997), tend to receive significantly less schooling than men (Meier and Rauch 2000: 267), and receive significantly less food intake and provision of medical care (Haddad et al. 1996).

One of the main remaining issues is whether and to what extent an increase in the demand for women's labor strengthens women's land rights in patrilineal communities. A closely related question is the extent to which discrimination against women in land transfers and schooling investments is attributable to social discrimination or to parental discrimination in such communities.

The extent to which land transfers and schooling are alternative means of wealth transfer must also be analyzed in depth. In Japan, where patrilineal inheritance had been practiced, it is commonly understood that the eldest son inherited farmland from his father, whereas younger sons received more schooling in order to find work in nonfarm activities, particularly in large cities such as Tokyo. This anecdotal evidence supports the substitutability of land inheritance and schooling, even though daughters were generally discriminated against in both land inheritance and schooling in Japan.

In our view, land inheritance and schooling can be close substitutes if educated women are favorably treated in nonfarm jobs. In other words, we believe that women have a comparative advantage in nonfarm jobs (as in the Philippines) if they do not face barriers to entry and wage discrimination in nonfarm activities. If this is the case, and if parents are indeed egalitarian, daughters would be more likely to receive more education and less land than do sons. Needless to say, this hypothesis is untested and, hence, needs to be examined in different locations under different inheritance systems.

The above discussions suggest the importance of the structure or the competitiveness of nonfarm labor markets as a determinant of intergenerational wealth transfers in rural settings. In this connection, we have to admit that a major shortcoming of this study is the lack of detailed analyses of nonfarm jobs, with the possible exception of the Philippine case study. During our field surveys in Sumatra and Ghana, which were implemented as part of a comparative study of land tenure and the management of land and trees in Asia and Africa (Otsuka and Place 2001), we paid primary attention to land inheritance issues, because they were highly complex. In consequence, we failed to investigate the types of nonfarm jobs held by the male and female members of farm households; whether men and women were treated equally or unequally in these jobs; and what differences in nonfarm wage earnings resulted from male and female household members' different levels of schooling over their life cycles. We must address these critically important analytical issues in the future, in order to gain a deeper understanding of intrahousehold equity issues.

Policy Implications

Our three-country study suggests that efforts to improve the distribution of income and resources between men and women in rural areas will not be successful without policies to improve women's income-earning abilities and opportunities. In particular, we advocate policies (1) to extend and strengthen schooling systems in rural areas; (2) to promote competition in nonfarm labor markets so as to eliminate discrimination against women; (3) to reform property rights systems, in general, to be more equitable toward women; and (4) to develop agricultural technologies that increase the returns to female labor, whether through increased demand or increased labor productivity. We would emphasize that in what follows there is no conflict between policies to enhance the efficiency of investments in land and human capital and policies to promote gender equity.

Improve Schooling Systems in Rural Areas

Increasing women's educational attainment is an important part of any long-term strategy to improve gender equity in rural areas. Because of imperfect credit markets, investments in schooling are constrained by income flows and the ownership of assets that can be used as collateral. In fact, according to a recent study of the schooling progression of children in sample households in the Philippines (Estudillo, Sawada, and Otsuka 2002), annual income is a critical determinant of investment in the additional schooling of children. This implies that the social rates of return to schooling investment exceed private rates of return, which is more likely to be the case for women (this is consistent with the international evidence reviewed in Schultz [2002]). Therefore, policy support for schooling investment in children, in general, and daughters, in particular, can be justified on both efficiency and equity grounds. Although the gender gap in schooling has closed in the Philippines and Sumatra sites, it continues to be an issue in rural Ghana, as in other poor and isolated areas in other developing countries. Approaches to promoting gender equality in education have revolved around (1) reducing prices and increasing physical access to services; (2) improving the design of service delivery; and, (3) investing in time-saving infrastructure (King and Alderman 2001; World Bank 2001).

Reducing prices and increasing physical access to educational services are important because parents' decisions to invest in girls' education are more sensitive to the price of education than are their decisions to invest in boys' education. Since girls' schooling is more sensitive to direct and opportunity costs, policy interventions to promote female education such as school stipend programs, tuition subsidies, and scholarships for girls offer some of the most promising ways of reducing the cost of schooling.

Parents' demand for girls' education also appears to be more sensitive than is their demand for boys' education to the quality of schooling, the extent of learning, and teacher attitudes. To this end, training staff, reviewing and revising school curricula, and educating parents can all play important roles in ensuring that gender stereotypes are not perpetuated in the classroom and in the community. The attitudes of girls themselves are important. One reason that girls do so well in Philippine schools, for example, is that the formal education system reinforces socialization patterns for girls, emphasizing "responsibility," "patience," and "sacrifice." Given an educational system whose staff is predominantly female, girls find school more congenial than boys do (Bouis et al. 1998).

Finally, investments that reduce distance to school as well as investments in basic water and energy infrastructure can help female enrollment rates in part by reducing the opportunity cost of schooling for girls. Similarly, increasing access to local healthcare facilities reduces the time women and girls need to spend on in-home care for sick family members. These investments mean fewer interruptions to women's paid work and to girls' schooling. However, such interventions are not sufficient to promote the schooling of girls. It is critically important to raise the return to investments in girls' schooling. Our analyses, as well as those of others, show that returns to schooling are low in farm production. Returns to female schooling are even lower or negative. With such low returns, it is not surprising that resistance to investing in girls' education persists in many rural areas where there is inadequate access to nonfarm employment.

Remove Barriers to Female Participation in the Nonfarm Labor Market

In the long run, given the limited labor absorption capacity of the agricultural sector (David and Otsuka 1994), realizing the returns to female education will increasingly depend on women's ability to find nonfarm employment, not only formal employment in urban enterprises but also employment in small rural enterprises and informal service sectors. We have already seen in our Ghanaian case study how low or even negative private returns to women's schooling in agriculture may act as a deterrent to parental investment in girls' education. We have also seen how the higher probability of obtaining nonfarm employment has gone hand in hand with girls' higher educational attainment in the Philippines. Thus, increasing competition and reducing barriers to female entry to nonfarm labor markets will be key to reducing the difference between social and private rates of return, and to enabling women themselves to realize the returns to their education.

Some of the barriers to entry can be removed through legislation that prohibits explicit discrimination against women. But some of the other barriers lie in the opportunity cost to women of participating in the nonfarm labor market. Women already tend to work longer hours than men, when both productive and domestic work are considered (McGuire and Popkin 1990), and in virtually all countries women perform a disproportionate share of household maintenance and care activities (World Bank 2001). Investments in time-saving infrastructure can reduce women's opportunity costs of participating in the labor market.

Lack of adequate childcare is one of the principal barriers to female employment, particularly in the nonfarm sector (Deutsch, Duryea, and Piras 2001). Much of the occupational segregation that is seemingly "voluntary" actually occurs because a lack of childcare services impels women to choose sectors that permit work and childcare to be combined. Women pay for this increased flexibility by being consigned to the informal sector or to jobs with lower wages. Various studies have demonstrated that access to affordable childcare increases female labor force participation and earnings (Deutsch 1998; Lokshin, Glinskaya, and Garcia 2000). There is a perception that childcare is not a relevant issue in developing countries owing to the ample supply of substitutes for mothers' time, but it has become increasingly important as more women work in the nonfarm sector and in urban areas. Indeed, it is often older daughters who bear the costs of mothers' labor force participation by taking care of younger siblings and dropping out of school.

Policies also need to change the way employers and educators think about women's employment. Hard numbers must be used to dispel myths about the expense of employing women. For example, recent research by the International Labour Organization (ILO) provides evidence from four Latin American and Caribbean countries that the "extra costs" of employing women—such as maternity leave or childcare—turn out to be quite insignificant (ILO 2001). Indeed, bearing these costs in the short run reduces the long-run cost of absenteeism and job turnover, and permits firms to retain more experienced women workers. Social marketing campaigns can be designed to convince employers that "pigeonholing" or underpaying female employees not only is a loss for the employees involved, but also makes the firm less productive and competitive. Educators at all levels need to encourage girls, particularly girls of indigenous or minority groups, to pursue studies in nontraditional areas. Employers and employees alike must also remember that education does not stop once one leaves school, and that job-related training, both pre- and in-service, can enable women to participate more effectively in the labor market.

Finally, in order to promote competitive labor markets, policies to strengthen market competition among enterprises should be adopted. Those enterprises that discriminate against women are less likely to survive in competitive market environments. Moreover, it is important to recognize that the promotion of competitive labor markets will stimulate investments in the schooling of female children. Here, too, there is no trade-off between efficiency and gender equity.

Reform Property Rights Systems

The reform of property rights systems and the legal framework is crucial to attaining gender equity. Because our study sites have either matrilineal or bilateral systems, it can be argued that our study is unduly optimistic about achieving gender equity in asset ownership. Gender equity, particularly in asset ownership, is much more difficult to achieve in patrilineal areas, where women's property rights are inherently weaker. Thus, reform of statutory laws is necessary to strengthen women's entitlements and to increase the enforceability of their claims over natural and physical assets. Gender disparities in natural and physical capital persist partly because the legal framework supports property rights systems that are biased against women (Quisumbing and Meinzen-Dick 2001).

Land titling is often mentioned as a solution to gender disparities in land rights. However, land titling is feasible only if land rights are sufficiently individualized; many programs have failed, largely owing to premature implementation. Titling programs will become feasible once communal land tenure institutions are sufficiently individualized—they have been found to be popular and sustainable in areas of high market and property rights development such as central Kenya (Migot-Adholla et al. 1993). If titling programs are implemented, they must pay special attention to the gender issue. If men are traditionally owners of land, as in western Ghana, land titling may strengthen their land rights at women's expense. For land titling to be fair, men and women should be equally qualified to acquire titles, or titles could be awarded jointly to men and women.

Women should be able not only to hold a title to land but also to inherit land. Judging from the experience of Ghana, the promulgation of the Intestate Succession Law, which stipulates how property should be bequeathed to the spouse, children, and other family members, is likely to be an effective policy option. It should facilitate less gender-biased land inheritance systems in customary land tenure areas. However, its effectiveness depends on women's knowledge of the provisions of the law and their ability to enforce their claims in court. Although improving women's land rights is conducive to both increased gender equity and production efficiency, it is not enough. Transferring ownership of land to women is unlikely to raise the productivity of women farmers if access to and use of other inputs remains unequal. These other constraints faced by women must also be addressed.

Develop Technologies to Increase Returns to Women's Labor

Because returns to education are higher in the nonfarm sector, the task remains to improve the incomes of those who remain in the agricultural sector. To this end, agricultural research can be directed toward technologies to increase the returns to women's labor. In labor-abundant economies, such as those of Asia at the time of the Green Revolution, this could take the form of labor-intensive technologies that increase the demand for women's labor. In labor-constrained economies, the technologies could be ones that make women's labor more productive—such as technologies to improve the efficiency of food processing or fuel collection. These technologies could also consist of new crops that are more profitable and offer a higher return to women's labor, such as agroforestry with commercial trees in hilly or agriculturally marginal areas. As with any type of intervention, the introduction of new technologies should take into account the existing division of rights, resources, and responsibilities within the household and the possibility that the intervention may alter this distribution, often in ways contrary to the intended result. There are numerous examples of project failure because early attempts to target technologies and programs to women did not recognize that women are not isolated economic actors (Quisumbing et al. 1998). For instance, when irrigation was introduced in The Gambia in the early 1980s to raise yields, commercialize rice production, and increase women's share of household income, community initiatives ended up reducing women's income. Yield increases transformed rice from a private crop under the control of women to a communal crop under the control of men (von Braun and Webb 1989; Dey 1981). Nor are women, as a group, homogeneous. Heterogeneity is demonstrated by, for example, differences in class and caste, tenure status, life-cycle stage, spousal seniority, headship, and household composition. All of these are sources of variance that may be greater than women's common interests (Meinzen-Dick et al. 1997).

It is worth emphasizing that the adoption of new profitable technologies and farming systems requires long-term investments, such as irrigation infrastructure, terracing, and tree planting. According to a recent study of land tenure institutions and natural resource management by Otsuka and Place (2001), efforts to invest in land improvement strengthen individual land rights. This implies that the development of new technologies and farming systems that enhance the returns to women's labor may contribute not only to the efficient use of land and other resources but also to strengthening the land rights of women. This possibility is supported by our Ghana study. It must also be pointed out that the development of agroforestry in place of shifting cultivation benefits both the local and the global environment by reducing soil erosion and increasing carbon sequestration.

It is important that women are empowered to benefit from the increased value of their time. The development literature is replete with stories of interventions that aimed to increase women's income-earning capabilities, raise the return to labor, or even improve the productivity of women's crops, but that failed because they did not take into account intrahousehold dynamics as well as possible resistance from men (Dey 1981; von Braun and Webb 1989). We have already shown that gender equity is not incompatible with productive efficiency. Increasing women's educational attainment, strengthening women's rights to property, removing barriers to women's participation in the labor market, and developing technologies that increase the returns to women's labor all work together to raise women's economic and social status either by improving women's opportunities outside the home or by increasing their bargaining power within the family.

References

Adams, Jr., R. 1996. Remittances, income distribution and rural asset accumulation. Food Consumption and Nutrition Division Discussion Paper No. 17. International Food Policy Research Institute, Washington, D.C.

Agarwal, B. 1994. *A field of one's own: Gender and land rights in South Asia.* Cambridge, U.K.: Cambridge University Press.

————. 1997. Editorial: Re-sounding the alert—Gender, resources and community action. *World Development* 25 (9): 1373–1380.

Alcantara, A. 1994. Gender roles, fertility, and the status of married men and women. *Philippine Sociological Review* 42 (1–4): 94–109.

Alderman, H., J. Hoddinott, L. Haddad, and C. Udry. 1995. Gender differentials in farm productivity: Implications for household efficiency and agricultural policy. Food Consumption and Nutrition Division Discussion Paper No. 6. International Food Policy Research Institute, Washington, D.C.

Andersen, J. N. 1962. Some aspects of land and society in a Pangasinan community. *Philippine Sociological Review* 10 (1): 41–48.

Anderson, T. L., and P. J. Hill. 1990. The race for property rights. *Journal of Law and Economics* 33 (1): 177–197.

Angelsen, A. 1995. Shifting cultivation and deforestation: A study from Indonesia. *World Development* 23: 1713–1729.

Awusabo-Asare, K. 1990. Matriliny and the new intestate succession law of Ghana. *Canadian Journal of African Studies* 24 (1): 1–16.

Barker, R., and R. Herdt. 1985. *The rice economy of Asia.* Washington, D.C.: Resources for the Future.

Barlow, C., and S. K. Jayasuriya. 1984. Problems of investment for technological advance: The case of Indonesian rubber smallholders. *Journal of Agricultural Economics* 35: 85–95.

Barlow, C., and Muharminto. 1982. The rubber smallholder economy. *Bulletin of Indonesian Economic Studies* 18 (1): 86–119.

Becker, G. S. 1974. A theory of social interactions. *Journal of Political Economy* 82 (6): 1063–1093.

Becker, G. S., and N. Tomes. 1979. An equilibrium theory of the distribution of income and intergenerational mobility. *Journal of Political Economy* 87 (6): 1153–1189.

————. 1986. Human capital and the rise and fall of families. *Journal of Labor Economics* 4: S1–S39.

251

Behrman, J. R. 1988. Intrahousehold allocation of nutrients in rural India: Are boys favored? Do parents exhibit risk inequality aversion? *Oxford Economic Papers* 40 (1): 32–54.

———. 1997. Intrahousehold distribution and the family. In *Handbook of population and family economics,* ed. M. R. Rosenzweig and O. Stark. Amsterdam, The Netherlands: North-Holland.

Behrman, J. R., and A. Deolalikar. 1995. Are there differential returns to schooling by gender? The case of Indonesian labor markets. *Oxford Bulletin of Economics and Statistics* 57 (1): 97–117.

Behrman, J. R., and J. C. Knowles. 1999. Household income and child schooling in Vietnam. *World Bank Economic Review* 13 (2): 211–256.

Behrman, J., and L. Lanzona. 1989. The impact of land tenure on time use and on modern agricultural technology use in the rural Philippines. Paper presented at a conference on family, gender differences and development, Economic Growth Center, Yale University, New Haven, Conn., U.S.A., September 4–6.

Behrman, J., R. Pollak, and P. Taubman. 1982. Parental preferences and provision for progeny. *Journal of Political Economy* 90 (1): 52–73.

———. 1986. Do parents favor boys? *International Economic Review* 27 (1): 33–54.

Bernheim, D., A. Shleifer, and L. H. Summers. 1985. The strategic bequest motive. *Journal of Political Economy* 93 (6): 1045–1076.

Binder, M. 1998. Family background, gender and schooling in Mexico. *Journal of Development Studies* 35 (2): 54–71.

Binswanger, H. P., and M. R. Rosenzweig. 1984. Contractual arrangements, employments, and wages in rural labor markets: A critical review. In *Contractual arrangements, employment and wages in rural labor markets in Asia,* ed. H. P. Binswanger and M. R. Rosenzweig. New Haven, Conn., U.S.A.: Yale University Press.

———. 1986. Behavioral and material determinants of production relations in agriculture. *Journal of Development Studies* 22 (3): 503–539.

Boadu, F. 1992. The efficiency of share contracts in Ghana's cocoa industry. *Journal of Development Studies* 29 (1): 108–120.

Boserup, E. 1970. *Woman's role in economic development.* London: Allen & Unwin.

Bouis, H. 1991. The determinants of household-level demand for micronutrients: An analysis for Philippine farm households. International Food Policy Research Institute, Washington, D.C. Photocopy.

Bouis, H., and L. J. Haddad. 1990. *Effects of agricultural commercialization on land tenure, household resource allocation, and nutrition in the Philippines.* Research Report No. 79. Washington, D.C.: International Food Policy Research Institute.

Bouis, H., and C. Peña. 1997. Inequality in the intrafamily distribution of food: The dilemma of defining an individual's "fair share." In *Intrahousehold resource allocation in developing countries: Models, method and policy,* ed. L. Haddad, J. Hoddinott, and H. Alderman. Baltimore, Md., U.S.A.: Johns Hopkins University Press.

Bouis, H., M. Palabrica-Costello, O. Solon, D. Westbrook, and A. B. Limbo. 1998. *Gender equality and investments in adolescents in the rural Philippines.* Research Report No. 108. Washington, D.C.: International Food Policy Research Institute.

Butcher, K., and A. Case. 1994. The effect of sibling sex composition on women's education and earnings. *Quarterly Journal of Economics* 109 (3): 531–563.

Cameron, L., J. Malcolm Dowling, and C. Worswick. 2001. Education and labor market participation of women in Asia: Evidence from five countries. *Economic Development and Cultural Change* 49 (3): 459–477.

Couch, K., and T. Dunn. 1997. Intergenerational correlations in labor market status: A comparison of the United States and Germany. *Journal of Human Resources* 32 (1): 210–232.

David, C. C., and K. Otsuka. 1994. *Modern rice technology and income distribution in Asia*. Boulder, Colo., U.S.A.: Lynne Rienner.

David, F. 1994. The roles of husbands and wives in household decision-making. *Philippine Sociological Review* 42 (1–4): 78–93.

Deaton, A., and C. Paxson. 1998. Economies of scale, household size, and the demand for food. *Journal of Political Economy* 106 (5): 897–930.

Deere, C. D. 1982. The division of labor by sex in agriculture: A Peruvian case. *Economic Development and Cultural Change* 30 (4): 795–812.

Deere, C. D., and M. Leon. 1982. *Women in Andean agriculture: Peasant production and rural wage employment in Colombia and Peru*. Women, Work, and Development Series No. 4. Geneva: International Labour Office.

Demographic and Health Survey. 1992. *Indonesia Demographic and Health Survey 1991*. Jakarta, Indonesia: Central Bureau of Statistics.

Deolalikar, A. 1993. Gender differences in the returns to schooling and in school enrollment rates in Indonesia. *Journal of Human Resources* 28 (4): 899–932.

Deutsch, R. 1998. *Does child care pay? Labor force participation and the earnings effects of access to child care in the favelas of Rio de Janeiro*. IDB Working Paper 384. Washington, D.C.: Inter-American Development Bank.

Deutsch, R., S. Duryea, and C. Piras. 2001. Labor markets and employment. In *Empowering women to achieve food security, 2020 FOCUS*, ed. A. R. Quisumbing and R. S. Meinzen-Dick. Washington, D.C.: International Food Policy Research Institute.

Dey, J. 1981. Gambian women: Unequal partners in rice development projects. *Journal of Development Studies* 17 (3): 109–122.

———. 1985. Women in African rice farming systems. In *Women in rice farming*, ed. International Rice Research Institute. Brookfield, Vt., U.S.A.: Gower Publishers.

Diaz, C. P., M. Hossain, T. R. Paris, and J. S. Luis. 1994. Adding value in rice production: A study on utilization of rice biomass and by-products in rainfed lowlands in Central Luzon. *Philippine Journal of Crop Science* 19 (3): 127–140.

Doss, C. R. 1996a. *Women's bargaining power in household economic decisions: Evidence from Ghana*. University of Minnesota Staff Paper P96-11. Minneapolis, Minn., U.S.A.: University of Minnesota.

———. 1996b. Testing among models of intrahousehold resource allocation. *World Development* 24 (10): 1597–1609.

Dwyer, D., and J. Bruce. 1988. *A home divided: Women and income in the third world*. Stanford, Calif., U.S.A.: Stanford University Press.

Efron, B. 1979. Bootstrap methods: Another look at the jackknife. *Annals of Statistics* 7 (1): 1–26.

Errington, F. K. 1984. *Manners and meaning in West Sumatra: The social context of consciousness*. New Haven, Conn., U.S.A.: Yale University Press.

Estudillo, J. P., and K. Otsuka. 1999. Green revolution, human capital and off-farm employment: Changing sources of income among farm households in Central Luzon, 1966–94. *Economic Development and Cultural Change* 47 (3): 497–523.

————. 2001. Has green revolution ended? A review of long-term trends in MV adoption, rice yields, and rice income in Central Luzon, 1966–99. *Japanese Journal of Rural Economics* 3: 51–64.

Estudillo, J. P., M. Fujimura, and M. Hossain. 1999. New rice technology and comparative advantage in rice production in the Philippines, 1966–94. *Journal of Development Studies* 35 (5): 162–185.

Estudillo, J. P., A. R. Quisumbing, and K. Otsuka. 2001a. Income distribution in rice-growing villages during the post-green revolution periods: The Philippine case, 1985 and 1998. *Agricultural Economics* 25 (1): 71–84.

————. 2001b. Gender differences in land inheritance and schooling investments in the rural Philippines. *Land Economics* 77 (1): 130–143.

————. 2001c. Gender differences in land inheritance, schooling and lifetime income: Evidence from the rural Philippines. *Journal of Development Studies* 37 (4): 23–48.

————. 2001d. Gender differences in wealth transfers and expenditure allocation: Evidence from the rural Philippines. *Developing Economies* 39 (4): 366–394.

Estudillo, J. P., Y. Sawada, and K. Otsuka. 2002. Gender, household income, and child schooling: A study of rural villages in the Philippines, 1985–2002. Foundation for Advanced Studies on International Development, Tokyo. Photocopy.

Fafchamps, M., and A. R. Quisumbing. 1999. Human capital, productivity, and labor allocation in rural Pakistan. *Journal of Human Resources* 34 (2): 369–406.

————. 2002. Control and ownership of assets within rural Ethiopian households. *Journal of Development Studies* 38 (2): 47–82.

Farmer, A., and J. Tiefenthaler. 1995. Fairness concepts and the intrahousehold allocation of resources. *Journal of Development Economics* 47 (2): 155–178.

Fegan, B. 1982. The social history of a Central Luzon barrio. In *Philippine social history,* ed. A. W. MacCoy and C. de Jesus. Honolulu: University Press of Hawaii.

Fei, J., G. Ranis, and S. Kuo. 1978. Growth and family distribution of income by factor components. *Quarterly Journal of Economics* 92 (1): 17–53.

Filmer, D. 1999. The intrahousehold allocation of schooling and preventive care: Estimates from Ghana. Unpublished paper. World Bank, Washington, D.C.

Foster, A., and M. Rosenzweig. 1996. Technical change and human capital returns and investments: Evidence from the green revolution. *American Economic Review* 86 (4): 931–953.

Garg, A., and J. Morduch. 1998a. Sibling rivalry and the gender gap: Evidence from child health outcomes in Ghana. *Journal of Population Economics* 11: 471–493.

————. 1998b. *Sibling rivalry.* Working Paper. Princeton, N.J., U.S.A.: Woodrow Wilson School, Princeton University.

Gatti, R. 1999. A cross-country analysis of fertility determinants. World Bank Development Research Group, Washington, D.C.

Gockowski, J., B. Nkamleu, and J. Wendt. 2001. Impact of resource use intensification for the environment and sustainable technology systems in the central African rainforest. In *Tradeoffs or synergies: Agricultural intensification, environment and economic development,* ed. D. R. Lee and C. B. Barrett. Wallingford, U.K.: CAB International Publishing.

Gouyon, A., H. de Foresta, and P. Levang. 1993. Does jungle rubber deserve its name? An analysis of rubber agroforestry systems in Southeast Sumatra. *Agroforestry Systems* 22: 181–206.

Gray, L., and M. Kevane. 1999. Diminished access, diverted exclusion: Women and land tenure in Sub-Saharan Africa. *African Studies Review* 42 (2): 15–39.

Greene, W. H. 1997. *Econometric analysis,* 3rd ed. Englewood Cliffs, N.J., U.S.A.: Prentice-Hall.

Guyer, J. 1980. *Household budgets and women's income.* African Studies Center Working Paper No. 28. Boston, Mass., U.S.A.: Boston University.

Haddad, L. J., J. Hoddinott, and H. Alderman H., eds. 1997. *Intrahousehold resource allocation in developing countries: Methods, models, and policy.* Baltimore, Md., U.S.A.: Johns Hopkins University Press.

Haddad, L. J., C. Peña, C. Nishida, A. R. Quisumbing, and A. Slack. 1996. Food security and nutrition implications of intrahousehold bias: A review of literature. Food Consumption and Nutrition Division Discussion Paper No. 19. International Food Policy Research Institute, Washington, D.C.

Hallman, K. 2000. Mother–father resource control, marriage payments, and girl–boy health in rural Bangladesh. Food Consumption and Nutrition Division Discussion Paper No. 93. International Food Policy Research Institute, Washington, D.C.

Hauser, R., and H.-H. Daphne Kuo. 1998. Does gender composition of sibships affect women's educational attainment? *Journal of Human Resources* 33 (3): 644–657.

Hayami, Y., and M. Kikuchi. 1982. *Asian village economy at the crossroads.* Baltimore, Md., U.S.A.: Johns Hopkins University Press.

————. 2000. *A rice village saga: Three decades of green revolution in the Philippines.* London: Macmillan.

Hayami, Y., and K. Otsuka. 1993. *The economics of contract choice: An agrarian perspective.* Oxford, U.K.: Clarendon Press.

Hayami, Y., A. R. Quisumbing, and L. Adriano. 1990. *Toward an alternative land reform paradigm: A Philippine perspective.* Quezon City, Philippines: Ateneo de Manila University Press.

Heckman, J. 1979. Sample selection bias as a specification error. *Econometrica* 47 (1): 153–161.

Heckman, J. J., and T. E. MaCurdy. 1980. A life cycle model of female labor supply. *Review of Economic Studies* 47 (1): 47–74.

Hill, A., and E. M. King. 1995. Women's education and economic well-being. *Feminist Economics* 1 (2): 1–26.

Hill, P. 1963. *The migrant cocoa-farmers of southern Ghana: A study in rural capitalism.* Cambridge, U.K.: Cambridge University Press.

Hoddinott, J., and L. Haddad. 1995. Does female income share influence household expenditures? Evidence from Côte d'Ivoire. *Oxford Bulletin of Economics and Statistics* 57 (1): 77–96.

Honoré, B. 1992. Trimmed LAD and least squares estimation of truncated and censored regression models with fixed effects. *Econometrica* 60 (3): 533–565.

Hsiao, C. 1986. *Analysis of panel data.* Econometric Society Monographs No. 11. Cambridge, U.K.: Cambridge University Press.

Humana, C. 1992. *World human rights guide,* 3rd ed. New York: Oxford University Press.

ILO (International Labour Organization). 2001. *2000 labour overview.* Lima, Peru: ILO Regional Office for Latin America and the Caribbean.

IRRI (International Rice Research Institute), ed. 1985. *Women in rice farming.* Brookfield, Vt., U.S.A.: Gower Publishers.

————. 1997. *Sustaining food security beyond the year 2000.* Los Baños, Philippines.

Jamison, D., and L. Lau. 1982. *Farmer education and farm efficiency.* Baltimore, Md., U.S.A.: Johns Hopkins University Press for the World Bank.

Jatileksono, T. 1994. Varietal improvements, productivity change, and income distribution: The case of Lampung, Indonesia. In *Modern rice technology and income distribution in Asia,* ed. C. C. David and K. Otsuka. Boulder, Colo., U.S.A.: Lynne Rienner.

Jolliffe, D. 1998. Skills, schooling and household income in Ghana. *World Bank Economic Review* 12 (1): 81–104.

Kaestner, R. 1997. Are brothers really better? Sibling sex composition and educational achievement revisited. *Journal of Human Resources* 32 (2): 250–284.

Kahn, J. S. 1980. *Minangkabau social formations: Indonesian peasants and the world economy.* Cambridge, U.K.: Cambridge University Press.

Karoly, L. 1994. Money for nothing? Remittances by migrants in the Malaysia Family Life Surveys. Paper presented at the Econometric Society Annual Meetings, Washington, D.C., January 1995. RAND Corporation, Santa Monica, Calif., U.S.A. Photocopy.

Kato, T. 1982. *Matriliny and migration: Evolving Minangkabau traditions in Indonesia.* Ithaca, N.Y., U.S.A.: Cornell University Press.

Kennedy, E. 1989. *The effects of sugarcane production on food security, health, and nutrition in Kenya: A longitudinal analysis.* Research Report No. 78. Washington, D.C.: International Food Policy Research Institute.

————. 1991. Income source of the rural poor in Southwestern Kenya. In *Income sources of malnourished people in rural areas: Micro-level information and policy implications,* ed. J. von Braun and R. Pandya-Lorch. Working Paper on Commercialization of Agriculture and Nutrition No. 5. Washington, D.C.: International Food Policy Research Institute.

Kennedy, E., and P. Peters. 1992. Household food security and child nutrition: The interaction of income and gender of household head. *World Development* 20 (8): 1077–1085.

Kevane, M., and L. C. Gray. 1999. A woman's field is made at night: Gendered land rights and norms in Burkina Faso. *Feminist Economics* 5 (3): 1–26.

Kevane, M., and B. Wydick. 2001. Social norms and the time allocation of women's labor in Burkina Faso. *Review of Development Economics* 5 (1): 119–129.

Khandker, S. R. 1990. *Labor market participation, returns to education, and male-female wage differences in Peru.* Policy Research and External Affairs Working Paper No. 461. Washington, D.C.: World Bank.

Kikuchi, Y., ed. 1989. *Philippine kinship and society.* Quezon City, Philippines: New Day Publishers.

King, E., and H. Alderman. 2001. Education. In *Empowering women to achieve food security, 2020 FOCUS,* ed. A. R. Quisumbing and R. S. Meinzen-Dick. Washington, D.C.: International Food Policy Research Institute.

King, E. M., and M. A. Hill. 1993. *Women's education in developing countries: Barriers, benefits, and policies.* Baltimore, Md., U.S.A.: Johns Hopkins University Press.

King, E. M., and L. A. Lillard. 1987. Education policy and schooling attainment in Malaysia and the Philippines. *Economics of Education Review* 6: 67–181.

Klasen, S. 1999a. Does gender inequality reduce growth and development? Evidence from cross-country regressions. Background paper for Engendering Development. World Bank, Washington, D.C. Available online at <http://www.worldbank.org/gender/prr/klasen.pdf>.

————. 1999b. Malnourished and surviving in South Asia, better nourished and dying in Africa: What can explain this puzzle? Paper presented at the annual meeting of the European Society of Population Economics, University of Munich, Germany.

Knowles, J. C., and R. Anker. 1981. An analysis of income transfers in a developing country. *Journal of Development Economics* 8 (2): 205–266.

Kochar, A. 1999. Evaluating familial support for the elderly: The intrahousehold allocation of medical expenditures in rural Pakistan. *Economic Development and Cultural Change* 47 (3): 621–656.

————. 2000. Parental benefits from intergenerational coresidence: Empirical evidence from rural Pakistan. *Journal of Political Economy* 108 (6): 1184–1209.

Lanzona, L. 1998. Migration, self-selection and earnings in the Philippines. *Journal of Development Economics* 56 (1): 27–50.

Lastarria-Cornhiel, S. 1988. Female farmers and agricultural production in El Salvador. *Development and Change* 19: 585–615.

————. 1997. Impact of privatization on gender and property rights in Africa. *World Development* 25 (8): 1317–1333.

Lavy, V. 1996. School supply constraints and children's educational outcomes in rural Ghana. *Journal of Development Economics* 51 (2): 291–314.

Lele, U. 1986. Women and structural transformation. *Economic Development and Cultural Change* 34 (2): 195–221.

Leones, J. P., and S. Feldman. 1998. Nonfarm activity and rural household income: Evidence from the Philippine micro data. *Economic Development and Cultural Change* 46 (4): 789–806.

Levine, N. E. 1987. Differential childcare in three Tibetan communities: Beyond son preference. *Population and Development Review* 13 (2): 281–304.

Lokshin, M. M., E. Glinskaya, and M. Garcia. 2000. *Effect of early childhood development programs on women's labor force participation and older children's schooling in Kenya.* Washington, D.C.: World Bank.

Lopez, C. 1902. Women in the Philippines. In *Anti-imperialism in the United States, 1898–1935,* ed. J. Zwick, *Woman's Journal* (January 29, 2001). Available online at <http://boondocksnet.com/wj/wj_19020607.html>.

Lucas, R. E. B., and O. Stark. 1985. Motivations to remit: Evidence from Botswana. *Journal of Political Economy* 93: 901–918.

McElroy, M. B. 1990. The empirical content of Nash-bargained household behavior. *Journal of Human Resources* 25: 559–583.

McElroy, M. B., and M. J. Horney. 1981. Nash-bargained household decisions. *International Economic Review* 22: 333–350.

McGuire, J., and B. Popkin. 1990. *Helping women improve nutrition in the developing world: Beating the zero-sum game.* World Bank Technical Paper No. 114. Washington, D.C.: World Bank.

Malhotra, A. 1997. Gender and the timing of marriage: Rural–urban differences in Java. *Journal of Marriage and Family* 59 (2): 434–450.

Maluccio, J. 1998. Endogeneity of schooling in the wage function: Evidence from the rural Philippines. Food Consumption and Nutrition Division Discussion Paper No. 54. International Food Policy Research Institute, Washington, D.C.

Medina, B. 1991. *The Filipino family: A text with selected readings.* Diliman, Quezon City: University of the Philippines Press.

Meier, G., and J. R. Rauch. 2000. *Leading issues in economic development,* 7th ed. Oxford, U.K.: Oxford University Press.

Meinzen-Dick, R., L. R. Brown, H. Sims Feldstein, and A. R. Quisumbing. 1997. Gender, property rights, and natural resources. *World Development* 25 (8): 1303–1316.

Menchik, P. 1980. Primogeniture, equal sharing, and the U.S. distribution of wealth. *Quarterly Journal of Economics* 94 (2): 299–316.

Mensch, B. S., and C. B. Lloyd. 1998. Gender differences in the schooling experiences of adolescents in low-income countries: The case of Kenya. *Studies in Family Planning* 29 (2): 167–184.

Michon, G., and H. de Foresta. 1995. The Indonesian agroforest model: Forest resource management and biodiversity conservation. In *Conserving biodiversity outside protected areas: The role of traditional agro-ecosystems,* ed. P. Halladay and D. A. Gilmour. Gland, Switzerland: The World Conservation Union (IUCN).

Migot-Adholla, S. E., G. Benneh, F. Place, and S. Atsu. 1993. Land, security of tenure, and productivity in Ghana. In *Searching for land tenure security in Africa,* ed. J. W. Bruce and S. E. Migot-Adholla. Dubuque, Ia., U.S.A.: Kendall/Hunt Publishing Company.

Miralao, V. 1997. The family, traditional values and the sociocultural transformation of the Philippine society. *Philippine Sociological Review* 45 (1–4): 189–215.

Mollel, N. 1986. An evaluation of the training and visit (T&V) system of agricultural extension in Muheza District, Tanga Region, Tanzania. M.S. thesis. University of Illinois, Urbana, Ill., U.S.A.

Moock, P. 1976. The efficiency of women as farm managers: Kenya. *American Journal of Agricultural Economics* 58: 831–835.

Morduch, J. 2000. Sibling rivalry in Africa. *American Economic Review* 90: 405–409.

Mukhopadhyay, S. 1991. *Adapting household behavior to agricultural technology in West Bengal, India: Wage labor, fertility, and child schooling determinants.* Economic Growth Center Discussion Paper No. 631. New Haven, Conn., U.S.A.: Yale University.

Nagarajan, G., A. R. Quisumbing, and K. Otsuka. 1991. Land pawning in the Philippines: An exploration into the consequences of land reform regulations. *Developing Economies* 29 (2): 125–144.

Otsuka, K. 1991 Determinants and consequences of land reform implementation in the Philippines. *Journal of Development Economics* 35 (2): 339–355.

————. 2002. Efficiency and equity effects of land markets. Paper presented at the workshop for Handbook of Agricultural Development, Bretton Woods, N.H., U.S.A., September 29–October 1, 2002.

Otsuka, K., and F. Place. 2001. *Land tenure and natural resource management: A comparative study of agrarian communities in Asia and Africa.* Baltimore, Md., U.S.A,: Johns Hopkins University Press.

Otsuka, K., V. G. Cordova, and C. C. David. 1992. Green revolution, land reform, and household income distribution in the Philippines. *Economic Development and Cultural Change* 40 (4): 719–741.

Otsuka, K., F. Gascon, and S. Asano. 1994. "Second-generation" MVs and the evolution of Green Revolution: The case of Central Luzon, 1966–90. *Agricultural Economics* 10 (3): 283–295.

Otsuka, K., S. Suyanto, T. Sonobe, and T. P. Tomich. 2001. Evolution of customary land tenure and development of agroforestry: Evidence from Sumatra. *Agricultural Economics* 25 (1): 85–101.

Pitt, M. M., and M. R. Rosenzweig. 1990. Estimating the intrahousehold incidence of illness: Child health and gender inequality in the allocation of time. *International Economic Review* 31: 969–989.

Pitt, M. M., M. R. Rosenzweig, and M. N. Hassan. 1990. Productivity, health, and inequality in the intrahousehold distribution of food in low-income countries. *American Economic Review* 80 (5): 1139–1156.

Pittigrew, J. 1986. Child neglect in rural Punjabi families. *Journal of Comparative Family Studies* 17 (1): 63–85.

Place, F., and P. Hazell. 1993. Productivity effects of indigenous land tenure in Sub-Saharan Africa. *American Journal of Agricultural Economics* 75 (1): 10–19.

Place, F., and K. Otsuka. 2001a. Population, land tenure, and natural resource management: The case of customary land areas in Malawi. *Journal of Environmental Economics and Management* 41 (1): 13–32.

————. 2001b. Tenure, agricultural investment, and productivity in customary tenure sector of Malawi. *Economic Development and Cultural Change* 50 (1): 77–100.

————. 2002. Land tenure systems and their impacts on agricultural investments and productivity in Uganda. *Journal of Development Studies* 38 (6): 105–128.

Psacharopoulos, G. 1985. Returns to education: A further international update and implications. *Journal of Human Resources* 20 (4): 583–604.

————. 1994. Returns to investment in education: A global update. *World Development* 22 (9): 1325–1343.

Pyatt, G., C. Chen, and John Fei. 1980. The distribution of income by factor components. *Quarterly Journal of Economics* 95 (3): 451–473.

Quisumbing, A. R. 1994. Intergenerational transfers in Philippine rice villages: Gender differences in traditional inheritance customs. *Journal of Development Economics* 43 (2): 167–195.

————. 1996. Male–female differences in agricultural productivity: Methodological issues and empirical evidence. *World Development* 24 (10): 1579–1595.

————. 1997. Does parental gender preference pay off? Migration and child–parent transfers in rural Philippines. International Food Policy Research Institute, Washington, D.C. Photocopy.

Quisumbing, A. R., and B. de la Brière. 2000. Women's assets and intrahousehold allocation in Bangladesh: Testing measures of bargaining power. Food Consumption and Nutrition Division Discussion Paper 86. International Food Policy Research Institute, Washington, D.C.

Quisumbing, A. R., and J. A. Maluccio. 2003. Resources at marriage and intrahousehold allocation: Evidence from Bangladesh, Ethiopia, Indonesia, and South Africa. *Oxford Bulletin of Economics and Statistics* 65 (3): 283–328.

Quisumbing, A. R., and R. S. Meinzen-Dick. 2001. Overview. In *Empowering women to achieve food security, 2020 FOCUS,* ed. A. R. Quisumbing and R. S. Meinzen-Dick. Washington, D.C.: International Food Policy Research Institute.

Quisumbing, A. R., and K. Otsuka. 2001. Land inheritance and schooling in matrilineal societies: Evidence from Sumatra. *World Development* 29 (12): 2093–2110.

Quisumbing, A. R., E. Payongayong, and K. Otsuka. 2001. Intergenerational wealth transfers in western Ghana: A study of gender differences in land inheritance and schooling investment. International Food Policy Research Institute, Washington, D.C. Photocopy.

Quisumbing, A. R., E. Payongayong, J. B. Aidoo, and K. Otsuka. 2001a. Women's land rights in the transition to individualized ownership: Implications for the management of tree resources in western Ghana. *Economic Development and Cultural Change* 50 (1): 157–182.

———. 2001b. Agroforestry management in Ghana. In *Land tenure and natural resource management: A comparative study of agrarian communities in Asia and Africa,* ed. K. Otsuka and F. Place. Baltimore, Md., U.S.A.: Johns Hopkins University Press.

Res, L. 1985. Changing labor allocation patterns of women in rice farm households: A rainfed rice village, Iloilo Province, Philippines. In *Women in rice farming,* ed. International Rice Research Institute. Brookfield, Vt., U.S.A.: Gower Publishers.

Robertson, A. F. 1982. *Abusa:* The structural history of an economic contract. *Journal of Development Studies* 18: 447–478.

Rosenzweig, M. R. 1980. Neoclassical theory and the optimizing peasant: An econometric analysis of market family labor supply in a developing country. *Quarterly Journal of Economics* 374 (1): 31–55.

———. 1986. Program interventions, intrahousehold distribution, and the welfare of individuals: Modeling household behavior. *World Development* 14 (2): 233–243.

Rosenzweig, M. R., and K. Wolpin. 1985. Specific experience, household structure, and intergenerational transfers: Farm family land and labor arrangements in developing countries. *Quarterly Journal of Economics* 100 (Supplement): 961–987.

———. 2000. Natural "natural experiments" in economics. *Journal of Economic Literature* 38: 827–874.

Sahn, D., and H. Alderman. 1988. The effects of human capital on wages, and the determinants of labor supply in a developing country. *Journal of Development Economics* 29 (2): 157–183.

Saito, K., D. Spurling, and H. Mekonnen. 1994. *Raising the productivity of women farmers in Sub-Saharan Africa.* Discussion Paper No. 230. Washington, D.C.: World Bank.

Sajogyo, P. 1985. The impact of new farming technology on women's employment. In

Women in rice farming, ed. International Rice Research Institute. Brookfield, Vt., U.S.A.: Gower Publishers.

Schultz, T. P. 1990. Women's changing participation in the labor force: A world perspective. *Economic Development and Cultural Change* 38 (3): 457–488.

———. 2002. Why governments should invest more to educate girls. *World Development* 30 (2): 207–225.

Schultz, T. W. 1964. *Transforming traditional agriculture.* New Haven, Conn., U.S.A.: Yale University Press.

———. 1975. The value of the ability to deal with disequilibria. *Journal of Economic Literature* 13 (3): 827–846.

Shorrocks, A. 1983. The impact of income components on the distribution of family income. *Quarterly Journal of Economics* 98 (2): 310–326.

Sikapande, E. 1988. An evolution of the training and visit (T&V) system of agricultural extension in Eastern Province, Zambia. M.S. thesis, University of Illinois, Urbana, Ill., U.S.A.

Skoufias, E. 2001. PROGRESA and its impacts on the human capital and welfare of households in rural Mexico: A synthesis of the results of an evaluation by IFPRI. Report. International Food Policy Research Institute, Washington, D.C. May be downloaded at <http://www.ifpri.org/themes/progresa.htm>.

Smith, L., and L. Haddad. 2000. *Explaining child malnutrition in developing countries. A cross-country analysis.* Research Report No. 111. Washington, D.C.: International Food Policy Research Institute.

Smith, L. C., U. Ramakrishnan, L. Haddad, R. Martorell, and A. Ndiaye. 2003. *The importance of women's status for child nutrition in developing countries.* Research Report No. 131. Washington, D.C.: International Food Policy Research Institute.

Stark, O., and R. Lucas. 1988. Migration, remittances and the family. *Economic Development and Cultural Change* 36 (3): 465–481.

StataCorp. 2001. Stata Statistical Software: Release 7.0. Stata Corporation, College Station, Tex., U.S.A.

Strauss, J. A., and D. Thomas. 1995. Human resources: Empirical modeling of household and family decisions. In *Handbook of development economics,* ed. T. N. Srinivasan and J. Behrman. Amsterdam, The Netherlands: North-Holland.

Suyanto, S., T. P. Tomich, and K. Otsuka. 2001a. Land tenure and farm management efficiency: The case of paddy and cinnamon production in customary land areas of Sumatra. *Australian Journal of Agricultural and Resource Economics* 45 (3): 411–436.

———. 2001b. Land tenure and farm management efficiency: The case of smallholder rubber production in customary land areas of Sumatra. *Agroforestry Systems* 52 (2): 145–160.

———. 2001c. Agroforestry management in Sumatra. In *Land tenure and natural resource management: A comparative study of agrarian communities in Asia and Africa.* Baltimore, Md., U.S.A.: Johns Hopkins University Press.

Swamy, A., S. Knack, Y. Lee, and O. Azfar. 2001. Gender and corruption. *Journal of Development Economics* 64: 25–55.

Texler Segal, M. 1986. *Land and labor: A comparison of female- and male-headed households in Malawi's smallholder sector.* WID Forum Paper X. East Lansing, Mich., U.S.A.: Michigan State University.

Thomas, D. 1990. Intrahousehold resource allocation: An inferential approach. *Journal of Human Resources* 25 (4): 635–664.

———. 1994. Like father, like son, like mother, like daughter: Parental resources and child height. *Journal of Human Resources* 29 (4): 950–988.

Thomas, D., and C. Chen. 1994. *Income shares and shares of income.* Labor and Population Working Paper 94-08. Santa Monica, Calif., U.S.A.: RAND Corporation.

Thomas, D., D. Contreras, and E. Frankenberg. 2002. Distribution of power within the household and child health. RAND Corporation, Santa Monica, Calif., U.S.A. Photocopy.

Udry, C. 1996. Gender, agricultural production and the theory of the household. *Journal of Political Economy* 104 (5): 1010–1046.

UNDP (United Nations Development Programme). 2000. *Human development report.* New York: Oxford University Press.

UNESCO (United Nations Educational, Scientific and Cultural Organization). 1999. *UNESCO statistical yearbook.* Paris.

Unnevehr, L., and M. Lois Stanford. 1985. Technology and the demand for women's labor in Asian rice farming. In *Women in rice farming,* ed. International Rice Research Institute. Brookfield, Vt., U.S.A.: Gower Publishers.

Von Braun, J., and P. Webb. 1989. The impact of new crop technology on the agricultural division of labor in a West African setting. *Economic Development and Cultural Change* 37: 513–534.

Von Braun, J., D. Puetz, and P. Webb. 1989. *Irrigation technology and commercialization of rice in the Gambia: Effects on income and nutrition.* Research Report No. 75. Washington, D.C.: International Food Policy Research Institute.

Weir, F. A. 2001. *Centennial history of Philippine independence, 1898–1998.* Available online at <http://www.ualberta.ca/~vmitchel>.

World Bank. 2001. *Engendering development through gender equality in rights, resources, and voice.* A World Bank Policy Research Report. Washington, D.C.: World Bank.

Yang, D. 1997. Education and off-farm work. *Economic Development and Cultural Change* 45 (3): 613–632.

Index

Page numbers for entries occurring in figures are followed by an *f;* those for entries occurring in notes, by an *n;* and those for entries occurring in tables, by a *t.*

Adams, R., Jr., 57

Africa, 6; farming systems in, 9, 14; illiteracy rates in, 20, 21f; North, 5; primary enrollment rates in, 22f; secondary enrollment rates in, 23f; size of cultivation area by gender, 17t; Sub-Saharan, 1, 2, 5, 6, 10, 11t, 181; tertiary enrollment rates in, 24f. *See also specific countries*

Agarwal, B., 2

Age distribution: in the Ghana study, 230, 231, 233, 234–35t, 236; in the Philippines study, 50, 51, 76–77t, 78, 80, 81, 83, 86, 87, 99, 100, 101, 102t, 103, 104t, 105, 107; in the Sumatra study, 153, 154, 158, 169, 170, 172t, 173t, 174

Agricultural income. *See* Farm income

Agricultural labor. *See* Farm labor

Agricultural technology, 51–52, 245, 248–50

Agriculture: dualistic systems, 9–10; extensively cultivated systems, 9, 134; gender issues in, 9–14; intensively cultivated systems, 9, 134; production function studies, 13–14

Agroforestry areas, 8, 19, 116, 137, 139, 148t, 149t, 150t, 151t, 163, 238, 243, 249; consumption expenditures in, 169, 171, 172t; income from, 154, 161; inherited, 133, 134t, 140–41t, 142–43t, 145; labor in, 128, 129t; land tenure institutions, 117, 122–25

Akans, 2, 13, 19, 25t, 26, 122n9, 181, 185, 186, 187, 190; consumption expenditures in, 230, 232t; gender discrimination in, 213, 214t, 224; land inheritance in, 208, 209,

212; landownership in, 196, 197, 198t, 199t, 228; schooling in, 194, 195t, 196, 212; socioeconomic characteristics of, 188

Alcantara, A., 110

Alcohol, expenditures on, 4, 5; in Ghana, 231, 232t, 233, 234–35t; in the Philippines, 98, 99t, 103

Alderman, H., 14, 29

Allocated land, 38, 183, 186, 187, 188, 190, 197, 233; gender equity and, 200, 204, 206–7t, 209; ownership inequality, 227, 228t, 229

Altruistic transfer motives, 7, 34, 36, 39–41

Ancestral land, 120–21, 124

Andhra Pradesh, India, 11t

Anker, R., 41

Appropriated community land, 186, 190, 227, 228t, 229

Aquino administration, 109

Arroyo administration, 109

Aseda (thanksgiving) ceremony, 188n6, 197n11

Asia, 249; Central, 1; East, 1, 5, 27; farming systems in, 9, 10; farm labor inputs in, 11t; illiteracy rates in, 20, 21f; primary enrollment rates in, 22f; secondary enrollment rates in, 23f; South, 1, 2, 5, 6, 9, 109, 244; Southeast, 1, 2, 5; tertiary enrollment rates in, 24f; West, 5. *See also specific countries*

Bangladesh, 5, 110, 111–12

Bargaining power, 112, 137, 145, 169, 230

Beans, 13

263

Matrilineal inheritance, 2, 3, 12, 19, 33,
115–17, 133, 135, 136, 238, 243, 248;
property concepts and, 120–22; schooling
and, 139, 145; shift from, 129–30, 162.
See also Uterine matrilineal inheritance
Mature cocoa fields, 183, 184, 185t; 186;
income from, 215, 216–17t, 219; labor in,
12t, 190, 191, 192t
Medina, B., 103
Mekonnen, H., 13
Melayu Jambi, 116, 117
Middle Region, Sumatra, 12, 18f, 19, 25–26,
33, 116
Migrants: in Ghana, 185, 186, 196, 204, 227,
228; in the Philippines, 74, 111
Minang, 120n5, 122n10
Minangkabau, 116, 117, 120, 145
*Modern Rice Technology and Income
Distribution in Asia* (David and Otsuka), xvii
Moock, P., 13
Morduch, J., 205
Motivations for bequests or transfers
—altruistic, 7, 34, 36, 39–41
—efficiency, 8, 62, 88, 134, 197, 237, 245
—egalitarianism, 3, 7–8, 10, 33, 34–35, 37,
237, 239, 240, 243, 244; in Ghana, 212,
225, 226, 227, 229, 232, 233, 236; in the
Philippines, xvii, 63, 72, 85, 86, 87, 89, 92,
97; in Sumatra, 133, 135, 136, 145–46, 147,
163, 164, 174
—equity, 8, 134, 197, 245
—nonaltruistic, 8
Mukhopadhyay, S., 27

National Program for Education, Health and
Nutrition (PROGRESA) (Mexico), 6
Nepal, 10, 11t
Nigeria, 16, 17t
Non-Akans, 244; consumption expenditures
in, 232t; gender discrimination in, 213,
214t, 224; land inheritance in, 204–5, 209,
212; landownership in, 196, 197, 198t,
199t, 228; schooling in, 194, 195t; social
discrimination in, 226; socioeconomic
characteristics of, 188
Nonaltruistic transfer motives, 8
Nonfarm employment, 237, 240, 244–45; in
Ghana, 241, 242, 246; in the Philippines,
xvii, 7, 33, 54, 59, 60, 62, 79, 83, 88; policy
recommendations for, 245, 246–48; in
Sumatra, 26, 146, 159, 160

Nonfarm income, 25
—in Ghana, 220, 228, 229, 233
—in the Philippines, 1, 29–32, 35–37, 60,
73–84, 85, 86–87, 88, 242; determinants of,
73–83; inequality of, 89–92, 111; sources
of, 55–57
—schooling and, 27–33
—in Sumatra, 130–31, 167, 168
Nuclear families, 121

Otsuka, K., 29, 32, 36, 100, 115, 123, 157,
219, 249
Owner-cultivators: in Ghana, 182, 183; in
the Philippines, 47, 49, 70t, 73, 74, 75, 76t,
82t, 101

Paddy fields, 3, 12, 18f, 19, 33, 35–37,
116–17, 137, 139, 146, 147, 151t, 243;
consumption expenditures and, 169, 171,
172t; income from, 158, 160, 161, 162;
inherited, 133, 134t, 140–41t, 142–43t, 144,
145; labor in, 128–29, 130; ownership
inequality, 167; size of, 118. *See also*
Lowland paddy fields; Rice; Upland paddy
fields
Pakistan, 7, 103, 107
Panay Island, Philippines, 3, 45, 46–47, 49,
50–51, 52–53; agricultural technology in,
51–52; characteristics of households, 50t;
consumption expenditures in, 98, 99t,
104–5t; factor shares in rice production,
54–55; farm labor in, 12t; household
income in, 55–57, 76–77t, 90, 91t; nonfarm
employment and earnings in, 80t, 81–82t;
number of sample households in, 48t; per
capita expenditures in, 102–3t; schooling in,
94t, 95–96t
Parental discrimination, 33, 200, 201–2, 205,
212–13, 232, 233, 237, 238, 239, 240, 244.
See also Gender discrimination; Social
discrimination
Parents, old age support of, 3–4, 18, 62
Parents' generation, 15, 16, 22–24; in Ghana,
19, 183, 194, 195t, 196, 239t; in the
Philippines, 48, 57–58, 239t; in Sumatra,
118, 131, 132, 133, 134t, 163, 239t
Partible inheritance, 16–17, 60
Paternal landholdings
—in Ghana, 196; consumption expenditures
and, 230, 232, 234t, 235t; gender equity
and, 204, 205, 206t, 207t, 208, 210t, 211t

About the Authors

Agnes R. Quisumbing is a senior research fellow in the Food Consumption and Nutrition Division of the International Food Policy Research Institute (IFPRI), Washington, D.C. She works on gender and intrahousehold issues, land tenure, and long-term economic mobility. Prior to joining IFPRI, Agnes was an economist at the World Bank, Washington, D.C., a visiting fellow at the Economic Growth Center, Yale University, U.S.A., and an assistant professor at the School of Economics of the University of the Philippines.

Jonna P. Estudillo is an assistant professor at the School of Economics of the University of the Philippines. Prior to her current position, Jonna was a faculty fellow at the Foundation for Advanced Studies on International Development, Tokyo, Japan, and a postdoctoral fellow at Tokyo Metropolitan University, Japan, and the International Rice Research Institute, Los Baños, the Philippines. Her research has focused on income distribution, poverty, technological change, and gender issues.

Keijiro Otsuka was a visiting research fellow in the Environment and Production Technology Division at the International Food Policy Research Institute, Washington, D.C., during 1993–98, and a professor of economics at the Tokyo Metropolitan University, Japan, until 2001, when he joined the Foundation for Advanced Studies on International Development in Tokyo as a professorial fellow. Having been selected as a chairman of the board of trustees at the International Rice Research Institute, Los Baños, the Philippines, Keijiro's current research interests include the transferability of the Green Revolution in Asia to Africa.